AF147902

Celebrity and Mediated Social Connections

Neil M. Alperstein

Celebrity and Mediated Social Connections

Fans, Friends and Followers in the Digital Age

Neil M. Alperstein
Department of Communication
Loyola University Maryland
Baltimore, MD, USA

ISBN 978-3-030-17901-4   ISBN 978-3-030-17902-1   (eBook)
https://doi.org/10.1007/978-3-030-17902-1

© The Editor(s) (if applicable) and The Author(s), under exclusive licence to Springer Nature Switzerland AG 2019
This work is subject to copyright. All rights are solely and exclusively licensed by the Publisher, whether the whole or part of the material is concerned, specifically the rights of translation, reprinting, reuse of illustrations, recitation, broadcasting, reproduction on microfilms or in any other physical way, and transmission or information storage and retrieval, electronic adaptation, computer software, or by similar or dissimilar methodology now known or hereafter developed.
The use of general descriptive names, registered names, trademarks, service marks, etc. in this publication does not imply, even in the absence of a specific statement, that such names are exempt from the relevant protective laws and regulations and therefore free for general use. The publisher, the authors and the editors are safe to assume that the advice and information in this book are believed to be true and accurate at the date of publication. Neither the publisher nor the authors or the editors give a warranty, express or implied, with respect to the material contained herein or for any errors or omissions that may have been made. The publisher remains neutral with regard to jurisdictional claims in published maps and institutional affiliations.

Cover credit: gilaxia/E+/Getty Images

This Palgrave Macmillan imprint is published by the registered company Springer Nature Switzerland AG
The registered company address is: Gewerbestrasse 11, 6330 Cham, Switzerland

For Spencer and Gabriel

PREFACE

For over 20 years I have been studying the imagination, in particular the ways in which celebrities—modern-day goddesses and gods—enter into our nocturnal dreams, daydreams, fantasies, stream of consciousness and related self-talk. I had the good fortune to study with John Caughey, an anthropologist who after spending time in India and Micronesia returned to the United States to focus on contemporary American culture. His 1984 book *Imaginary Social Worlds* has been a major influence on my scholarly work, and I learned from him ethnographic methods that provide a gateway into my informants' inner worlds. Much of my scholarship has in the past focused on advertising, as it is the one form of modern communication that has clear intent to sell or at the very least influence the consumer. If those years of research taught me one thing, it was not to take what we see before us—what's on the surface—for granted. The real work is below the surface, and getting there is no easy chore. There is great resistance, as there should be, to allow one to enter into what has been a very private sphere. I am indebted to more than 500 people who over the years have recounted their dreams to me, reported the thoughts they arrested during media consumption and told me stories of how what they gleaned from media consumption entered into their private thoughts and fantasies as well as their everyday discourse. I was never interested in decision-making or influence, the site of much advertising research, as I was in mapping the relationship between media consumption and our private world.

Along the way, something happened, which I might describe as a watershed moment that changed the way people consume media and the related ways in which we process its content, sloughing off most of it as a result of overload, but internalizing some of it as a way of making sense of our everyday lives. That change, of course, is digital media: social media, apps, games and related technologies like the smartphone and more recently digital assistants and virtual toys. The major questions raised in this book, and additional ones to which I attempt to provide some answers, are what happens when media is with us pretty much all of the time, and even monitors our sleep (Fitbit); what happens when communication that used to be one way becomes interactive and perhaps many to many; and what happens to the imagination when what used to be our private world spills out without filters in the form of tweets, messaging, comments, likes and dislikes? Most importantly, I think, with regard to the latter, is there still room for the imagination when the world we live in is becoming more virtual, driven by digital assistants, augmented and virtual reality, and the like that call on us to extend our inner world into the outer public world, as we are called upon to respond quickly, viscerally? I think there is good news and bad news to be had, but I won't give away the conclusions here—you'll have to read the book. I can hear your internal musings now; your reactions to my unwillingness to give you the punch line. You might keep it to yourself, or you might want to take to twitter. Everything is possible in this new world of mediated social connections in which our insides are turned outward, as what used to be our stream of consciousness now streams our consciousness in public.

When I first began researching the imagination, my orientation was based on the theoretical model regarding imaginary social relationships we form with unmet media figures. There is nothing particularly new about the influence of celebrities, as the idea of emulation was the basis during the early part of the twentieth century for the use of theatrical performers and then movie stars in advertising. The repeated exposure through traditional media like radio and television, as well as gossip magazines, allowed actors and other entertainers, sports figures and political figures to become a part of individuals' everyday lives. However, with the emergence in the 1990s of a Web 2.0 24-hour participatory culture, the nature of our social connection to media has arguably intensified between the individual and the celebrity, in terms of how celebrities may model behavior and how individuals manage their own identities and learn how to operate in their own social world. New mobile technologies and content delivery systems, such as Facebook, Snapchat, Instagram, Pinterest and Twitter, have brought about changes in the ways we relate to

celebrities, as individuals redefine what it means to be a fan, friend or follower, including the possibility of achieving an actual connection to a
celebrity, as we move from the "illusion of intimacy" to what may be
referred to as the "possibility of interaction." Additionally, social media
require a higher level of disclosure on the part of the celebrity. As a result,
issues around both intimacy and authenticity arise. Both the idea of imaginary relationships and the changing nature of digital media have implications for the ways individuals communicate in the second decade of the
twenty-first century, digital media being just one component in a broader
referent system through which we make, unmake and remake meaning in
our everyday lives. Accompanying the new rules for the ways in which
celebrities operate in the new media system is the phenomenon of self-
branding and in that the advent of micro-celebrities. Now pretty much
anyone can play at the game of participatory media, perhaps with the end
goal of becoming a star. But let's just say, for now, that it is complicated,
as fans, friends and followers communicate along with celebrities and
micro-celebrities within the celebrity-industrial complex.

Establishing and conducting a mediated connection with a celebrity is
an idea that grew out of television research in the 1950s based on observations by British researchers Horton and Wohl regarding what they termed
parasocial interactions between viewers and media personalities who
looked out of the TV set at the viewer, giving the impression that the
viewer was being spoken to directly. The parasocial nature of the interaction was media centric, as Horton and Wohl did not track how that parasocial interaction traversed the point of media consumption to enter into
other aspects of everyday life. In the early 1990s I first wrote about the
ways in which advertising served as a mediating force in imaginary social
relationships that held the potential to both stabilize and destabilize the
relationship. Such imaginary relationships continued off the screen,
extending Horton and Wohl's original idea. I explored this phenomenon
in my book *Advertising in Everyday Life*. My theoretical orientation conceives of individuals as active participants in making sense of their everyday
lives through, among other things, the use of celebrities. This position is
consistent with a cultural studies approach rooted in conceptualizing audiences as active rather than passive dupes of the media industry. I credit
individuals with a sense of intelligence as well as a sense of humor and
skepticism as they find pleasure and meaning in the dynamic process of
creating, maintaining and perhaps dissolving imaginary relationships with
celebrities.

It has become evident with the emergence of digital media that the nature of imaginary relationships changed. First, the media through which we consume and more recently produce content has changed. Second, many people feel compelled to always be connected to media, another indicator of a shift in consumptive habits. Third, the interactive nature of digital media also signals a cultural shift in which participation is not an option. And fourth, what used to remain inside our heads has now been extended into our technologically based world. Contemporary life is mediated by technology in ways that have altered the nature of what it means to be social. As played out on social media, in particular, changes in technology are accompanied by a shift in cultural expectations regarding what is appropriate and what is not appropriate. By way of example, I recall one of my informants recounting a story where she chastised a friend for actually calling her on her mobile phone when, as she said, the friend should have merely texted her back. In other words, texting is appropriate; talking, not so much. As a result of cultural shifts, the nature of social connection on and through digital media has changed in unprecedented ways. In the world of digital media, we may be more influenced by weak social connections than by those people with whom we have a strong relationship. Connection becomes more ephemeral in this era of digital media. I therefore have titled this book *Mediated Social Connections* as a way of advancing the ideas of parasocial interaction and imaginary social relationships in the age of digital media.

In *Celebrity and Mediated Social Connections: Fans, Friends and Followers in the Digital Age*, I map onto the path that fans take as they go about their daily lives sometimes engaging with celebrities, micro-celebrities, and other friends and followers. The book begins with the idea of what Horton and Wohl described in 1956 as a parasocial relationship in which a TV talk show host figuratively reached out to the audience member and in a pseudosocial manner spoke directly to her or him and extends that idea into the world of social media, which has turned the notion of a one-way relationship with a celebrity on its proverbial head. The possibility of direct interaction and the illusion of intimacy between fan and celebrity and celebrity and fan opens up the possibility to play out a fantasy within a mediated environment that may feel real or authentic, but may ultimately be illusory. Beyond the possibility of literally engaging with a celebrity, fans may become voyeurs as they witness a celebrity's interactions with others and perhaps other celebrities. There is also the opportunity for the fan to circulate the meanings they find in celebrity postings on the web, modify those meanings through memes, for example, or alter those meanings in significant ways through their own participation in the world of digital media. We take Siri and Alexa for granted, but they along with augmented and virtual reality as well as robotics represent the next tectonic shift that has implications for our outer, as well as our inner, worlds. All of this is placed within the context of a shift in our understanding of reality itself, as the concept is fractured in light of not only augmented or virtual reality, but also the perceptions that digital media fosters a mediated reality that extends from the really real to the almost real to the unreal. In other words, "real" has taken on multiple meanings and such meaning can be applied to relationships we create and maintain through digital media and beyond.

This book breaks new ground with regard to the parasocial nature of relationships with people we don't actually know as a function of our engagement with technologies that allow us to jack in, blurring the lines between fantasy and reality. This critical examination of our mediated everyday lives presents a paradox in which our digital lives are benefited by mediated connections while detracting from our analog relationships, as a result of which we engage in illusory connections that may impinge on our imagination. Digital media have altered our imagination to the extent that our perceptions of what is real and not real have been altered. Digital media and related technologies have changed the way we are learning to deal with the ever-shifting lines between fantasy and reality. We still utilize celebrities and we use micro-celebrities and other participants engaged in digital media, but the ways in which we connect with and to those media have been extended. Yes, we still fantasize about celebrities and other media figures and include them in our imaginary inner worlds, but we also seek to engage with and about them in a more interactive manner. I hope the chapters that follow help to illuminate the changes that are taking place and provide some guidance regarding those changes and their implications for our society and culture.

The topics covered in the following chapters are intimately related, but admittedly they are wide in scope. While the broad theme revolves around the role that digital media plays in our everyday lives, the central thesis, however, focuses on the changing nature of relationships. I think of this book as a watercolor painting. Unlike oil paintings where dark colors are applied first and lighter ones follow, watercolor works just the opposite. So, it is with a broad brush stroke that I begin to layer this book; each chapter, however, adds greater background and detail. It is only when you step back from the book that you see the ways in which the translucent quality of each chapter forms a coherent story of mediated social connections in the digital age. Chapter 1 serves as an introduction to the paradox of our digital existence, setting forth the thesis of the book, which, simply put, is that social media is not very social, at least not very social based on our historic understanding of what it means to be social. Social networks, as demonstrated throughout this book, are based on loose connections and tend toward weak ties. Social media platforms ushered in as new communication media have us staring in the mirror of narcissism, sending ephemeral messages that whiz by like shooting arrows into the air and not caring where they land or if they land at all. There are times when we do care, like when a celebrity responds to an Instagram post or tweet. For a time a fan's social status is elevated. And, because celebrities and micro-celebrities are so engrained in our mediated popular culture or rather our popular culture is so engrained in our social media, we get to be voyeurs as celebrities use digital media to reach out to one another, as fans become privy to inside information. This makes us feel good. As well, we gain a sense of closeness when intimate details are shared or exclusive content about a celebrity's life emerges. Over time we feel like we really know them. Chapter 2 extends the theory of imaginary social relationships to consider the impact that digital media have on our imagination—daydreams, reverie, mind wandering, fantasies and nocturnal dreams. Anthropologist John Caughey coined the term imaginary social relationships, which he described as one-sided relationships in which the individual knows a great deal about the celebrity, but the relationship is not mutual. Caughey's theoretical model suggests individuals utilize imaginary social relationships with celebrities as a way to shape their own identities and their feelings about themselves. Chapter 3 takes a step back in time to consider how children are inculcated into a world of digital technologies, whether it be apps, games or websites. When very young children receive their first teddy bear or other projected object, they psychologically begin to engage with a mediated world. Teddy bears notwithstanding, today children engage with what is being referred to as the Internet of Toys (as opposed to the Internet of Things), in which case an electronic object like Furby, in its latest iteration, learns to respond to a child. Robotic toys are becoming more commonplace, especially those based on artificial intelligence. We know that imaginary relationships are ways for children and perhaps adults to elaborate upon, that is act out, real experiences. The question addressed in this chapter has to do with what happens when the "real" relationship is with a robotic toy. Chapter 4 considers the role of celebrities in selling their own branded products and products they endorse through the use of social media, as Twitter, Facebook, Instagram, Snapchat as well as dedicated websites become forums through which celebrities can communicate with their fans in order to promote the purchase of products and services. The chapter focuses on celebrities like Kim Kardashian, Lady Gaga and Justin Bieber as exemplars of the use of social media as an advertising and promotional vehicle. Such buying opportunities presented by celebrities allow the fan to "label" themselves as a fan and craft an identity based on attitudes and values put forth by the celebrity. Chapter 5 takes a critical look at the phenomenon of micro-celebrities that has been fostered by a Web 2.0 culture that encourages user-generated content (UGC). In order to exemplify how micro-celebrities operate, the chapter follows travel vloggers who have acquired a significant fan base that helps to support their adventures. Along the way these travel vloggers sometimes get caught between the authenticity and sincerity required of them and the world of commerce that allows them to continue their adventures. Chapter 6 moves from the world of micro-celebrity to the role that bona fide celebrities play in the world of direct-to-consumer prescription drug advertising (DTCA). Direct-to-consumer prescription drug advertising is the fastest-growing form of advertising, topping $6 billion in expenditures in 2016. Celebrities play a key role in promoting prescription medications, including entertainers, actresses and actors, sports figures and political figures. This chapter provides an overview of the ways in which direct-to-consumer prescription drug advertising (DTCA) has moved from its beginning in print and television to include forays into social media platforms, what is referred to as eDTCA. The chapter investigates the role of celebrity spokesperson and ePatients in the context of promoting prescription drugs. Chapter 7 looks at contemporary social and political movements that have been fueled by digital media. The chapter investigates how celebrities participate in the Me Too movement, and it looks at the ways in which ordinary individuals, like the Parkland High School teens, who were by unfortunate circumstance drawn into the limelight and quickly learned to navigate the tempestuous waters of social media. Chapter 8 offers an ethnographic interview of an informant who is engaged in a mediated social connection with an Olympic ice-dancing couple. The interview illustrates how what may begin in legacy media leads to information seeking on the Internet and onward to establishing mediated connections with celebrities and like-minded individuals. Sometimes those mediated connections lead to actual social relationships. This book paints in layers of increasing detail how dependence on digital media and related technologies impacts relationships with people we don't actually know, but with whom we may feel a sense of closeness. The closeness we feel is a function of the mediated social connections that fans, friends and followers develop with celebrities in contexts as varied as commerce, social issues and culture on a global scale.

Baltimore, MD, USA   Neil M. Alperstein

Acknowledgments

I am indebted to many people who have helped me arrive at this point in my academic career of observing culture and learning from those around me who have generously contributed to this project. I would like to thank especially John Caughey, PhD, with whom I studied as a graduate student, and it was through John that I was first introduced to the concept of imaginary social relationships. His model has become the bedrock of much of my research, and I am eternally grateful to him for leading me down this intellectual pathway. I am indebted to my colleagues at Loyola University of Maryland's Department of Communication and the graduate program in Emerging Media of which I am the founding academic director. I am grateful for the support, in particular, of Elliot King, PhD, a colleague and partner for the past 25 years. We have forged a friendship and intellectual bond that has nurtured our academic interests in digital media and online education. I have said many times in the past that I would not be here if it were not for my wife Nancy whose life-sustaining efforts brought me back from near oblivion, and it was through her gallantry that I have survived the ravages of cancer; indeed I have thrived to live another day. I want to give special acknowledgment to Elaine Bourne Heath, PhD, who many years ago mentored me and nurtured me as a teacher and scholar. I will always be indebted to you and cherish the role you played in my early career. I would also like to thank my parents who allowed me to wallow in my own boredom to the extent that it stimulated my imagination and opened up my imaginary social worlds. Several of the ideas in this book were germinated in my musings on the blogsite Medium. com. There I have written on myriad topics that, like this book, reflect my eclectic tastes in popular culture. I thank all who have engaged with those blog posts, several of which are based on my scholarly research. The conversation doesn't have to stop at these pages, as you can find me on various social media platforms including my website www.mediatedsocialconnections.com. At Palgrave Macmillan, I am indebted to Shaun Vigil, Senior Editor, Cultural, Media, and Communication Studies, who commissioned this book, and to Glenn Ramirez for managing the production of this book. I thank the anonymous reviewers for their critical feedback and to others who have offered their critical commentary. I would also like to thank Camille Davies, Editor, Cultural, Media, and Communication Studies. And I would like to thank the production team at SPi Content Solutions, SPi Global, in particular I want to thank Project Manager Sarulatha Krishnamurthy.

CONTENTS

LIST OF FIGURES

LIST OF TABLES

CHAPTER 1

Introduction: Mediated Social Connections: Place, Imagination and Togetherness

In June 2010, Jonathan Metz, a Connecticut man, caught his left arm in the basement furnace while attempting to repair the boiler. Being stuck and having 12 hours to reflect on his ordeal, Metz asked himself "What would MacGyver do?"[1] By calling on a well-known television character, Metz was able to come to a decision: amputate the arm. When Metz invoked MacGyver, he was invoking a media figure—someone Metz did not actually know—in order to make a life-altering decision. In fact, MacGyver isn't a real person; rather, he is a character from a television program. And while this may be an extreme example, it serves to illustrate the important role that celebrities, including the characters they play, perform in a mediated culture. Similar to the ways in which spirits may have guided members of traditional societies, in contemporary society, celebrities not only guide us to make important decisions but serve as role models, mentors, teachers, best friends, love interests, father or mother figures, and brother, sister or cousin figures; in other words, we form social relationships with people we do not actually know. Relationships such as these, formed through media consumption, may begin in early childhood, where deep feelings that may develop can endure, oftentimes lasting decades, perhaps a lifetime.[2]

Establishing and conducting a parasocial relationship with a celebrity is an idea that grew out of early television research based on observations of parasocial interactions between viewers and media personalities who appeared to look out of the television at the viewer, giving the impression

© The Author(s) 2019
N. M. Alperstein, *Celebrity and Mediated Social Connections*,
https://doi.org/10.1007/978-3-030-17902-1_1

that the viewer was being spoken to directly.[3] In fact, as television execu-
tives realized that audiences were developing emotional connections to
performers, those performers were encouraged to adopt personality characteristics that would imbue them to their fans.[4] In the 1980s anthropologist John Caughey coined the term imaginary social relationships that he
described as one-sided relationships in which the individual knows a great
deal about the media figure but the relationship is not mutual.[5] And in the
early 1990s I first wrote about the ways in which advertising served as a
mediating force that held the potential to stabilize as well as destabilize the
imaginary social relationship.[6] With the addition of media experiences
extending from legacy formats like television, radio and print, we entered
into an era 30 years ago of the World Wide Web and digital media through
which to connect to others, including celebrities. In the early 2000s came
the ability through Facebook and later Twitter to connect with friends,
current and past, as well as acquaintances or other like-minded individuals,
and media figures. Although with the latter, who may be more like Stanley
Milgram's familiar strangers, connection is most likely voyeuristic.[7] And
yet more recently platforms like Instagram and Snapchat, among other
social media platforms, are impacting the ways in which people present
themselves to one another. This is a mediated world of reciprocity in which
celebrities provide a model of communication in the ways in which they
reach out to fans and the ways in which fans attempt to interact with celebrities. This chapter explores the nature of mediated social connections in
an era of digital media. The mediated world of familiar strangers advanced
to consider parasocial interaction between the TV screen and the individual and on to imaginary social relationships in which the connection
extended to our inner worlds. With regard to mediated social connections,
both the nature of what it means to be social and the nature of connection
have changed. This chapter frames the discussion of those changes within
three concepts: place, imagination, and sociality or togetherness. The
chapter describes the ways in which individuals develop mediated social
connections, and it addresses the changing nature of those connections
brought on by newer ways of communicating through digital media.

PLACE, IMAGINATION AND TOGETHERNESS

There was a time when media consumption was location bound. By this I
mean that if you wanted to watch a movie, you had to do so in a theater.
If you wanted to watch television, you would have to be sitting in a

particular room where the TV was located. With digital media and related technologies we are no longer bound to the location where the communication might have otherwise occurred. For example, you no longer have to watch the news on your TV when you can be pretty much anywhere watching or reading the news as long as you have an Internet connection and app on your smartphone. Having established that locative media allow us to make content transportable, the notion of place also refers to the ways in which media allow us—encourage us—to be in more than one place in our mind at a time, promoting movement through multiple realities. This applies to both consumption of fixed media and locative media, as we are no longer talking about technology but what the mind does with media content. Moving through multiple realities may refer to consuming multiple media simultaneously, and it may refer to the kind of finger surfing we do when shifting among social media platforms. In addition, we can be physically here in the present and there, meaning mentally elsewhere, at the same time. Based on the content we consume, the experience becomes layered, based on the mediated social connections we conduct with others, some of whom we may know, but others we know about, like celebrities.

Celebrity as a Practice

Marwick and boyd define celebrity as a practice, using terms like "celebrity practitioners" or "famous people" to avoid the binary implications of the noun.[8] Here I am thinking about the term celebrity more expansively to include media figures like a sports person, an actor, even the character they may play or a pop singer. While we recognize many celebrities because of their talent as singers, performers or athletes, there are other so-called celebrities who demonstrate no particular talent but have become noteworthy for other reasons. It is important to include micro-celebrities, individuals who are likely to be ordinary people but who do extraordinary things that they document on social media. Celebrities, micro-celebrities and media figures are terms that are often used interchangeably; however, there are distinguishing features that will be critically analyzed in this book. Additionally, anyone who engages with social media operates in the same or at least similar manner as do celebrities. Anyone can have a Facebook or Instagram account or a Twitter feed. Of note, however, are issues related to authenticity and sincerity and the seemingly different requirements for celebrities and micro-celebrities and the rest of us. There is the related issue of sociality or togetherness, which refers to the changing nature of our social world including strong and weak social connections to others, like the superficial nature of having many hundreds of "friends" on Facebook. We increasingly live in a world in which being together with others is simulated through the use of technology rather than through actual social interaction. As Massachusetts Institute of Technology (MIT) social psychologist Sherry Turkle so aptly put it, we are alone together. However, the innate need for connection and intimacy drives us toward mediated social connections, and it is the desire to experience the emotional connection to others through social media that keeps us coming back for more. The authenticity of relationship that we seek is not a state of being; rather it is questionable whether through the use of social media individuals can experience authentic connections or whether those connections remain illusory.

EVERYDAY ROUTINES AND MEDIA EXPERIENCES

Driving an automobile in a routine manner is analogous to the ways in which people navigate through much media consumption, and it illustrates how people can mentally be in two places at once. Consider the following scenario: you drive to work or school just about every day—what we might call a routine experience. Oftentimes you arrive at the location only to ask "How did I get here? I don't remember driving here." Such an important yet routine activity like driving to the same place every day promotes a shift from what we are supposed to be doing (in this case paying attention to pedestrians and other drivers) to thinking about other things. In a sense, we are in two places at once: here in the present driving and mentally elsewhere thinking about other things. We understand the importance of remaining mentally present while driving, and yet we are so well practiced at this task—driving routinely to school or work—that many of us find our minds wandering. If we can so easily employ an attention strategy while driving an automobile that allows for thinking about other things (hopefully without causing an accident), media consumption that involves little risk—watching, listening or reading, perhaps simultaneously with multiple media—presents opportunities to turn away from what is before us and engage in our imaginary worlds. The fluidity with which we move between what is before us and our imagination is important to the ways in which we use media, but the ways in which people utilize digital media may vary as the requirements for finger surfing or using a keyboard or mouse are different from passively watching television, listening to the radio or reading a magazine or book. While people create their own regular route through legacy media along the way, elaborating in their own minds about what they are reading, hearing or seeing, use of digital media requires a greater degree of attention and interactivity.[9] In a less interactive media environment, the regular route through media provides the opportunity for a fan to shift from attending to the medium before them to their stream of consciousness thinking or fantasy as they have learned over time to fluidly move from the medium or content to elaboration in their own minds based on that which is salient or relevant. This may not be the case with digital media that not only draw our attention but also require participation even at a minimal level, like pressing a "like" button.

When considering particular media figures, like celebrities, such shifting between medium and imagination allows individuals to invoke a particular celebrity from among one's personal subset of celebrities depending on one's consumptive state of mind. And, by traveling along a metaphoric route in which the fan routinely seeks out the latest news on a gossip website, follows a celebrity on Twitter, a YouTuber or Instagrammer, views the latest Snaps or reads their Facebook wall, the relevant content becomes intertwined so that the lines between objective reality and the imaginary become blurred to the point where the difference does not seem to matter, what the social philosopher Jean Baudrillard referred to as hyperreality. As the character Cypher from the movie *The Matrix* says, "I know this steak doesn't exist. I know that when I put it in my mouth, the Matrix is telling my brain that it is juicy and delicious. After nine years, you know what I realize? Ignorance is bliss."[10] In a somewhat similar manner, individuals are able to easily shift between multiple realities, energizing the imagination and encouraging engagement in imaginary social worlds. The inner imaginary world of the individual is a culturally rich environment inhabited only partially by celebrities, as the era of digital media has opened up the practices of digital media to anyone who wants to participate and engage, assuming they have access to an Internet connection and appropriate technology. Celebrities and media figures not only appear in our fantasies, daydreams and stream of consciousness, they also appear in our nocturnal dreams.[11] However, celebrities play an important part in the broader mediated referent system in that people often invoke a celebrity outside of media consumption during social conversations, self-talk or as Jonathan Metz did when making a life-altering decision, which extends the use of celebrities and media figures into everyday life.

The shift in place refers to both the turn inward within our own imaginations and the ways in which we shift from one content platform to the next or one medium to the next, including simultaneous consumption of multiple media. Place, in this sense, also refers to the ways in which media are available in contexts other than the comfort of one's living room: screens are everywhere and they go with us or seem to follow us everywhere we travel. Therefore the stimuli that encourage us to shift between what is before us and our imaginary world can be invoked at any time and any place.

Hyperreality

The late French social philosopher Jean Baudrillard saw the coming of a postmodern world in which simulations became a reasonable substitute for reality. The willingness to accept a simulation as a reasonable substitute for something real needs to be distinguished from the inability to distinguish what is real from that which is simulated. As we move into the era of robotics, digital assistants, virtual, augmented, immersive and mixed reality, the two positions are often confused; however, Baudrillard believed in the former. In the 1970s he described the blurring between what is real and fiction as hyperreality. For example, a family visiting the French pavilion at Disney's Epcot Center in Florida can experience "authentic" French food and purchase "authentic" French merchandise. The experience is such that some visitors have been known to say they no longer feel the need to visit France, as the Epcot experience is a reasonable-enough substitute. A writer for the Disney blog says of the French pavilion: "From the romantic architecture to the wonderful aromas that float gently throughout the shops, I'm transported to another place every time I visit."[12]

The Pokemon Go phenomenon of 2016 serves as an example of hyperreality at work in which players, youngsters and adults alike view imaginary characters in an augmented reality experience in real contexts that had them, in a couple of incidents, falling off a cliff and getting shot.[13] The CEO of the company Niantic that created Pokemon Go claims that augmented reality is better than virtual reality because it is "far more interesting and promising—for technology and, really, for humanity."[14] The ways in which people interact with both Pokemon Go and eating or shopping at the French pavilion at Epcot are examples of simulacra and simulation, terms closely associated with Baudrillard's hyperreality. Pokemon characters are not real, but players treat the characters as if they were real. Eating or shopping at the French pavilion at Epcot is a simulation of a real world experience. Even the term "real life" has garnered a new acronym, RL, and in that becomes another version of reality along with virtual, augmented, immersive and mixed reality. Hyperreality can be viewed through the lens of media, ranging from more traditional forms like movies and television, and extended to include the use of smartphones to engage with virtual, augmented, immersive and mixed reality. It can also be associated with particular forms of content, like a television program, a film, an advertisement or a simulated experience like a visit to Epcot Center. As well, the concept can be extended to consider mediated culture.

Mediated Culture

The advent in 1988 of photo-altering software like Photoshop ushered in an era in which celebrity retouching became automated. This mediation of celebrity images, especially in advertisements, promoted and exploited the hyperreal world that Baudrillard was envisioning. One of the advertisements in the Dove Real Beauty advertising campaign, titled *Evolution*, turns hyperreality on its head by letting the consumer become an insider.[15] The commercial literally depicts the use of photo-altering software to demonstrate how advertising manipulates and distorts images.[16] This is an example of hyperreality taking a postmodern turn, as in Goffmanesque terms the commercial merges the "backstage" with the "frontstage." As for effects, criticism ranges from the images of ultra-thin models, for example, that may lead to depression because what is being depicted is unattainable, to whether consumers react by rejecting those images through a form of cultural resistance. A study of the ways in which women respond to the idealized images on the social media platform Pinterest concluded that in the process of comparing themselves to idealized images, respondents presented a more complex set of reactions than one might expect.[17] While there was extreme admiration, there was also disdain. In other words, human beings are more complex in the ways in which they respond to idealized images such as those of celebrities. Therefore, it is not just that everyone buys into the hyperreal; although some people certainly do, others may reject the images of celebrities or for that matter they may simultaneously admire and/or reject some particular aspects of those images.

It's important to emphasize that Baudrillard's concept of hyperreality wasn't just about our inability to distinguish between reality and the simulation, as it considered that hyperreality reflected our acceptance of the simulated as a reasonable replacement for reality. What this means is that by teaching youngsters, for example, to be more discerning when it comes to distinguishing between reality and simulation is naïve. For example, as part of its noble self-esteem project, Dove through a multimedia effort tries to teach young women the differences between Photoshopped beauty (a simulation) and real beauty, the latter being the theme of a long-running advertising campaign. It is paradoxical that it takes a marketing and advertising campaign, something we would usually associate with promoting hyperreality, to address the very issue that it is trying to ameliorate by playing against celebrity culture. At base, to play against what we know to be the way things are is a standard creative technique that is used by advertisers to gain and keep attention, as it invites elaboration on the part of the consumer of that content. The divergence from the expected leads to the unexpected "ah ha" moment. Culture, generally speaking, is something we do—it is a social practice—not something we are likely to learn abstractly, at least not directly through media. Culture making is to a great extent an unconscious process. Consider something as simple as learning to brush your teeth. In Western culture, as a child one receives minor instruction in oral hygiene, but once a child "gets it," brushing becomes a routine cultural practice. It's not something to think about—you just do it. Similarly, we come to mediated culture through similar means, as we are inculcated into a society that watches screens or listens to audio. It's what we do, and we quickly adapt to newer forms of technology delivering content, whether it be through smartphones or purveyors of celebrity content on the Internet. Dove's Real Beauty website quotes an 11-year-old girl saying what she wants to be when she grows up. Becky says: "Famous!" Such a response is not isolated, as it has become an acceptable vocational aspiration for both boys and girls—to become celebrities. Role models for fame without talent or credential abound and digital media have moved the culture in the direction of the hyperreal. The Dove Real Beauty Project reports "25% of young American women would rather win America's Next Top Model than the Nobel Peace Prize." And the project also reports the results of a study that suggests that "more than half the girls they interviewed felt pressure to look like a celebrity."[18] Desire to become famous for fame's sake and to look like a celebrity are outcomes of living in a culture that promotes simulation; this is especially the case with the young who are more vulnerable to such influences. The MTV program "Made" is a good example of mediated transformation of a fan's identity into a singer, athlete, dancer and skateboarder, among other possibilities.

On the other hand, it is important to understand that effects are not automatic or linear, as in cause and effect, as it can also be demonstrated over time that people can learn through experiences with and through various media to be more discerning.

Yearning for Authenticity

Digital media have changed the social landscape enormously, partially because of the proliferation and availability of technological devices and platforms through which people can connect with one another. With regard to celebrities, along with the emergence of social media is a set of requirements that parallel the ways in which ordinary people communicate: creating the feeling of direct address in the guise of greater intimacy between the celebrity and fan, opening up opportunities for fans to directly interact with the celebrity and providing opportunities to purchase endorsed products. Celebrities who wish to create a bond with their fans and followers through digital media must operate within the code of authenticity. Reflecting on all the "fakeness" around us, in their 2007 book titled *Authenticity: What Consumers Really Want,* Gilmore and Pine claim that we have reached "toxic levels of inauthenticity."[19] The types of inauthenticity to which they refer include emails from people we don't know or don't feel we can trust, and news from untrustworthy sources rather than professional journalists and so-called friends from Facebook. Paradoxically, it is this loss of trust that has individuals yearning for authenticity. Using Google nGram, the word authenticity's appearance in books peaked in 1806 and except for a brief blip upward in 1826, the word experienced a downward trend until it reached an upward peak in 2006, around the time that social media platforms began to proliferate.[20]

And, it was a few years later that novelist Jonathon Franzen critically claimed, "inauthentic people are obsessed with authenticity"[21]—often cited as a basis for understanding the limits of social connections is the Dunbar Number that Robin Dunbar created in the 1990s based on his studies of monkeys and apes. Dunbar calculated that humans should be able to maintain relationships with roughly 150 people at a time, but in reality intimate friendships were much fewer. The implications suggest that connections with many hundreds if not thousands of friends and followers must be inauthentic.

If authenticity and sincerity are important attributes of creating and maintaining a social media presence, it is important to distinguish between what the ancient Greeks might have referred to as the naturalistic sense of an authentic self and the contemporary version of a normative self that emerged from the Romantic period. In the former, we are believed to have an essential nature; however, with the latter, authenticity is something we may search for, a quest of sorts. If authenticity is part of a journey—a never-ending one—then we need to consider a process-oriented approach, the authenticating self.[22] As Marwick and boyd point out, with social media like the micro-blogging site Twitter, there is no place to hide, as what takes place on the "stage" of social media is closer to real time if not in real time.[23] Is that what is meant by the authenticating self? In a social media world that lacks norms, perhaps because of its newness—as a culture we are still finding our way with regard to determining what is right or wrong, good or bad, to post on social media—individuals who violate expectations may be publicly shamed; in other words, some aspect of their authentic self has been exposed. This is the topic of Jon Ronson's book *So You've Been Publicly Shamed* that deals with the consequences of people who have crossed the ethical or moral line on social media; in some cases, they have lost their jobs.[24] On the other hand, violating expectations may be seen as a form of authenticity; in other words, it is the violation that makes the action more real. We tend to operate in the space between authentic and inauthentic, and it is through this ambiguity that marketers may purposefully exploit the confusion. Examples of the inauthentic/authentic beyond digital media include craft beer and farm-to-table restaurants, and extend to the tiny house movement.[25] Admittedly, these are tangible items that are marketed, but what about social media? The way we present ourselves on and through social media—or perhaps I should say promote ourselves—is through conscious self-branding. In other words, we present ourselves on social media in the same manner that marketers promote products.

Celebrity scholar P. David Marshall describes personas as an accoutrement or mask added to the self in order to achieve some sort of completion and satisfaction in the public world. In other words, the persona is not about the authentic self, as I have been describing it, but rather about the way in which the self links to the personal, which Marshall suggests is a public form of identity. He theorizes that we have come to a point where there is "a pandemic obsession with constructing personas," adding that this manifests in "the constant preening of the presentation of the self."[26] As an example of persona building or in this case re-construction, in one of his essays, "Stephen Colbert Reveals His True Self," Marshall points to the shift that took place when comedian Stephen Colbert ended his run on The Colbert Report that aired on the Comedy Central cable network to take over the coveted role of host of the long-running Late Show on the CBS television network. Colbert in making the transition had to shed his identity as a pseudo–right wing talk show host to project an alternative version of himself, although perhaps not his "real" or "authentic" self, despite disclosures about his religious beliefs, upbringing and home life, although it represented a new construction of self. Marshall states: "With Colbert, converting his public persona to a real television talk show host demands some sort of dropping of his current masked identity, which paradoxically is how his audiences and the public now perceive him."[27]

With regard to celebrities, in order to lend an atmosphere of authenticity, social media provide the possibility of increased confidence that the celebrity is who she or he claims to be, as well as the verification or documentation of authenticity through two key markers: first, the absence of privacy; and second, spontaneity. However, we know that social media, because of its performative nature, lacks spontaneity, as it is a highly constructed environment for anyone who uses it, including celebrities. The illusion engendered by celebrity tweets, for example, provides a glimpse into the inner life of the celebrity, while at the most basic level fans want assurances that the person tweeting or posting to their Facebook wall is who they claim to be. Authenticity is a term that is often bandied about when it comes to social media use by celebrities and other media figures. But it may be that fans or followers simply do not care whether or not it is the "real" celebrity with whom they are communicating. Some communication professionals have suggested that authenticity is a key component of effective communication, as if authenticity makes the celebrity believable—more trustworthy—and in that more credible as spokespersons for brands. Implied in such a position is that celebrities or other influencers are not believable, and we therefore come at this from a position of ambiguity or disbelief.

The book *Advertising in Everyday Life* presents the position that the marketplace is not as stable or controlled as marketers would like it to be. The system, from manufacturer to distribution to retail to promotion, is fraught with varying levels of volatility. It is the marketer that seeks to control each stage of the marketing process. Advertising has historically been a means to control aspects of promotion since the advertiser can control the message and select the medium in which the message will appear. The advertiser can, furthermore, specify a page or time slot when an ad is to appear. And, they can select a celebrity spokesperson or "real life" spokesperson with whom to align the brand. These are all attempts at control. Control has, however, always been a bit of an illusion, and digital technologies and social media platforms have made that desire all the more complicated; authenticity is one aspect of attempting to control the marketplace. The inability of media-related industries to control a text, no matter what form it is in, creates tension and as such becomes one of the elements that brings audiences pleasure as they work to figure out—that is, measure—the celebrity or influencer against what they know or believe they know. A 2017 survey of 2000 individuals in the United States, United Kingdom and Australia concludes that consumers feel they can spot a professionally manufactured image as opposed to one that was generated through user-generated content (UGC).[28] There is the famous statement: "You can fool all the people some of the time and some of the people all the time, but you cannot fool all the people all the time," which may apply to celebrities and other media figures. It is important to emphasize that even UGC is contrived and in that performative—there is pleasure for fans to be had trying to figure all this out. Ideologically this places the fan or follower, as isolated individual, squarely within the neo-liberal worldview, a belief system in which our engagement and participation produce culture. The degree to which that culture is shared remains to be seen, as there is great variability regarding the ways in which individuals use media in their everyday lives.

PERFORMATIVE NATURE OF DIGITAL MEDIA: THE AUTHENTIC SELF VERSUS AUTHENTICATING SELF

In the 2012 Woody Allen movie *To Rome with Love*, academy award winner Roberto Benigni portrays "an ordinary, middle-class Roman plunged arbitrarily into a swirl of media celebrity, hounded by paparazzi and breathlessly interviewed on talk shows."[29] In the movie a TV news reporter, for example, asks him how he likes his toast in the morning and other very mundane questions. For a time, however, he transcends his ordinariness— someone without exceptional talent or abilities—to become a celebrity. He is, in other words, an authentic person placed in exceptional circumstances. Based on the same theme, another character in this movie, Giancarlo, in his everyday life sings in a very professional operatic voice; however, he can only perform in the shower. In order to accommodate the reluctant singer, Allen who portrays a concert promoter in the movie, produces an opera in which the character, played by a genuinely talented opera singer (in real life), performs onstage, but in an absurd twist, in a shower. Both of these instances are send-ups regarding the meaning and significance of celebrity culture in contemporary society. In the first instance, celebrity comes without the requirement of skill, talent or accomplishment; in the second, celebrity comes from talent, but only when the backstage (the shower) is merged with the frontstage. This is not the first time Allen has toyed with notions of celebrity culture. There is a famous scene in the movie *Annie Hall* in which media critic Marshall McLuhan appears from behind a poster to castigate a professor standing in line behind the Allen character, loudly pontificating about McLuhan. And in the movie *The Purple Rose of Cairo*, the character played by actor Jeff Daniels literally steps out of a movie screen to run away with Mia Farrow's character, a movie fan who is sitting in the theater's audience. These movies raise questions regarding authenticity and the place of celebrity in contemporary society. Who qualifies as a celebrity? Does one have to have talent or is being famous for the sake of being famous enough? How does the nature of celebrity affect our understanding of the authentic self versus the authenticating self? Such questions extend to consider what is real versus what is fake and, in line with that, who is authentic or deceitful in contemporary mediated culture?

Kayfabe

The first time I heard of the term Kayfabe, was when I saw it mentioned in a *New York Times* interview with venture capitalist Peter Thiel. It was suggested that Thiel learned the term, which refers to staged events that are offered up as real or true, from the wrestler Hulk Hogan, whose lawsuit against the online publication Gawker Thiel bankrolled. According to the *New York Times* article, "Using two wrestling terms he learned, Mr. Thiel says that many people assumed Mr. Trump, who was then a candidate for President, was "kayfabe" — a move that looks real but is fake. But then his campaign turned into a "shoot" — the word for an unscripted move that suddenly becomes real."[30] It is ironic that these two terms gleaned from a "sport" (heavy on the quotes) that is understood to be fake, but nevertheless fans accept as real enough to be entertaining, should guide aspects of our lives beyond mere entertainment. In this digital age the distinction between what is real and what is not has become blurred. In fact as has been pointed out in this chapter, the distinctions between the two no longer seem relevant.

Breaking Through the Wall

There has always been a metaphoric wall between the celebrity and fan, and as such the connection or relationship was mediated, taking place within the imagination. An exception might be when one attended a concert or other performance. Although in the presence of the celebrity, there is likely no physical connection, no greeting or talk, it might, however, be possible to obtain an autograph before or after the show or, better yet, a selfie with the celebrity. However, much of what we might identify as a social connection is left to thought and fantasy. In the heavily mediated world in which we spend a good deal of our everyday lives, the distinctions between reality and fantasy, exemplified in *The Purple Rose of Cairo* mentioned earlier, become so intertwined that those differences don't mean much; we learn to easily glide between the two worlds. In other words, we live in a world where reality is just one stop on a continuum that ranges from pure fantasy to that which is really real, and everything in between.

Another example of the blurring between celebrity and fans is demonstrated in *Sofia Coppola*'s movie *The Bling Ring*, based on Nancy Jo Sales' reporting of a true story, in which a group of California youngsters broke into the homes of several celebrities to steal their, well, bling (jewelry). The teens' caper was rooted in their desire to become like the celebrity they were robbing, one of the traits of an imaginary social relationship, and it exemplifies the blurring of the lines between reality and fantasy. In yet another example in the movie by actor Joseph Gordon-Levitt *Don Jon*, a young man is tempted to mediate his addiction to Internet pornography with an authentic relationship. Again, we are placed at the intersection of reality and fantasy, or perhaps the intrusion of one into the other. And then there is Spike Jones' foray into imaginary social worlds in the movie *Her* in which Theodore, a socially alienated writer played by actor Joaquin Phoenix, falls in love with his new operating system, which, unlike Apple's Siri, sounds quite human (she is played by actress Scarlett Johansson) and responds intuitively to Theodore's endearment. These are contemporary examples, but we can also look back at Harvey, a 1950 movie starring actor Jimmy Stewart in which his character maintains an imaginary social relationship with a life-size rabbit, Harvey—a relationship he prefers over actual human relationships. It is somewhat ironic that the mythical Hollywood dream factory becomes the primary purveyor of lessons about reality and fantasy.

THE FRONTSTAGE AND BACKSTAGE COLLAPSE

One of the differences between the imaginary social world established and maintained through traditional media and digital media is that with the latter, sometimes under some circumstances individuals can break through the imaginary wall to actually connect with celebrities or other media figures. This was the case of Genie Bouchard, the professional tennis player who posted a tweet in which she declared Atlanta would win the 2017 Super Bowl. A fan tweeted back "If Patriots win we go on a date?" to which she responded "yes" (see Fig. 1.1). As it turns out the Patriots did win the Super Bowl; she did live up to the bet.[31]

The late sociologist Erving Goffman utilized a dramaturgical metaphor to describe frontstage and backstage behavior. The metaphor, even though he developed it in the late 1950s, is applicable in today's era of digital media. The frontstage might describe, in social media parlance, the "performance" one posts on a platform like Facebook, for example; usually one spins a positive light on one's life through words and/or pictures. Historically, the backstage is where the real interaction was located—life with all its warts. Today, however, the distinction between the two has become blurred.[32] Digital media offer a new set of requirements: creating the feeling of direct address in the guise of greater intimacy between the person posting and the viewer, reader or listener, opening up opportunities to interact and perhaps providing opportunities to purchase endorsed products. Celebrities, micro-celebrities or other social influencers intending to create a bond with their fans, followers or friends through digital

Fig. 1.1 Direct message between a celebrity and fan

media platforms must operate within a code of authenticity. But what does that code tell us about digital culture? First, much of our interaction is really nothing more than voyeurism; we get to "see" others in action close up, like Kim Kardashian tweeting to one of her sisters. By that I mean we get to witness the conversation that celebrities engage in with others, perhaps other celebrities. For example, fans get to witness a long-standing Twitter "war" between rapper Kanye West and pop star Taylor Swift, the penultimate moment of which might have been the appearance in a music video of Swift in bed with West and his wife Kim Kardashian; the lyrics made reference to "we might still have sex."[33] As it turns out, the "people" in the video weren't real at all, but were wax figures. With social media like micro-blogging site Twitter, as Marwick and boyd point out, there is no backstage.[34] Therefore, there is no place for the celebrity in this instance to metaphorically rehearse; what takes place on the "stage" of social media. But we should not be deluded into thinking that just because there has been such collapse between the front and backstages this equates with authenticity, which many perceive to be a cornerstone of successful communication, that is, a mechanism of control on social media platforms.

Authenticity, or rather the performance thereof, leads to self-consciousness, which is to suggest that celebrities and other users of social media have to maintain self-awareness as they continually develop their presentational selves—a new requirement of the culture. Self-consciousness takes us out of the realm of the imaginary. That leaves two choices: either to yearn for days in which we could be less self-conscious, like when we were children, or to live within the irony of a faux-authentic culture.[35] As authenticity is being appropriated by the culture industries, thus establishing a new set of cultural requirements, it creates tension as performed authenticity displaces the imagination. In a world dominated by newer media, authenticity serves to displace the imaginary and in its stead promotes the self-conscious act of faux authenticity. Authenticity or lack thereof may represent the yin and yang of contemporary mediated culture; as such, it may also be the cause of much psychological stress. Individuals can offer resistance, but such resistance becomes part of a cultural struggle between the nostalgic yearning for innocence, and in that the lack of self-awareness, and the self-consciousness promoted by today's mediated culture. The feeling of needing to be "on your game," coming up with and posting clever memes, for example, or presenting your manufactured self on a YouTube video or Instagram photo takes a lot of work.

REALITY–FANTASY CONTINUUM

The theory of hyperreality extends to the issue of fake news, which likely had an impact on the 2016 U.S. presidential election and elections in other countries as well. The problem has grown in intensity to the point that several countries—Malaysia and the Czech Republic in particular—have launched efforts to teach citizens to discern the differences between real and fake news. But as Baudrillard would suggest, for many people the differences—for various reasons—just don't matter, because reality is a contested space that is subject to negotiation. Thomas de Zengotita explores the reality-fantasy continuum in his book *Mediated: How the Media Shapes Your World and the Way We Live in It*, in which the author claims that the opposite of real isn't fictional, but rather optional. What he means is that at one end of the continuum, reality is something that must be dealt with; it's not optional. And the freer we are from a mediated world, the more real our world is. One example of the rejection of a mediated environment would be digital media resistance. de Zengotita would agree with Baudrillard's assessment that the simulations that we enjoy are mediated, a term he derives from McLuhan's idea that media stands between us and reality; in other words, media mediates "the way we experience the world." de Zengotita refers to a number of different ways in which reality is depicted: not real to almost real to really real.[36] He describes reality as something that is optional, available in different versions or variations. He presents a spectrum or range of reality in the following:

- Real real
- Observed real
- In-between real real and observed real, edited real real
- Edited observed real, staged real
- Edited staged real
- Staged observed real unique
- Staged observed real repeated

And he described the other end of the spectrum to include the following:

- Staged realistic
- Staged hyperreal
- Overtly unreal realistic

- Covertly unreal realistic, in-between overtly and covertly unreal realistic
- Real unreal
- Unreal real[37]

Within such variations we can begin to think of reality as existing on a continuum. Reality therefore is not an absolute, but rather something that individuals approach tactically. In this era where technologies are portable, with us and on all the time, much of what we consume is mediated, based not only on de Zengotita's long list but also on McLuhan's famous and widely quoted phrase "the medium is the message." Our personal reality is mediated or rather negotiated through the multiple lenses of realities available to us. Sherry Turkle goes so far as to suggest we have two bodies: our physical one and our "technobody," the result of which is a loss of perspective between what is real and what is virtually real.[38] People seek to create authenticity as they pursue the same understanding within others as well. In other words, authenticity is an important part of being human, but as we extend our humanness, we have to ponder what it is like to live in a mediated world that offers extended versions of reality in all the variations listed above. Therefore, how are we to understand parasocial interaction and related imaginary social relationships in an era where truth and falsity blend within varying stages of reality?

MAY I HAVE YOUR ATTENTION PLEASE?

There was a time when celebrities merely sought to be noticed, but they did so at a distance through appearances in legacy media—television, movies and magazines, and perhaps as characters in books. In this age of digital media, the tables have to some degree been turned on their proverbial head, as fans seek to connect to celebrities through Instagram direct messaging or similar features on Twitter and other platforms. Getting the attention of a celebrity is an art form, as some celebrities are likely to have hundreds of thousands if not in some cases many millions of followers. Some celebrities don't follow fans at all, while others will follow many, perhaps hundreds of thousands of fans. On the one hand, it is easy to see with millions of followers that it is unlikely that a celebrity has the wherewithal to respond directly to fans, and it is clearly understood that many celebrities hire individuals and firms to "handle" their social media for them. As Kotenko reports, "You'd have to be particularly witty or obscenely offensive to catch the eye or ire of a celeb, and you'd have to catch them at just the right moment when they've got nothing better to do than scroll through their Instagram account's recent activity."[39] On the other hand, celebrities because of the nature of the entertainment business spend a lot of time waiting around, and so there are opportunities to engage directly with their fans and followers. It is this general understanding that actually promotes an interesting conundrum: we understand that the celebrity may not be the person responding or they most likely will not respond at all, and there is the possibility that they may engage with their fans/followers through some sort of direct messaging. This leads to the "possibility of interaction" that fuels the celebrity-fan social connection. Marwick and boyd, writing about Twitter, state that "There is no singular formula for celebrity practice; it consists of a set of learned techniques that are leveraged differently."[40] Have you ever tweeted at a celebrity, social influencer or media figure, perhaps direct-messaged them? Did they direct-message you back? As you are most likely a follower, did they follow you back? How might that feel, to be followed or messaged? There is little question that it is an uplifting experience for the fan who may for a period of time feel like a celebrity herself or himself.[41] Direct messaging with micro-celebrities involves a slightly different set of requirements or expectations. As the micro-celebrity is likely managing their social media accounts, there is greater assurance that it is the micro-celebrity that is responding, not a hired hand. This distinction is important as it relates to the issue of authenticity. There is an acceptance that with celebrities the messaging may be "fake" in that it might come from someone other than the celebrity herself or himself, or even a bot. But with micro-celebrities the "fakeness" of social media is diminished and the feelings of closeness enhanced. But we delude ourselves if we think the world of the micro-celebrity is any more authentic than that of the celebrity: each of these is a highly manufactured world, constructed through performance that is both contrived and in most instances indirect. By indirect, I mean that while there is the "possibility of interaction," there most likely isn't any direct interaction.

The variations of reality that are available to us suggest that there will be a multiplicity of responses or reactions to the same content, as evidenced through YouTube comments, for example. As such one individual may feel love or admiration toward a particular media figure and another may express disdain. As individuals move between the subjectively real and fantastic, Beverland and Farrelly identify three cues that convey authenticity: control, connection and virtue.[42] First, the researchers describe control as the desire to master one's environment, especially when individuals are working toward self-improvement or self-reliance, which may come from testing the system. Second, connection refers to being part of a community with like-minded others. The collective nature of a fan community, what Gruzd and colleagues refer to as imagined community, would illustrate this point.[43] Third, the researchers refer to virtue as an act of being true to your set of values. This can be seen time and again when fans take on a critical posture regarding what they may see as a celebrity's immoral behavior. Variations are based on personal interests that have been honed over time or visceral reactions in the immediate, as people sometimes degrade celebrities when they cross an ethical or moral line, like selling out for material gain or commercial interests. James Carey's seminal work regarding the ritual view of mass communication has application to the "world" constructed by computer-mediated communication and social media.[44] We can no longer look at communication as a dyad in which there is online and offline communication—the lines are irrevocably blurred between the two. Sherry Turkle, in her book *Alone Together*, describes how everyday digital rituals create a paradox—we are extensively networked and connected, yet deeply self-directed and alone.[45] From a practical point of view, those YouTube comments referred to earlier are mostly like shooting arrows into the wind. Individuals may be connected to a network in the sense that they have watched the same video, but the comments are to the greatest extent self-directed. In this way individuals use their social media presence in order to gain control over their own thoughts and beliefs and in that to better understand themselves within the everyday world in which they live. The ways in which individuals make their way through mediated environments is a social practice, which is to say that individuals employ various tactics that they use in order to make sense of their mediated experiences: they may post or re-post, reply or comment, like or dislike (thumbs up or down). Michel de Certeau described these as "tactics of consumption," which he referred to as the "ingenious ways" in which we deal with everyday life.[46] While de Certeau was not referring to digital media, his ideas do apply. And, as de Certeau was considering various aspects of everyday life, we too can consider consuming media as an aspect of everyday life. Moreover, we can also include the post-mediated experiences of everyday life in which the content that we consume carries over into other things: conversations, thoughts, stream of consciousness, daydreams or nocturnal dreaming, as from time to time we think about or even dream about celebrities and other new media figures. As well, media consumption opens up the possibility to establish and maintain an imaginary social relationship with a celebrity.[47] de Certeau introduced the term "textual poacher" to describe the ways in which individuals appropriate meanings that they glean from media content. By appropriation, he is referring to making the content one's own. He offers the following analogy: Appropriating a media text is like renting an apartment. The apartment may belong to someone else, but the renter will arrange the furniture in order to make the dwelling his or her own. Such appropriation can take place within an individual's inner world of thought, self-talk and imaginings as they continue to make sense of what they consume and through their parasocial interaction. However, within the digital media environment appropriation may be extended outward in the form of reactions or responses posted to a media site, like YouTube comments. Because of the amount of time individuals spend with media, be it traditional media like television or digital screens like smartphones, the significance of the place of media in various aspects of our everyday lives cannot be underestimated.

What is missing from contemporary life that encourages individuals to move between their subjective reality and in that groping for a sense of what is authentic and their imaginary world, sometimes pursuing relationships with imagined others? David Giles, a psychologist who has written extensively on this subject, points out that the imaginary relationship fulfills the inner need for affiliation and companionship.[48] Marwick and boyd would support the idea that affiliation is important. But they maintain that affiliation is a reflection of unequal status. In the instance where Taylor Swift and Kanye West carry on their Twitter war for all to see, it is between two celebrities. Fans can carry on a parallel conversation, but it is just that, parallel not a direct engagement with the celebrity. Having said that, fans do create their own interconnected clusters within the celebrity network where they do process the conversations to which they are privy. It is a strange form of affiliation, but affiliation nonetheless. Perhaps this parallel universe creates the illusion of connection. In a related sense, one reason why fans participate in imaginary relationships can be explained by the concept of anomie, the personal alienation that results from a breakdown in societal norms. When individuals cannot find their place in society without clear rules, they may look to others—in this case, celebrities and other media figures—to help guide them. Aloneness and feelings of alienation may indeed be key motivators for fans to engage in mediated social connections with celebrities.[49] The digital media environment provides an ideal social sphere for individuals to cling ever so tightly to celebrities as one suitable replacement for traditional relationships in order to find friendship, moral grounding and advice, just to name a few ways in which celebrities fill the gap in everyday social life. But this level of intimacy is at a distance—mediated—perhaps it is nonetheless satisfying. Through the use of digital media, the difference between an imaginary relationship and an actual one is extended, as social media have the unique ability to convey a sense of connectedness when communication is perceived as sincere, which separates it from the ways in which fans connect to celebrities through legacy forms of media, for example, television. Authenticity and sincerity are qualities that are usually assigned to non-media relationships. In this sense, reading a magazine article about a celebrity does not require the same amount of personal investment as a tweet.[50] In other words, digital media provide opportunities more so than legacy media to interact with media figures and to delve deeper into the more private aspects of their lives; participation in social media demands greater disclosure on the part of those that participate. And, as has been pointed out, mediated social connections may result in greater recognition for the fan. In this way fans communicate not necessarily directly with, but along with, celebrities and their social networks.

An important aspect of the individual's meaning-making system is not so much about whether or not the celebrity is trustworthy, as a certain amount of gamesmanship is acceptable in the authenticating process. Part of the game of celebrity and micro-celebrity is that of routinely presenting themselves in the media. It is their routine presence that over time leads to a sense of certainty. Certainty in this sense does not relate to trust, but assurance that the celebrity will be there. This may seem superfluous, but in a world that lacks certainty where relationships come and go or exist on a superficial plane, routine postings on social media lend a great deal of assurance about the celebrity, influencer or media figure and their network. Certainty has to be measured against a sense of skepticism that also operates within mediated social connections, as there is a natural tension that exists between the mediated connection based on the possibility for interaction and the illusion of intimacy. After all, the mediated social connection is just that, one rooted in a fantasy as opposed to one based on reason or rationality or for that matter objective reality. Therefore the individual's willingness to make the leap beyond reason is indicative of the likelihood that the fan will seek affiliation, closeness or identification with others.

Even when the development of a mediated social connection is inspired through traditional media experiences, such relationships are marked by volatility. In that sense appearances in television advertisements, for example, provide a signal to the fan that the celebrity primarily known for appearing in movies is moving up the ladder of success or conversely that the celebrity's career is on the wane. As the imaginary relationship is one-sided, the relationship operates within the fan that must work through the tension. Should something happen that might signal a lack of certainty, a failed relationship, immoral or illegal activity, poor performance or a career misstep that causes a shift, perhaps questioning the validity of the relationship, the fan can easily move on.[51] We need look no further than the spate of Hollywood figures, prominent news reporters, TV hosts, politicians and corporate types who have fallen from grace because of their egregious involvement in sexual harassment and abuse. A fan standing outside the NBC Today studios reported the shock of learning the news about Matt Lauer's firing. She referred to Lauer as an "icon." "But, I appreciate the fact that they are trying to clean up the workplace for women, especially," she added. "But I am shocked. I mean he seems like such an upstanding guy."[52] Finsterwalder et al. raise the question as to whether transgressive celebrities can redeem their standing among fans. They maintain that those fans engaged in an imaginary social relationship are more likely to forgive the celebrity as such imaginary relationships are similar to those of actual friends, whom people may also be more likely to forgive.[53] The researchers cite cyclist Lance Armstrong, actress Kristen Stewart and golfer Tiger Woods as examples of celebrities working to redeem themselves. In this sense, engagement in an imaginary social relationship is quite dynamic, fueled by the 24-hour news cycle brought about by content providers like TMZ.com or PerezHilton.com, among many others. Fans weave a web as they traverse the Internet clicking from a search engine to gossip blog to a celebrity's Facebook page, Instagram account and onward. There is more than a rhythmic dance going on with regard to the pseudo-physical experience—performative friendship—of moving from web address to web address, or television to web, as individuals grow more comfortable with simultaneous media use. There is an intertextual quality to the experience as news, information and product promotion on one website feeds off of and builds on information gleaned from another to create a dance of elaboration in the mind through which the individual constructs an interior social world. Elaboration refers to thoughts, fantasies and self-talk in which individuals engage as they consume media and afterward. Within the boundaries of this pseudo-social interaction, individuals engage in identity formation as they engage with the imaginary, extending the borders between objective reality and the imaginary. As such sometimes the inner world leaks out in the form of tweets, re-tweets, comments and direct messaging. The space in between is where culture does its work, as the individual judges and evaluates others and themselves within a social media system that paradoxically connects people to celebrities that we do not know who offer the illusion of social connection and make us feel closer to our authentic self, as we move from self-consciousness to unconscious interior worlds. It is in this way that authenticity does not equate with reality, and, conversely, reality in all its variations does not equate with authenticity.

CONCLUSION

This chapter explored three principles that guide mediated social connections with celebrities and the ways in which newer digital media impact mediated social connections—place, imagination and togetherness. These concepts help to explain how mediated connections work in Western culture and some of the work fans and followers do within those pseudo-relationships. Our ability to be, in our minds, in more than one place at a time enables individuals to fluidly move through a complex media environment that is both fixed and mobile. As such we are both our bodies and our technobodies, as technology becomes an extension of ourselves. The imaginary worlds we create through fantasy, stream of consciousness thinking, daydreaming and nocturnal dreams demonstrate how celebrities, micro-celebrities and media figures become intertwined in everyday life and sometimes in decision making. And, while some individuals appear to have hundreds of friends through myriad web connections, fans use of likes or dislikes, @replies or comments on social media in reality are ways of maintaining those weakened social connections in greater isolation. We may participate in networks, but those networks are loose and the connections weak as we communicate not with the group, but rather within clusters, by merely shooting proverbial arrows into the wind or thinking to ourselves in order to confirm that the world is as it should be.

Our earliest understanding of celebrities was based on the notion of emulation. That is why in the early part of the twentieth century, celebrities began to appear—as they still do—in advertising. The development of media like radio and television, as well as gossip magazines, what we now

refer to as legacy media, allowed the relationships with celebrities to proliferate and become a part of people's everyday lives. We thought about,
dreamed about and spoke to one another about celebrities, as they make
great fodder for gossip and as we find other uses for them in the course of
everyday life. With the development of the Internet 30 years ago and the
World Wide Web 25 years ago, along with the emergence of a participatory culture in the 1990s, individuals gained the ability to create their own
content that held out the possibility of connecting directly with the celebrity, communicating along parallel lines or perhaps even becoming a celebrity, like some Instagrammers or YouTube stars. Newer social media have
brought about additional changes as fans begin to redefine what it means
to be a friend, teacher or lover including the possibility of achieving a personal connection with a celebrity. In a quest for authenticity, social media
require of users a higher level of disclosure and interactions that hold out
the possibility of actual connection, extending the notion of an imaginary
social relationship as it evolves into a mediated social connection. But
these are not absolutes, as mediated social connections happen for some of
the people some of the time, but imaginary social relationships are ubiquitous. Can you name ten media figures? Can you then identify one from
your list that has significant meaning to you, perhaps one you greatly
admire? The range of experience with celebrities may be superficial or
deep and abiding, and sometimes we forgive their transgressions. But the
networks through which they and we engage are what we have in today's
mediated world where the mobile device has become an extension of our
physical being: it's always on and always near us. Fear of missing out
(FOMO) is our anxiety; it keeps Millennials, in particular, checking their
mobile devices 157 times a day.[54] Belief in what is real or not is hard to
come by these days; however, for the broader culture mediated social connections provide a means by which individuals can grapple with topics,
issues, products and people that are of interest to them. Mediated social
connections serve a purpose as we move from the subjectively real to the
imagined and back again. In this chapter I have laid the groundwork for
understanding the shift that has taken place as fans, friends and followers
began to engage with digital media. Chapter 2 provides greater context to
the shift in our relationship to celebrities that has taken place with the
advent of digital media. It explores historically how notions of celebrity
have changed and it delves deeper into the theoretical underpinnings of
how imaginary social relationships evolve in the age of digital media to
become mediated social connections.

NOTES

1. Reported by CBS News 2010. What Jonathan Metz went through has been described as a MacGyver moment. The web is replete with examples of such moments, which are defined as a time when you "improvised an excellent solution to a problem using non-traditional materials, techniques, or tools." (http://sqlblog.com/blogs/kevin_kline/archive/2010/03/29/mac-gyver-moments.aspx)
2. Hoffner, C. (2008). Parasocial and Online Social Relationships. In *The Handbook of Children, Media and Development*, edited by Sandra Calvert and Barbara Wilson, Chichester, West Sussex, UK: Blackwell Publishing Ltd.
3. Horton, D. & Wohl, R. (1956). Mass Communication and Para-social Interaction: Observations on Intimacy at a Distance. *Psychiatry*, 19, pp. 215–29.
4. Rojek, C. (2016). *Presumed Intimacy: Para-Social Relationship in Media, Society and Celebrity Culture*. Cambridge, UK: Polity Press.
5. Caughey, J. L. (1984). *Imaginary Social Worlds: A Cultural Approach*. Lincoln, NE: University of Lincoln Press.
6. Alperstein, N. (1991). "Imaginary Social Relationships with Celebrities Appearing in Television Commercials." *Journal of Broadcasting & Electronic Media* 35 (1): 43–58. During the subsequent years I have conducted ethnographic interviews with more than 500 individuals regarding the nature of their imaginary relationships.
7. Milgram, S. (1971). The frozen world of the familiar stranger, an interview with Carol Tavris. *Psychology Today*. 8:1, pp. 70–80.
8. Marwick, A. & boyd, d. (2011). To See and Be Seen: Celebrity Practice on Twitter. *Convergence: The International Journal of Research into New Media Technologies* 17(2), pp. 139–158. DOI: https://doi.org/10.1177/1354856510394539.
9. Some television programs, like NBC's *The Voice*, have created apps and encouraged social media use during consumption of the program in an attempt to keep attention focused on the program even if and when viewers turn away from the TV screen to focus on the smartphone screen.
10. The Matrix. (1999). Sci Fi Quotes.net. Retrieved from: http://scifiquotes. net/quotes/122_Ignorance-Is-Bliss
11. In a survey of this phenomenon, Barbara Vann and I performed a content analysis of more than 200 dreams. More than half the respondents reported dreaming of a celebrity, and perhaps as important celebrities who were represented in respondents' dreams shed their celebrity role (although they were recognized as a celebrity) to become a friend of the dreamer. Alperstein, N. and Vann, B. (1997). Star gazing: A socio-cultural approach to the study of dreaming about media figures. *Communication Quarterly*, 45:3.

12. Miller, S. (March 24, 2016). A World Showcase of Unforgettable Shopping at Epcot – France Pavilion. Disney.Go.com. Retrieved from: https://disneyparks.disney.go.com/blog/2016/03/a-world-showcase-of-unforgettable-shopping-at-epcot-france-pavilion/
13. Humphries, M. (July 17, 2016). Two Pokemon Go players fall off a cliff, while two more are shot at. Retrieved from: http://www.geek.com/tech/two-pokemon-go-players-fall-off-a-cliff-while-two-more-are-shot-at-1662203/
14. Johnson, E. (September 19, 2016). "Why Pokémon Go's John Hanke says augmented reality is better than virtual reality." Recode.net. Retrieved from: http://www.recode.net/2016/9/19/12965508/pokemon-go-john-hanke-augmented-virtual-reality-ar-recode-decode-podcast
15. Dove Evolution Advertisement. (n.d.). Retrieved from: http://selfesteem.dove.us/Articles/Video/Evolution_video_how_images_of_beauty_are_manipulated_by_the_media.aspx
16. Evolution. YouTube.com. Retrieved from: https://www.youtube.com/watch?v=iYhCn0jf46U
17. Alperstein, N. (2015). Social Comparison of Idealized Female Images and the Curation of Self on Pinterest. *The Journal of Social Media in Society*, 4:2, December. Retrieved from: http://www.thejsms.org/index.php/TSMRI/article/view/82/57
18. Dove Real Beauty Project. (n.d.). Celebrity culture: Sorting the real reality from hyper reality. Retrieved from: http://selfesteem.dove.us/Articles/Written/Celebrity_culture_sorting_the_real_reality_from_hyper_reality.aspx
19. Gilmore, J. & Pine, J. (2007). *Authenticity: What Consumers Really Want.* Mass: Harvard Business Review Press. p. 43.
20. Google nGram. (n.d.). Authenticity. Retrieved from: https://books.google.com/ngrams/graph?content=authenticity&year_start=1800&year_end=2016&corpus=15&smoothing=3&share=&direct_url=t1%3B%2Cauthenticity%3B%2Cc0
21. Hempel, J. (February 6, 2012, February 6). Three Degrees of Reid Hoffman. *Fortune.* 165:2, pp. 22–24.
22. Fuller, S. (n.d.). Authenticity, Reality and Being. IAI News. Retrieved from: https://iainews.iai.tv/articles/authenticity-reality-and-being-auid-615
23. Marwick & boyd point out there is no backstage. Therefore, there is no place for the celebrity to metaphorically rehearse. Marwick, A. and boyd, d. (2011). "To See and Be Seen: Celebrity Practice on Twitter." *Convergence.* 17(2), pp. 139–158.
24. Cooke, R. (March 15, 2015). So You've Been Publicly Shamed and Is Shame Necessary? review – think before you tweet. The Guardian. Retrieved from: https://www.theguardian.com/books/2015/mar/15/publicly-shamed-jon-ronson-is-shame-necessary-jennifer-jacquet-review-think-before-you-tweet

25. Lieberman, C. (November 15, 2017). JStor Daily. Don't Buy into the Authenticity Scam. Retrieved from: https://daily.jstor.org/dont-buy-authenticity-scam/
26. Marshall, P. D. (2016). *The Celebrity Persona Pandemic*. Minneapolis: University of Minnesota Press.
27. Ibid., p. 12.
28. Stakla.com (2017). The 2017 Consumer Content Report: Influence in the Digital Age. Retrieved from: https://stackla.com/go/2017-consumer-content-report-influence-in-digital-age/
29. Scott, A. O. (June 21, 2012). When in Rome, Still an Anxious New York Intellectual: Woody Allen's Latest, "To Rome with Love." *The New York Times*. Retrieved from: http://www.nytimes.com/2012/06/22/movies/woody-allens-latest-to-rome-with-love.html
30. Dowd, M. (January 11, 2017). Peter Thiel, Trump's Tech Pal, Explains Himself. *The New York Times*. Retrieved from: https://www.nytimes.com/2017/01/11/fashion/peter-thiel-donald-trump-silicon-valley-technology-gawker.html
31. Cnn.com. (February 16, 2017). Eugenie Bouchard takes fan on date after losing Twitter bet. Retrieved from: http://edition.cnn.com/2017/02/16/tennis/eugenie-bouchard-super-bowl-date/
32. Goffman, E. (1956). *The Presentation of Self in Everyday Life*. New York: Random House Publishers.
33. Cosmopolitan magazine. (November 10, 2017). A timeline of Taylor Swift and Kanye West's feud. Retrieved from: http://www.cosmopolitan.com/uk/entertainment/news/a41965/taylor-swift-kanye-west-feud-timeline/
34. Marwick, A. & boyd, d. (2011). "To See and Be Seen: Celebrity Practice on Twitter." *Convergence*. 17(2), pp. 139–158.
35. Raisanen, M. (March 7, 2012). The Current Rage In Branding: Fake Authenticity Is Now A-Okay. Co.Design. Retrieved from: https://www.fastcodesign.com/1669220/the-current-rage-in-branding-fake-authenticity-is-now-a-okay
36. de Zengotita, T. (2006). *Mediated: How the Media Shapes Your World and the Way You Live in It*. Bloomsbury USA. p. 8.
37. Ibid., pp. 20–21.
38. Turkle, S. (1997). *Life on the Screen: Identity in the Age of the Internet*. New York: Simon & Schuster.
39. Kotenko, J. (January 13, 2016). This is why your Instagram idol will never, ever reply to you, The Daily Dot. Retrieved from: https://www.dailydot.com/debug/instagram-push-notifications-8m-followers/
40. Marwick, A. & boyd, d. (2011). To See and Be Seen. *Convergence: The International Journal of Research into New Media Technologies* 17(2), p. 144.
41. Ibid., p. 150.
42. Beverland, M. & Farrelly, F. (2010). The Quest for Authenticity in Consumption: Consumers' Purposive Choice of Authentic Cues to

Shape Experienced Outcomes. *Journal of Consumer Research*, 36:5 (February), pp. 838–856. Retrieved from: http://www.jstor.org/stable/10.1086/615047

43. Gruzd, A., Wellman, B., & Takhteyev, Y. (2011). Imagining Twitter as an Imagined Community. *American Behavioral Scientist*, 55:10, pp.1294–1318. Retrieved from: https://journals.sagepub.com/doi/abs/10.1177/0002764211409378

44. Carey, J. (1992). *Communication as Culture, Revised Edition: Essays on Media and Society*. New York: Routledge Publishers.

45. Turkle, S. (2011). *Alone Together: Why We Expect More from Technology and Less from Each Other*. New York: Basic Books.

46. De Certeau, M. (1980). *The Practice of Everyday Life*. California: The University of California Press.

47. Alperstein, N. (2003). *Advertising in Everyday Life*. New Jersey: Hampton Press.

48. Giles, D. 2002. "Parasocial interaction: A review of the literature and a model for future research." *Media Psychology*, 4, pp. 279–305.

49. Although they looked at the traditional medium of television, in particular favored television programs, Derrick et al. developed the social surrogacy hypothesis to explain how loneliness motivates individuals to engage in imaginary relationships. However, these researchers draw no conclusions as to whether the phenomenon is maladaptive or provides positive social support when needed. Derrick, J., Gabriel, S. & Hugenberg, K. (2009). Social surrogacy: How favored television programs provide the experience of belonging. *Journal of Experimental Social Psychology*. 45, pp. 352–362.

50. Marwick and boyd point out that an article appearing in a magazine does not require the same amount of disclosure by a celebrity as a post on Twitter (2011).

51. Gallagher, B.J. (March 18, 2010) Celebrities Behaving Badly. HuffPost.com. Retrieved from: https://www.huffingtonpost.com/bj-gallagher/celebrities-behaving-badl_b_311625.html

52. Norman, G. (November 29, 2017). Matt Lauer firing stuns 'Today' show viewers outside Rockefeller Center. FoxNews.com. Retrieved from: http://www.foxnews.com/entertainment/2017/11/29/matt-lauer-firing-stuns-today-show-viewers-outside-rockefeller-center.html

53. Finsterwalder, J., Yeeb, T., & Tombsc, A. (2017). Would you forgive Kristen Stewart or Tiger Woods or maybe Lance Armstrong? Exploring consumers' forgiveness of celebrities' transgressions. *Journal of Marketing Management*, 2017 33:13–14, pp. 1204–1229. https://doi.org/10.1080/0267257X.2017.1382553

54. Social Media Week. (May 31, 2016). Millennials Check Their Phones More Than 157 Times Per Day. Retrieved from: https://socialmediaweek.org/newyork/2016/05/31/millennials-check-phones-157-times-per-day/

CHAPTER 2

A Model of Mediated Social Connections

I am going to tell you a deep, dark secret. When I was 14 years old, Courtney Love was my idol. I got dressed every morning before high school by carefully layering ripped fishnets over purple tights, fastening the clasps on my vintage baby doll dress, combing out my peroxided hair, and adjusting my nose ring. The goal was this: if Courtney Love were to come to my high school and pick the coolest person there, she would surely pick me. It never occurred to me to wonder why she would be dropping by a small town in Rhode Island, or why, if she did so, she would hold some kind of high school fashion show. I knew only that I was dressing to impress. (Leah Carroll reflection on her review of the book Fame (Carroll, L. (December 27, 2010). From "The Iliad" to "Us Weekly": The History of Celebrity Gossip. The Atlantic. Retrieved from: https://www.theatlantic.com/entertainment/archive/2010/12/from-the-iliad-to-us-weekly-the-history-of-celebrity-gossip/67997/))

This fantasy is quite typical of an imaginary social relationship. It is one that is spawned by the mundaneness of living in a small town coupled with the possibility of attracting the attention—that is, being recognized by someone who is famous—of a celebrity. Whether it is fantasizing about being called up on stage to sing a few songs with Bruce at a Springsteen concert or imagining being invited to a celebrity's party to mingle with other famous people, such fantasies abound in the culture. However, they may go beyond mere fleeting reverie and are anything but trivial, cast aside like last night's dream, which, too, might have been about a celebrity. Our

© The Author(s) 2019
N. M. Alperstein, *Celebrity and Mediated Social Connections*,
https://doi.org/10.1007/978-3-030-17902-1_2

imaginary relationships serve real purpose beyond lifting us out of the doldrums, as celebrities and other media figures play important roles in our everyday lives. Although not focused on media or celebrity fantasies, the psychiatrist and psychoanalyst Ethel Person in her book *By Force of Fantasy* writes: "fantasy is as essential as air, forming the medium or the ether in which all the other activities of mind take place."[1] Placing celebrity in the context of fantasy, Tom Payne writes in his book *Fame: What the Classics Tell Us About Our Culture of Celebrity* that our relationship to celebrity or fame in contemporary society operates in similar fashion as it did in prior times, perhaps dating back to the ancient Greeks.[2] Payne draws analogies, for example, between Britney Spears shaving her head and Joan of Arc, and he relates actor Heath Ledger's death to Goethe's Faust. In other words, our connection to celebrity and fantasy is deeply rooted in culture.

In this chapter a model of mediated social connections will be explored as a contemporary extension of imaginary social relationships based on parasocial interaction with digital media. The chapter looks historically at the notion of celebrity, fame and media figures and uses as the starting point the theoretical model of imaginary social relationships proposed by John Caughey and the process of parasocial interaction developed by Horton and Wohl. The chapter provides an understanding of how these ideas may be applied to a world in which digital media change our relationship, not only to technologies, but also to people we may admire, like, love or perhaps hate—people we know about, but really do not know.

Fred Inglis writes in *A Short History of Celebrity* that the concept of fame was only beginning to be "recognized and talked about in public" in the eighteenth century and that the "effects and conditions of celebrity" included "public recognizability, the interplay of envy, admiration, generous acclaim, malicious denigration, prurient attentiveness, swift indifference."[3] To a great extent these conditions hold true today. Inglis distinguishes between fame and celebrity; the latter he suggests "is either won or conferred by the mere fact of a person's being popularly acknowledged, familiarly recognized, attended to, selected as a topic for gossip, speculation, emulation, envy, groundless affection, or dislike."[4] While there are some similarities between fame and celebrity, in contemporary society we tend to look at celebrity as a product of media. Daniel Boorstin, writing in his book *The Image: A Guide to Pseudo-Events in America*, described a celebrity as simply someone "known for their well knownness."[5] And offering a more contemporary view of celebrity, psychologist David Giles argues that fame was transformed through the development of media technology into celebrity. The proliferation of media—both legacy and digital media— gave rise to a concurrent increase in the number of celebrities; in other words, in contemporary culture, media and celebrity go hand in hand. It is fair to suggest, therefore, that with the development of the Internet—the first truly new medium in more than half a century—the potential for producing celebrities continues to grow as digital media platforms and technologies proliferate and more people generate their own content. And, since the introduction of the smartphone in the mid-1990s, we can take celebrities with us wherever we go; as such, celebrity has become portable as well as ubiquitous.

CELEBRITY AND NEW MEDIA FIGURES

Although the concept of being famous may have been around since the 1700s and the term celebrity may have slowly emerged along with the advent of mass communication, sometimes the term celebrity, as one who may have some talent—singer, actor, sports figure, among others—is extended to include media figures that may refer to someone like a journalist, corporate spokesperson, blogger or vlogger, or other micro-celebrity, and it may refer to someone who is thrust into the spotlight because of their connection to a news event. One such media figure would be Nadya Suleman, who was euphemistically referred to as the Octomom, because in 2009 she gave birth to octuplets and experienced a subsequent rise in notoriety.[6] But there are many other individuals who for a period of time become prominent in popular culture for myriad reasons, ranging from Bernie Madoff to Charles Manson and beyond. In the contemporary usage, the distinction between the terms famous, media figure or celebrity seems to matter little, as the term celebrity has become a generally understood way to categorize both those individuals who exhibit a special talent or quality and those who, like an astronaut returning from the space station, become famous for a time for what they have accomplished, and these individuals, perhaps because of what has happened to them, are thrust for a time into prominence as newsmakers. In sum, celebrity may be the broad term that refers to actresses and actors, musicians, athletes, politicians, writers, YouTube stars, newsmakers and fictional characters as well. However, when we see their celebrity play out on digital media, the term digital media figure might be appropriately applied.

Beyond defining celebrity, because celebrity is so closely intertwined with the development of media, what is of interest is how the nature of fan to celebrity relationship has changed with the development of newer technologies and social media platforms, like Instagram, Snapchat, Facebook, Twitter and Pinterest. It is perhaps obvious that in order to be a celebrity one must have fans, a shortened version of the word fanatics and followers. According to the *Merriam-Webster's* dictionary, the word fan showed up in the English language in the late seventeenth century, but it disappeared for the next 200 years—for unknown reasons—until its re-emergence in the nineteenth century. The word was used in reference to "devoted observer" or participants in sports.[7] We can see the devoted observer in the extreme when in 1947 Ruth Ann Steinhagen shot the Philadelphia Phillies first baseman Eddie Waitkus. According to her obituary, Ruth Ann had a penchant for falling in love with unattainable men. Her story, based on an imaginary relationship gone awry, was immortalized in Bernard Malamud's novel *The Natural*, later turned into a movie.[8] In an autobiographical sketch Steinhagen wrote:

> I used to go to all the ballgames just to watch him. We used to wait for them to come out of the clubhouse after the game, and all the time I was watching him, I was building in my mind the idea of killing him. As time went on, I just became nuttier and nuttier about the guy. I knew I would never get to know him in a normal way, so I kept thinking, I will never get him, and if I can't have him, nobody else can. Then I decided I would kill him. I didn't know how or when, but I knew I would kill him.[9]

Ruth Steinhagen's obsession extended beyond the extreme admiration that is highly acceptable and prized by celebrities, but it was more than being a fan, as Waitkus was her imaginary love interest. She was engaged in an imaginary social relationship. What makes fandom different in the era of digital media is the ability to interact with a new media figure, even if it is on the simplest basis of pressing the like button.

TACTILE TO SYMBOLIC CONNECTIONS

Scholars began to get a better understanding of fan-celebrity deeper connections when in the mid-1950s two British researchers introduced the concept of parasocial interaction. Parasocial interaction certainly predated Horton and Wohl's research, as people first began to attend sixteenth-century market fairs and theatrical performances that provided fairgoers with ample opportunities to engage their imaginations—something that continues to this day through the use of legacy media and into the use of digital technologies and social media platforms. Indeed magic and wonder have always been a part of performance and keys to understanding what drives us toward the inner world of imagination. Historian T. Jackson Lears points out that for centuries commerce was connected to a carnival atmosphere, the fantastic and the magical.[10] The early modern period (1500–1800) brought about the merger of the religious carnival and the market fair. "The market fair brought locally rooted townsfolk and peasants into contact with the exotic and the bizarre: with magicians and midgets, quacks and alchemists, transient musicians and acrobats; peddlers of soap from Turkey, needles from Spain, and looking-glasses from Venice."[11] As Western societies developed, the market fair gave way to the general store where, for example, one could scoop out a pound of crackers from the cracker barrel. The storeowner would simply dump soda crackers in a barrel, without packaging, logos and associated promotion. In other words, all crackers were created equal. And, consumers could see the crackers up close, perhaps even touch or taste them. As commerce grew there was a shift from a tactile environment where you could see and touch the crackers to one that was mediated. As such connections to goods became more symbolic: you could see the cloth of a dress in a late nineteenth-century magazine, but you could not touch it. Crackers were no longer in a barrel, but packaged and sealed for freshness. Packaging and the shift to a national distribution system, based on the development of the transcontinental railway in the United States led to a shift from the tactile connection (I can see or touch the crackers in the barrel) to a symbolic connection (I can see the sealed box of crackers with the brand or logo on the outside). As mass production began to allow for greater quantities of products that could be shipped across the United States, there was a need to distinguish one "brand" of cracker from another. In order to create distinction, advertising became a necessity. That is why toward the end of the nineteenth century we began to see the beginnings of branding, which led to the use of early celebrities, including silent film stars and professional athletes, in advertising. Lears states: "It wasn't until the early twentieth century that the rise of corporate advertising brought a disembodiment of abundance imagery, as the carnivalesque celebration of fleshly excess was streamlined into an exaltation of industrial efficiency, and the process of productivity became a model for the organization of everyday life."[12] The industrial efficiency to which Lears alludes relates to the symbolic nature of the celebrity system and the ways in which we align ourselves with celebrity images that serve as a symbolic short cut to being an insider. For example, the cinematographic qualities of much advertising or entertainment provides a magical backdrop, as scenes dissolve, fade or cut to another scene in a gauzy haze—although we take such mediated structures for granted, they do have magical qualities that can transport a person to another place. Advertising is a case in point, as promotional messages utilize creative techniques that encourage elaboration—thinking, stream of consciousness or fantasizing—but such commercial messages are created in such a way as to produce a particular interpretation of a message: buy this or that product or service. However, all advertising, as persuasively constructed as it is, is subject to aberrant readings. Looking at it another way, we may be beckoned into the magical world of advertisement, but we may not interpret it as given. Individuals may not give in to the preferred reading or interpretation of a commercial message, and that goes for celebrities who appear in such intentional media content. Paradoxically, advertising in particular utilizes magical qualities to induce fantasy, but as it does, we may enter into an imaginary world taking us away from the selling message. Advertising, because it is such a highly constructed environment, limited to short forms of 15, 30 or 60 seconds or a single page in print, with very specific intentions, is an extreme example, but the same goes for other media content without such specific intentions.

As we moved forward in time and with the development of digital media, particularly social media, at the point that we entered a Web 2.0 culture a shift took place whereby communication became interactive, specifically when individuals could directly participate in the conversation through likes or dislikes, comments or shares. As culture moved in the previous century from the tactile to the symbolic, in the current era of digital media, we have moved to a newer form of tactility. If the sensory feedback associated with tactility relates to touch, then the haptic feedback we get from engaging with technology is kinesthetic, like the vibration you feel through your iPhone, or through the touch of a keyboard, mouse or merely swiping. Tactile refers to the touch we sense on the surface when holding fabric, for example, but kinesthetic refers to the use of muscles, tendons, joints and fingers to gain feeling. Whether virtual, augmented, immersive or mixed reality will eventually return us to yet another version of tactile sensation remains to be seen. But what is left in this current haptic media environment is a way to "touch" celebrities through the "tools" given to us on social media platforms: direct messaging, commenting and liking, among others. In this manner, individuals have a voice in what is going on in the culture, although it may not feel very magical, as the Internet and apps provide the space and encourage people to play out their emotions online as opposed to in their heads. However, it's important to understand that both may exist simultaneously, as digital media experiences may extend from haptic activity to the imaginary. Often we hear about the lack of filters in social media: people act before they think, although in this instance, thinking as a rational process gives way to engagement experienced in the context of or after consuming media content through commenting and messaging, among other emotional outlets. The shift that began to take place in the early to mid-2000s with the development of social media and user-generated content (UGC) is one in which there is greater opportunity for fans, followers and friends to participate more fully in digital media and the lives of celebrities than they were in the past, often beyond the brief autograph signing that has been one way of directly interacting with a celebrity.

PARASOCIAL INTERACTION

British researchers Horton and Wohl in their 1956 scholarly article "Mass Communication and Para-social Interaction" first introduced the concept of parasocial interaction. The researchers posited that consuming media gave the illusion of an actual face-to-face relationship with a newsreader, talk show host or weather reporter, among others. Parasocial interaction was a concept that was one way with someone the individual does not know, between fan and celebrity. Such interaction can be viewed as the emotional response to a talk show host who might look directly into the camera and appear on the screen as if they were directly addressing the viewer. The key to parasocial interaction is the emotional identification with the media figure. This phenomenon can be seen when children are playing in front of a television: when someone in a commercial, for example, looks directly out of the screen as if delivering a message directly to the viewers, kids will look up from their play as if called to attention. But the phenomenon is not just based on a singular instance of direct address, as there may be a give and take as the performance continues to build through parasocial interaction. In the course of everyday mediated life, such parasocial interactions become routine behavior. Although as this was a mediated communication, there was no obligation on the part of the viewer to maintain a connection; however, the individual may elaborate in her or his own mind regarding the performer or performance, in which case a parasocial relationship might ensue. Of course, the so-called relationship was one way, one sided and non-dialectic, based on the illusion of intimacy. There is the possibility, as psychologist Charles Fernyhough describes in *The Voices Within*, that sometimes a celebrity or character can "get inside our head" and speak to us within an inner dialogue.[13] Predating the early days of television when Horton and Wohl developed their theory, radio performers would often sign off at the end of the program by directly addressing listeners. For example, Burns and Allen, a comedy team that transitioned from radio to television, would end with George Burns directing his partner to address the audience by saying: "Say Goodnight Gracie." And, conversely, fans of late night TV, at the end of the last talk show they've watched, will often say to the TV "good night Jimmy" in reference to Jimmy Kimmel (or any other late night TV host) as they did when Johnny Carson was the last person they saw before going to bed. The parasocial interaction in Horton and Wohl's conception primarily took place within the context of viewing, and such interaction becomes part of the routine of their everyday life. Predating Horton and Wohl's research on television and parasocial interaction, the sociologist Robert K. Merton wrote about singer and radio star Kate Smith's ability to raise tens of millions of dollars to support the American efforts in the Second World War. Her ability at persuasion was based, according to Merton, on the audience's emotional involvement and strong identification with the singer.[14]

It was not until 1984 that anthropologist John Caughey, in his book *Imaginary Social Worlds*, introduced the term imaginary social relationship to describe a similar phenomenon, but he extended the concept to consider that fans may carry the relationship beyond the viewing or listening experience into their everyday lives, perhaps embellishing it along the way. He included television and movie stars, and popular singers as well as politicians, fictional characters and news figures.[15] Like many anthropologists, Caughey spent time studying distant cultures: he spent time studying the cultures of Pacific islanders and in northern Pakistan. Among the things he recognized was the high regard that these non-Western cultures had for the imaginary, fantasies, stream of consciousness and nocturnal dreams. Upon his return to the United States he turned to American informants, including schizophrenic imaginary systems at a psychiatric ward. He continued to collect data from hundreds of informants whose imaginary experiences were distilled into his theoretical proposition that fans formed relationships with celebrities the fan did not actually know. These imaginary social relationships, he maintained, paralleled actual social relationships, especially with regard to the roles those celebrities could play in the everyday lives of fans. Vital to our understanding is that such relationships were taking place in the imagination of the individual; issues like authenticity and sincerity considered in Chap. 1 were not vital, as one could have an imaginary relationship with someone who was inauthentic. After all, this is a world of fantasy that extends from stream of consciousness to nocturnal dreams in which celebrities play a role; authenticity is not a necessary antecedent to forming an imaginary social relationship. The process through which fans engage with celebrities through media like television is similar to the ways in which audiences engaged with actors in the theater. Although in a theater we are members of an audience, when the lights go down, we are alone. We may be having a common experience, but that experience is quite subjective.

Through my own ethnographic research, I've been able to describe, for example, three potential ways in which fans invoke their imagination while they consume media: blanking, fading and lucid thinking. Blanking refers to the fan that literally blanks out or is swept away into their reverie as they watch television or a movie, for example. In this way the fan develops an attention strategy using cues from the screen—perhaps a celebrity—to cut to (to utilize the language of cinema) a scene in their own mind upon which they might elaborate internally. Within this process, fans feel the abrupt pull of reality as an additional cue (shift to commercial, shift back from commercial or change of scene) interrupts their train of thought. The second way in which fans connect to the imaginary during media consumption is by fading out and fading back in to pay attention to the screen, or perhaps something else draws them back. I am again invoking the language of cinema to describe the way in which fans more slowly lose consciousness regarding what is before their eyes, as they drift inward toward their own imaginary world. There may be a psychological discomfort about being "away" rather than a particular cue that draws the fan back to the screen. In the final process the fan is in a metaphoric sense in two places at once: they are aware they are watching some form of entertainment, but they are at the same time carrying out a fantasy in their own mind. I refer to this as lucid thinking, because the fan carries a level of self-awareness into the process. Such processes account for how we engage

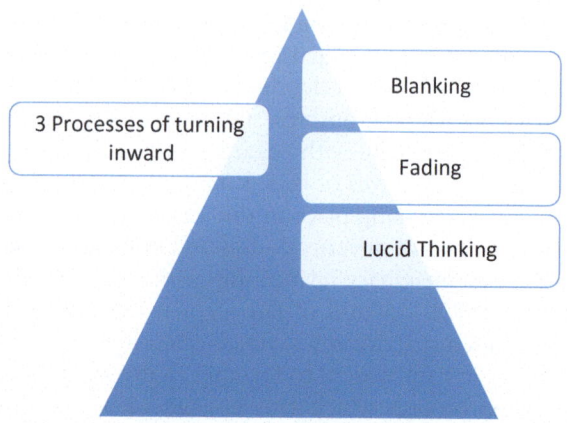

Fig. 2.1   Three processes of turning inward

in fantasy behavior in the context of media consumption. But it is important to point out that such reverie takes place outside of media consumption, as fans can invoke a celebrity at will. I point out these three processes to distinguish consuming legacy media from the ways in which we engage with social media via the Internet or through apps. Brain studies have described how watching television relaxes the brain, perhaps encouraging the kind of fantasy behavior I have described as like being in a hypnoidal state (Fig. 2.1).

However, when individuals utilize computers or smartphones or other forms of haptic technology they are active in the way they consume content, using their mouse or track pad, for example, to click from website to website, or use a controller, perhaps multitasking, or to make the process more complex multitasking with multiple media.[16] The difference between viewing television and using a computer or mobile device, the latter requiring active participation, coupled with the potential for simultaneous media use, suggests that the initial connection to celebrities or other new media figures in a social media world is rather complex, more so than with legacy media. In other words, consuming digital media, because platforms require participation of an active user, does not make for a relaxing experience conducive to fantasy behavior, as does a medium like television. This is not to suggest that fans do not engage in fantasy with regard to celebrities with whom they interact on the Internet through social media; rather, the process of fantasizing may merely be different, perhaps taking place away from the media experience as the fan basks in the glow of the previous interaction. For example, one may watch a YouTube video from beginning to end and have a similar experience as watching a television program or movie. However, they may upon completing their viewing scan to the bottom of the video to see the comments viewers or subscribers are making and perhaps along the way consider posting a comment of their own. They may also receive a reply or engage in the social network of the celebrity or micro-celebrity.

IMAGINARY SOCIAL RELATIONSHIPS

In the reflection on her attraction to Courtney Love described at the beginning of this chapter, Leah Carroll spoke about the guilt she felt over grunge singer Kurt Cobain's death in 1994: "So my special relationship to Courtney Love was a kind of mourning, an atonement for a terrible act I had been powerless to prevent. If I could not save Kurt, I could be best friends with Courtney, and dressing just like her would prove how right we were for one another." Carroll was not alone in her admiration of Kurt Cobain, projected through her desire to be close to Courtney Love. At that time, many others felt the same depth of loss, and unfortunately crisis centers were flooded with calls from fans that were contemplating the same fate. There were reports at the time of some fans that sadly took their own lives.[17,18] Copycat suicides notwithstanding, this example serves to illustrate the potential depth of feelings between a celebrity and a fan.

Beyond the spectator-text encounter, as Caughey referred to the point of consumption, he went on to say that once the TV program or movie ends, the individual might continue to "engage in certain imaginal interactions with the fictional character, as in dreams and daydreams."[19] In a seminal article "Gina as Steven," Caughey wrote of one of his informants, Gina, who spoke to him about a new attraction. This was not someone she had actually met, but as she described it, the relationship was quite intense. She was referring to Steven Seagal, the movie actor; actually, it was the fictional character he played in action films. It was odd, as Caughey described it, that Gina, who is a clinical social worker who in the past worked as a counselor at a center for victims of rape and domestic violence and who experienced nightmares about rape, would choose a character that is known for his violence. Beyond being physically attracted to Seagal, she described him as her hero, a strong protective male ally, more like an older brother figure. In Chap. 1, I described the experience of Jonathan

Metz who invoked the fictional character MacGyver to make a life-altering decision. In this way, Metz slipped out of his own identity and through strong identification with the character partially became the character. In Gina's case, Caughey says, she didn't identify with any of the women in his movies; rather she became him. Becoming Steven manifests in daydreams, stream of consciousness thought or nocturnal dreams. In the same way that Metz had his "MacGyver moment," Gina "pulls a Steven Seagal." In other words, Gina internalized the Steven Seagal character, viewing herself as someone who if wronged would seek justice and revenge. As someone who worked with abused female clients, in her fantasies, she had the ability to "fight against all these men." Caughey emphasizes the need to look at the connections between individuals and celebrities whether the connection is based on admiration, love, envy or hatred, as those connections are part of the individual's meaning-making system. It's also important to consider the individual's unconscious, as nocturnal dreams may play an important role in the complex web we weave between fantasy and reality based on multiple subject positions people inhabit. Nocturnal dreams are a controversial area, as J. Allan Hobson, professor of Psychiatry Emeritus at Harvard University, argues that dreams in the rapid eye movement (REM) state are formed by random neurochemical changes in the brain, although more recent research indicates a stronger connection to emotional states and dreaming that takes place outside of the REM state.[20] But others feel different about the meaning of dreams, including non-Western cultures that see great significance in dreams.

Although Caughey did not present it as such, a theoretical model emerged from his ethnographic research providing an understanding of how media figures, as he referred to celebrities, may display traits admirers would like within them, to develop or refine. The types of attraction that fans fall into include (see Fig. 2.2) physical attraction, social attraction and task attraction, in which case the fan may want to be like or perform like the celebrity, as was the case with Gina.

Fig. 2.2 Caughey's three types of attraction

Three Types of Attraction

Physical   Social   Task

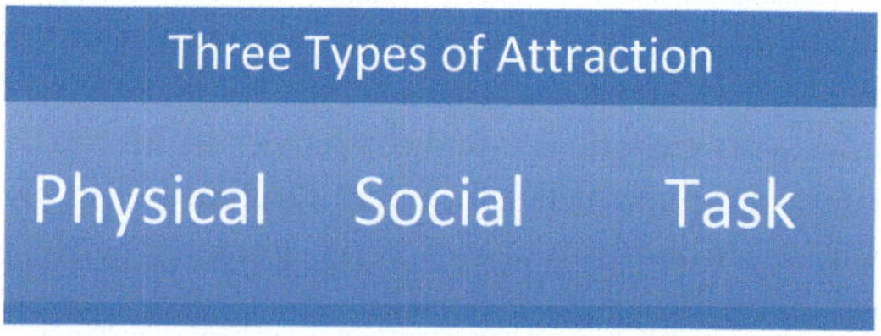

Implied in this model is a causal link between the celebrity's physical appearance, talents, or special abilities, the values they express and the attitudes they convey and the individual who seeks to bring their own self-image in line with that of the celebrity role model, mentor, teacher, friend, among other roles celebrities play in our everyday lives. In this way, the theoretical model that emerges suggests that individuals utilize imaginary social relationships with celebrities as a way to shape their own identities and their feelings. Perhaps what is most important is that imaginary social relationships operate in a similar manner to actual social relationships. Even in our own fantasies, we may talk (self-talk) to a celebrity mentor, for example, as a celebrity or character gets inside our head and speaks to us within an inner dialogue.

Stream of consciousness, self-talk and fantasizing are based on the premise that such activities are part and parcel of everyday life. Within the context of most media consumption, which is such a low-stakes activity, people may enter an altered state of consciousness; as Ien Ang suggests, fantasy can "create imagined worlds which can take us beyond what is possible or acceptable in the 'real' world."[21] I have observed the ways in which advertising—the most overtly persuasive form of communication—serves as a mediating force in imaginary relationships that held the potential to either stabilize or destabilize the relationship between celebrity and fan.[22] My theoretical orientation conceives of fans as active participants in making sense of their everyday lives through, among other things, the use of celebrities. This position is consistent with a cultural studies approach rooted in conceptualizing audiences as active rather than passive participants of the media industry. Henry Jenkins and danah boyd write about participatory culture as a form of activity that requires actual actions or behaviors that demonstrate participation, like writing fan fiction.[23] I use the concept of active audience to describe a participatory culture that takes place for the most part in the inner worlds of the individual. In this manner, we construct an interior social world for ourselves within which we interact with others in that world; sometimes those others are celebrities. I credit individuals with a sense of intellect as well as a sense of humor and skepticism as they find pleasure and meaning in the dynamic process of creating, maintaining and perhaps dissolving imaginary relationships with celebrities. Fantasizing, stream of consciousness and related self-talk are all private practices, as opposed to social practices that are public. These activities take place inside our head, but as our thoughts and fantasies are a product of the culture, sometimes we talk to celebrities and sometimes they talk to us. Paradoxically, fantasy behavior is not encouraged in Western culture, as it is often associated with being unproductive. What do we look for when we engage our stream of consciousness? Often it is self-confirmation that we receive through imaginary others, by winning their gratitude, admiration or envy. All of this remains true, but in an age of digital media, a shift has taken place as our interactive engagement with digital media is productive and performative.

THE ATTENTION ECONOMY

Today there is much talk about the attention economy, as digital media vie for our "eyeballs." There is an adage: where attention goes, money will follow. This accounts for the shift away from traditional media to newer platforms, including extended-reality (XR) technologies such as virtual, augmented, immersive and mixed reality.[24] The long tail of this shift has spawned one counter response in the form of banner blindness. Banner blindness refers to the learned ability to shift our attention away from messages that appear on the screen. As one study found, "We simply confirmed for the umpteenth time that banner blindness is real."[25] But there is another form of inattention that preceded banner blindness, as, in a similar fashion, individuals have learned not only to shift their focus to a part of a screen that doesn't include a banner ad—although there are several newer techniques that advertisers have developed to regain attention—but long before to turn their attention inward, you just can't see them do it, making such activity difficult to observe or measure. Among the reasons, shown in Fig. 2.3, why individuals turn inward when confronted with content, images or people is based on familiarity, comfort and escapism.

Repetition in advertising, in particular, is one of the cornerstones of effectiveness. That is to say, media planners know they have to broadcast a commercial or repeat a message somewhere between three and six times

Three Reasons why people turn inward	Familiarity
	Comfort
	Escapism

Fig. 2.3   Three reasons why people turn inward

before it registers with a viewer, reader or listener. Any exposure above that number may breed irritation. With regard to digital media, such repetition causes banner blindness. Although advertising is a special case, because it has persuasive intention, the same holds true for entertainment programming and the celebrities or characters they play with whom we may through repeated exposure become highly familiar. Paradoxically, repeated exposure encourages an individual to turn away; sometimes this means they turn their attention inward. It is ironic that the purveyors of content encourage, through escapist content and repetition, our involvement in fantasy activity. This might be referred to as escaping without leaving, but there are times when we do, based on these same principles of familiarity, comfort and escapism, literally get up and leave the room, perhaps to go to the bathroom or get something to eat, among other possibilities that interrupt the flow of communication. Also, because of the proliferation of screens and the ways in which screens are embedded in various aspects of everyday life, we may have some content before our eyes or ears while exercising, cooking or eating and working, among other activities. And, there is the issue of simultaneous media usage, as sometimes individuals may be working on their computer, playing video games or using their smartphone, for example, and have the television on in the background or similarly listening to music. The combination of all of these ways in which we utilize legacy and digital media in our everyday lives encourages inattention. Attention may be directed toward our inner world; however, that form of attention has gone largely unrecognized. As Caughey states, "In our (Western) society fantasy has traditionally been viewed in one of two ways. First, like stream of consciousness processes generally, fantasy has been seen as 'woolgathering,' unrealistic, unimportant waste of time—hence a trivial subject for research."[26] He acknowledges that fantasy has also been associated with psychopathic behavior.

In Chap. 1, I suggested that what drives people to want to get to know celebrities better, and in that more intimately through the use of social media, is a reflection of their own personal alienation many people feel when social structures and normative behaviors break down. The sociological concept of anomie advanced by French sociologist Emile Durkheim in the late 1800s is utilized to describe such personal alienation. As traditional institutions in the United States—the family, religion, education and government—become weakened, coupled with the highly mobile nature of modern society, individuals seek *terra firma* with regard to social relationships. Replacing an absent father or mother, a brother, sister or friend with a celebrity provides continuity in a social world in which people are increasingly isolated. Whether they are referred to as Stanley Milgram did as "familiar strangers" or as Chris Rojek calls them "second order relationships," celebrities become emotionally engaged with people we don't know. In the book *Alone Together*, MIT technology and society professor Sherry Turkle explores the power of technology to dramatically alter our social lives.[27] She describes a world in which actual social relationships are supplanted by electronic companions and social networking tools. For the present and next generation, their feelings of connectivity are placed against a reality of greater isolation. By relying on our self-imposed isolation, imaginary relationships with celebrities within a hyperreal environment of social media satisfy the basic human need for actual relationship.

MOVING THROUGH IMAGINARY WORLDS

When individuals shift from the objective world to their inner imaginary worlds they tend to elaborate in their thoughts about the past or they may anticipate the future. As they engage in this elaboration, the inner world becomes populated with places, objects and people, including celebrities. In Western society we hold dual beliefs that encourage and discourage the use of the imagination. Although a majority of children up to seven years of age develop an imaginary friend, after the age of seven such imaginary relationships are deemed inappropriate and are discouraged by parents and teachers.[28] There is the familiar story of the young student for whom a teacher sends a note home dismayed over the child's daydreaming during class, as illustrated by the song "Be Good Johnny" by the Australian pop group Men at Work:

> Off to school you go
> 'Don't you be a bad boy Johnny
> Don't you slip up
> Or play the fool'
> 'Oh no Ma, Oh no Da
> I'll be your golden boy
> I will obey ev'ry golden rule'
> Get told by the teacher
> Not to day-dream

There is culture at work here as daydreaming, that is imagining, is considered by Western standards nonproductive behavior; furthermore, a cornerstone of the capitalist economy is that people are taught never to be idle. Therefore, engaging in an imaginary relationship equates with nonproductive behavior by Western standards. The ways in which authority figures like bosses, teachers or parents disdain participating in imaginary social worlds—be they video games like World of Warcraft, Minecraft, a newer social reality platform like Sansar or mere imagining without media enhancement—provide a partial explanation as to why many people have difficulty admitting to engaging in imaginary social relationships as they show a side of themselves that is not consistent with dominant cultural beliefs or values. In response, we employ our weirdness censor when it comes to hiding from others that we engage our imaginations.[29]

To be clear, some imaginary relationships are pathological, as sometimes fandom can turn into fanaticism. Connections to celebrities exist on a continuum: at one end, we merely know about and perhaps are attracted to a celebrity or media figure; however, at the other end of the continuum, the fan may move beyond the imaginary to stalk or perhaps do worse as has been the case for predators like Mark David Chapman, who killed John Lennon, or John Hinckley, who attempted to assassinate President Ronald Reagan in order to impress actress and director Jody Foster. He wrote to Foster saying just before shooting Reagan:

> Jody, I'm asking you to please look into your heart and at least give me the chance with this historical deed to gain your respect and love. I love you forever. [signed] John Hinckley.[30]

There exist celebrity stalkers that are at the extreme end of the continuum of what Brian Spitzberg and Lawrence Cupach describe in their article "Fanning the Flames of Fandom" as "disordered forms of fandom" that reflect the darker side of the celebrity–fan relationship, making it difficult to discuss attraction to celebrities for fear of being labeled a stalker.[31] Perhaps this reluctance to admit to having a relationship with an imaginary other is understandable, as one of the paradoxes of contemporary Western culture is that, on the one hand, we prize imagination in art, literature and technological innovation, but, on the other hand, hold this aspect of the imagination in disdain, as would be the case with the daydreaming student. At the same time, parents encourage entry into the imaginary social world of celebrity worship in any number of ways. First, many young people have posters of their favorite celebrities hanging on their bedroom walls. Second, parents often accompany their teens and pre-teens to pop concerts simply because it is safer—from a parent's perspective—to have a youngster engage in an imaginary relationship than a real one. And third, engaging in such imaginary relationships at an early age is practice for conducting an actual relationship later in life; therefore, social learning may take place even though it is simulated or part of a pseudo-experience.

For most if not all of us who consume media, imaginary relationships are a part of our broader cultural experience. Whether we recognize it or not or are willing to discuss it or not, we all engage on some level or at some point on the continuum in an imaginary relationship. It is most common that the imaginary relationship takes the form of extreme admiration and what develops from that admiration is a friendship or other social role the celebrity or media figure may play in the life of the fan, follower or friend. As admiration grows in intensity and as the fan's connection may move along the continuum of meaning, it is possible that an imaginary love interest may form. While such an imaginary relationship is moved forward along the continuum, it is certainly well within the bounds of normal attraction. The love interest is usually something attributed to adolescent infatuation: the idol worship teen and pre-teen girls and boys display for their favorite pop stars. However, such fantasies may become deeper as they carry into post-adolescence and beyond.

A common imaginary relationship emerges when the celebrity serves as a role model or perhaps as a mentor and it is here that celebrity or social influencer appearances in advertising are likely to have greater impact. It would make sense that for the imaginary relationship to evolve—to move beyond attraction to role model or mentor—appearances in various media or repeated appearances in a serial program would provide opportunity if not encouragement for the developing relationship. Over time fans use celebrities in order to gratify particular needs they may have, like the need for entertainment, relaxation or information. Close identification suggests individuals sometimes want to be the celebrity, be with them or perhaps be like them as illustrated by a 1990s' commercial for Gatorade featuring the tagline "Be like Mike" in reference to Michael Jordan.[32] The tag later became a popular Internet meme (see Fig. 2.4).

Individuals, over time, may develop deeper feelings through pseudo-social interactions and develop corresponding strategies in which they carry those interactions into the rest of everyday life. The content derived

Fig. 2.4 Be like Mike Meme. (Be Like Mike Meme. (n.d.). Memegenerator.net)

from different media provides fuel for the relationship to develop. The individual's mediated referent system serves a useful purpose in everyday life, as the content of one medium or the content within one medium feeds into another. And, the media referent system is integrally connected to our social referent system in that media content is portable—we take it with us as we travel through everyday life and can invoke the imaginary at will. Individuals often gossip about celebrities, use celebrities to make critical evaluations of media content or use them to evaluate their own tastes or values against the values of others. Media content is often the subject of "water-cooler" talk and often the subject of self-talk, part of our internal dialogue.

WHEN CONSUMERS BECOME PRODUCERS

An exponential growth in the number of celebrities and media figures available to ordinary people suggests there are more choices and the potential to include—in one form or other—more of them in one's everyday life. The potential for an "ordinary" person to become, even if for a brief time, a celebrity has also increased with the development of participatory media like YouTube, where one can upload a performance of their own, hoping to attract an audience of followers. When we think of fans or for that matter the concept of fandom, oftentimes we think of groups of fans. And, fandom sometimes refers to the coalescing of those groups into productive entities, like fan clubs. In other words, the adoration that fans heap on celebrities may be part of a collective social experience, and it is through that experience that meaning is produced, along with membership. For example, the following are fan groups identified by their fan group name:

- Nicki Minaj—Barbies
- Rihana—The Navy
- Mariah Carey—Lambs
- Lady Gaga—Little Monsters
- Justin Bieber—Beliebers
- Paris Hilton—Little Hiltons

As an indication of how extreme admiration works as a function of an imaginary relationship, it was reported that after Kendall Jenner split with One Direction's Harry Styles, she posted a picture on her Instagram that said: "don't let boys be mean to u." Style's fans were so distressed that in one case a fan tweeted "@KendallJenner stay away!!!!!!!!!!!!!!! HE'S MINE." "May have to unfollow Kendall Jenner on insta, she makes me want to die," threatened another.[33] It's important to point out that this fan's venting took place not in her imagination but within the comment section of Instagram.

Social media are an ideal place for individuals to connect with other like-minded individuals around various topics or issues including celebrities that represent them. The social connections one makes, although they are mediated social connections, are certainly an important part of the fan experience, and so is the way in which fans utilize celebrities as a means of creating and modifying their personal identity, as would be the case of the fan who purchased an item of clothing they saw a celebrity wearing. And, it is important to point out that a fan is different from a friend or follower, and as such rather than forming a fan group, there may be clusters or crowds that might include admirers, haters and everyone in between. With regard to imaginary relationships with celebrities, however, for the most part these are private experiences, taking place inside one's head. Although there is a caveat, as sometimes individuals will choose to share aspects of their mediated social connections with others in the guise of what has come to be known as water-cooler talk. One of my informants, for example, reported speaking to a friend about the then relationship between Kristen Stewart and her at the time boyfriend. In response to her friend's text castigating Stewart for breaking up with her boyfriend she said:

> Well, you can't judge because you don't know all the facts. They could have been on the rocks for a while and it could have nothing to do with Rob.

The friend then responded:

Are you like her best friend now?

The informant, a woman in her early 20s, said:

I knew I had a problem. I knew more about her life than I did about my (real) friends, and I was defending her against the hatred of others.

Digital media have changed the ways in which imaginary relationships are conducted, as the one-way address of a medium like television has given way to the potential for two-way interaction through direct messaging on Twitter, for example. Although in the past fans were on occasion able to interact with celebrities by showing up at a book signing or after a concert or show to get an autograph, for example, such interaction was quite limited, isolated and bound by location.[34] The emergence of digital media represents a watershed moment that extends beyond internal interaction to consider the potential for two-way actual interaction. As an example of this engagement, Gayle Stever describes in her study of parasocial and social interaction with celebrities how pop singer Josh Groban utilized what she described as "grassroots interactions" including a fan website, attendance at radio station-sponsored events, backstage meet-and-greets, blogging, vlogging (video blogging), online chats, Twitter feed and Facebook page.[35] Best practices in the digital media environment dictate the use of several if not many communication channels or platforms, but social media also requires communication forms through which the celebrity and her or his fans may interact. Groban (or should I say Groban's "people") is one of many celebrities who uses Internet-based digital media to interact with their fans.

Similar to the ways in which individuals utilize texting on their mobile phone in order to control when they will respond to another's text and take the time to consider what they want to say, when it comes to imaginary relationships that are mediated by legacy or digital media, the individual believes they are in control. By that I mean the fan, friend or follower feels the power to begin and end the connection when they so choose. Furthermore, the relationship may be ended merely by switching channels when a particular celebrity appears or by avoiding a website or social media platform where the celebrity is likely to be present. In other words parasocial interaction is up to the individual. When compared to mobile phone texting, we can see a parallel in the ways in which individuals use social media in order to connect to others in a controlled manner, including celebrities. It is in this way that imaginary relationships converge with the ways in which we conduct actual relationships in a mediated world. Imaginary relationships begin to emerge through repeated exposure through different media, but at a certain point the follower through their proactive pursuit of news, information and gossip becomes a fan. The relationship may further develop away from media consumption when the fan thinks or fantasizes about the celebrity or finds reason to invoke the celebrity in a situation they deem warranted. And, the fan may attempt to interact with a celebrity or other fans of the celebrity, sometimes lauding the celebrity as fans connect with one another and sometimes to defend a celebrity against others who may denigrate the celebrity. In such instances the celebrity fills important gaps in the fan's social life, playing social roles that may otherwise not be available to them: giving advice, demonstrating how to do things or modeling social behavior that may be useful in their online experiences and in their actual social world. The fan gets to carry out this connection both within the mediated environment and in other aspects of their everyday life. There may be distinct advantages to using imagined others, even though imaginary relationships might be characterized as weak relationships; they still play a vital role contributing to the individual's well-being. The term "weak" should not be taken as a negative concept as Mark Granovetter described in his 1973 article "The Strength of Weak Ties," it is possible that even in an instance where a youngster may not take the advice of a parent, but more likely rely on a trusted friend, because there is greater social distance, and hence less dissonance, between the youngster and the imagined other than with a close relative.[36] The celebrity-fan relationship is analogous, as celebrities, paradoxically because of their distance—both physical and social—from the individual, allow the weak social connection to supersede that of one based on closeness. David Giles who has written extensively about parasocial relationships with celebrities could not anticipate in 2000 with the publication of his book *Illusions of Immortality* the shape of social media to come. While he considered such things as the death of television, he could not have foreseen our speeded-up culture that operates within a 24-hour always-on Internet or the proliferation of smartphones, apps, and virtual, augmented, immersive and mixed reality. Celebrities like Katy Perry, whose Twitter followers have topped 104 million, have achieved extraordinary popularity and learned to manage their fan base through the use of legacy as well as newer social media. Those weakened relationships play a vital role for individuals that create and maintain them in a social media world and beyond. In his more recent book *Twenty-First Century Celebrity*, Giles argues that some scholars have devalued mediated social connections based on the binary that relationships are either social (meaning real) or parasocial (meaning fake).[37]

PERSONAL CONNECTIONS MAY NOT BE AUTHENTIC, BUT MAY BE IMAGINARY

Throughout human history, Nancy Baym maintains in her book *Personal Connections in the Digital Age* that physical location was the basis for forming relationships; however, this is not so for relationships formed through social media as shared interest has replaced shared place.[38] One of the qualities of social interaction that fans seek through social media is a feeling of connectedness to a celebrity or media figure, but along with that connection we have been told that what is desired is an authentic encounter. The question remains: what do fans and celebrities have in common other than a common interest in the celebrity? In other words, what needs of the fan are gratified through a connection with a celebrity? Social connection is not directly tied to authenticity, begging the question: who is "selling" the idea that authenticity is a vital aspect of mediated social connections? The answer, I argue, is the media industry. While individuals may have a desire to know that whom they are connecting with is who they appear to be, but as we see with Chatbots and the acceptance of professionals who ply social media platforms on behalf of celebrities, ultimately authenticity is not of acute concern. Yes, fans would agree that it would be nice if they were messaging with the actual celebrity, but these other methods also provide a sense of satisfaction and gratification. Furthermore, within the context of social media, the fan operates within a network that includes other fans. Fan to fan communication is equally important and satisfying as it lends a sense of intimacy, and celebrity to celebrity communication through which the fan gets to see the celebrity communicating with other celebrities provides another outlet to encourage and enhance the mediated social connection.

If the formation of social identity is a performance, the venue in which that performance takes place is important. Since the mid-1800s Speakers' Corner in Hyde Park London has provided a venue for anyone to freely speak on any subject of their choosing. The connection between the speaker and a public space is extended in a world of social media where connections take place within a much broader virtual landscape. Although platforms like Twitter are corporate entities whose prime interest is not free speech, but generating advertising revenue, people nonetheless treat it as a public sphere of free expression. There are distinct differences, however: audiences on social media are diffused, and audiences at Hyde Park are simple.[39,40]

Social media is the stage for diffused audiences, as they don't have to be in a central location; technology allows the audience to be pretty much anywhere they have a connection to the Internet. However, in this application of sociologist Erving Goffman's concept of public performance, social media represent a staged social setting. Social media are not the theater or another public forum where social relationships are being conducted; rather, social media are the artificially constructed performative spaces where celebrities present a version of themselves to their fans. In her article "Browsing the Performative: A Search for Sincerity," Kate Hawkins distinguishes between performance and performative, a distinction useful to this discussion. Performance is something that happens in the present, but it is one that can be repeated; however, the experience of the performance will not be the same. We usually associate the idea of performance with something an artist created, but it may be applied to fans as well. In other words, fans can perform like celebrities through user-generated content (UGC). Performative, on the other hand, is an act of doing; it does not require an audience in the theatrical sense. The distinction becomes important when applied to social media: social media require one to navigate their terrain and as such require active participation; they utilize two-way communication, perhaps more as the celebrity and the fan or fans are involved in an interactive exchange of sorts. The idea that fans are sharing or collaborating with celebrities is an example of our own self-deception as we confuse the public space of the Internet with the private nature of the interaction with the celebrity who might be posting to Facebook or Instagram or tweeting a direct message to the fan or the fan who might be tweeting to a celebrity, in which case the fan merely acts as a voyeur, in other words a spectator to a performance. What is going on in social media is a highly constructed version of authenticity in which the self becomes commodified—packaged and sold to the fan-consumer. An interesting paradox emerges in which the celebrity through their performative act can never reveal their true self, but their repeated presence in social media suggests that they cannot conceal their true self. Where is the authentic? It is in the revelations of celebrities in the form of Tweets, Facebook Messenger and YouTube confessions through which one exposes their authenticating self as an example of performative sincerity. Whether there is a backstage in social media or not remains a question, as the merger between the back (rehearsal) and the front (performance) merges online to create an act of sincerity, or at least that is the way it is perceived. From Goffman's dramaturgic perspective, the act that a celebrity performs through social media is the kind of role-playing we would expect in any public space by two individuals.

I extend Goffman's ideas regarding the front and backstages as applied to social media to consider another stage in which the performance continues—the imagination. With television, or magazines for that matter, images are flattened—two-dimensional—however, the individual may inflate the image within their imagination in order to fulfill their own needs and desires in the form of a fantasy. Therefore to assume that the role the celebrity plays in the individual's thoughts and fantasies is unreal (a fantasy), and that the role the celebrity plays within social media is somehow real, denies the hyperreal nature of online space and the experience of the celebrity that extends beyond it. Fans may be active as opposed to passive in the ways in which they consume newer social media; however, the worlds they traverse are no more fixed or stable. Pop star Taylor Swift's dedicated app serves to illustrate how the immersion into a celebrity's mediated social world operates. In social media parlance, an app can serve as a stage, and as apps are locative media available on smartphones, the stage travels with you. In this example, an app was developed for pop singer Taylor Swift, called The Swift Life. According to its creator, the app is a dedicated social network, allowing fans to see pictures and videos and learn about news regarding the pop star. As well, they can communicate with each other and the singer through the use of what they are called Taymojis.[41] It's worth noting that pop singer Lady Gaga created an app for her fans that she refers to as Little Monsters.[42]

The interchange between the celebrity and the fan is important to promote the mediated social connection, but also of importance is the aspect of the interchange between the celebrity and fan that is reintegrated into the fan's everyday life. This might include a practical skill the fan learns from the celebrity, or other information they gleaned from the celebrity that may be useful in other aspects of the fan's life including confirmation of one's values. As well, in the case of Taylor Swift, she becomes portable (in your smartphone), with you at all times, along with her fan network with which you can interact. All of this becomes fuel for the imagination. In other words this interchange becomes internalized into the imaginary and then drawn upon in another social context through which the fan produces their personal meaning about or through the interchange. This could include learning to manage one's own mediated performance on social media, sometimes becoming what has been referred to as micro-celebrity in their own right as fans learn to perform like celebrities on social media.[43] And the fan's performance on social media might also lead to a feeling of newly acquired status gained through the direct communication to or from a celebrity and then communicated to others. In this way, fans participate in the celebrity's social network, but they also create their own social network that may interconnect with the celebrity's network or may operate in a parallel universe.

It is important to consider the difference between what legacy media provide in relation to the ways in which a fan invokes their imagination as they read a magazine article about a celebrity and then reintegrates some aspect of that experience into their everyday life and the ways in which they create and maintain mediated social connections with digital media. Marwick and boyd address the difference between experiences with consumption of legacy media, like magazines, and the experience of Twitter as an actual experience.[44] While these researchers maintain that a Twitter exchange is different from the experience and ties with and through legacy media, there is little evidence regarding what happens after media consumption that would suggest the difference is experienced when it becomes reintegrated into everyday life. The Twitter experience, although it is seemingly an actual experience, is performative and therefore it is one that is socially constructed.[45] The seemingly authentic or actual operates within the context of the imaginary, as the celebrity becomes recontextualized—leaps off the screen and into the mind—within the imaginary and as the imaginary spills back out into everyday life. The experience of the Twitter exchange is not the same as the purely imaginary exchange that takes place within the context of consuming legacy media. One difference might be the status that the fan feels in regard to the direct interchange with the celebrity, which is something that is not likely through legacy media, simply because others can't see it. Such status enhancement, which translates into feelings of emotional closeness—heightened intimacy—might be the motivation to carry that mediated social connection forward into a conversation with others, or it may provide support as one uses their mediated social connection in order to further enhance their own feelings of self-worth and perhaps internalize the experience as they craft their own identity as part of their own authenticating experience. Participating in social media exchanges even as a voyeur makes a fan or follower feel more of an insider than one would be if they were to read *People* magazine or gossip reported on a website, and if one were to consider oneself an insider that would certainly elevate their own social status should they choose to share their insider information and perhaps experience with others. The experience of watching, viewing or listening may begin in the world of legacy media and traverse online media to extend the experience to social networks, and there is the additional imaginary world of the individual or perhaps worlds that are populated with people, places and things from these other mediated worlds. We operate within multiple realities—those that are mediated as well as those that are not—and some of our experiences, both real and imagined, may be integrated into the everyday life of the individual.

Although they looked at the medium of television, in particular favored television programs, Jaye Derrick and colleagues developed the social surrogacy hypothesis to explain how loneliness motivates individuals to engage in imaginary relationships.[46] However, these researchers draw no conclusions as to whether the phenomenon is maladaptive or provides positive social support when needed. Newer social media provide opportunities more so than legacy media to interact directly with celebrities and with other fans and to delve deeper into the more private aspects of their lives, as participation in social media demands greater disclosure on the part of the celebrity, and in doing so provides a more integrative experience as the lines between social worlds of the online experience and the individual's imagination become blurred. The reality show star and entrepreneur Kim Kardashian utilizes the Internet and newer social media in a masterful way by maintaining a Facebook page and Twitter feed, among others.[47] She also maintains a dedicated web page, a blog and an online store, which in addition to selling products extends the conversation and perpetuates the dialogue between the celebrity and her fans. At the same time Kardashian is selling herself, she is also selling her line of clothing as well as brands like Skechers for whom she appeared in a 2011 Super Bowl commercial. In a sense, the fan can enter her world vicariously through traditional media, learn intimate details about her life on her cable program *Keeping Up with the Kardashians*, or on gossip websites, and engage more actively by reading her Twitter feeds or posts on her Facebook wall. Social media have a participatory quality in that a fan can actively retweet, comment, disseminate information or videos through their own social network, and ultimately purchase and wear products Kardashian promotes. The possibility of interaction through multiple channels enhances the illusion of intimacy experienced at a distance by the fan creating the potential to feel a sense of closeness, enhanced personal meaning and deeper emotions through the always available connection, allowing the fan to become a friend of Kim, be more like Kim or become Kim for that matter, as the fan herself presents her Kim "look" to the world.

Lady Gaga is another celebrity who uses social media to effectively connect with fans. To that end, her "team" created an app, Little Monsters, which states:

> Welcome home, Little Monsters. This is for us. All of us. Little Monsters is a place for all fans of Lady Gaga to gather, create, and to inspire. Share your passion and creativity in a community full of art, acceptance, monsters, and Gaga. Remember to be brave, be kind, be respectful and most importantly … be yourself![48]

A 20-year-old female informant who is of Italian heritage and attended Catholic school like Lady Gaga reflects on a storehouse of information she has gathered regarding her "friend" Lady Gaga and the similarities in their backgrounds:

> We come from such similar home backgrounds that I actually think we could be friends in real life. Making news everyday on Perez Hilton and X17 keeps me in the loop of the everyday life of Lady Gaga. Her outfits change almost as fast as her stories online do, with daily updates on her award show appearances, and shopping excursions.

The informant says that "by following your friends just as much as you follow Lady Gaga, she becomes one of your friends," in a way that makes this seem "real." The "friendship" with Lady Gaga is fully established through acquisition and integration of information through multiple media sources. The possibility of interaction can be actual, not imaginary, as a fan or follower may send an @reply to a celebrity who may in turn send an @reply to a fan's Twitter page as a means to "perform connection and availability, give back to loyal followers, and manage their (celebrity's) popularity"[49] This, of course, takes the relationship, for a time, beyond the imaginary, and it is not particularly unique to digital media, as there are a growing number of ways, like meet and greet events, in which fans gain access to celebrities. The mediated world of Twitter, Facebook, blogs and the like constitute an alternative reality, which is socially constructed through relationships, hierarchies and roles that shift along with news, information and gossip about the celebrity. In other words, there is a social hierarchy within Twitter that may render the fan a mere observer or voyeur as the celebrity confines her or his tweets to others within their inner circle. Nevertheless, there is pleasure in being a voyeur observing the interchange between a celebrity and her inner circle.

A celebrity may create a sense of intimacy by allowing the fan or follower to eavesdrop by reading tweets that are intended to be between the celebrity and individuals in their social circle, like Kim Kardashian tweeting to one of her sisters. By allowing a fan to vicariously follow such microblogging interchanges, the fan feels like an insider. The concept of togetherness introduced in Chap. 1 suggested that the kinds of feelings that fans develop with celebrities through legacy media are amplified and made more complex through social media. However, managing the social distance between the celebrity and fan is the responsibility of the celebrity for whom their personal brand and the promotion of products and services is at stake. As digital media feed the illusion of greater intimacy, the various roles celebrities play in everyday life continue to extend the nature of all the relationships individuals have with people they actually know and people they do not know, many Facebook "friends" and Twitter "followers" among them. As of 2009, the average Facebook user had 120 "friends," more for women than men.[50] The paradox of togetherness suggests that as our online social sphere grows, the distance between actual and imaginary relationships diminishes. The huge number of Facebook friends some users of that social network maintain belies the strength of those relationships. Imaginary relationships with celebrities created and maintained in social media are based on weak ties; however, as has been pointed out, weaker ties are not necessarily negative when it comes to relationship hierarchies. As Granovetter points out, weak ties are important to one's social integration as they "serve crucial functions in linking otherwise unconnected segments of a network."[51]

MEDIATED SOCIAL CONNECTIONS: A BLENDED VIEW

How do we reconcile the more passive process of consuming legacy media and the related opportunities to engage with during media consumption and afterward in imaginary worlds with the more active process of consuming social media platforms on portable technologies—locative media—with more haptic qualities that employ kinesthetic responses that may diminish the ability to enter or delay entrance to imaginary worlds? In Chap. 1, I wrote about the routine nature of media consumption with regard to legacy or traditional media; media consumption rituals involve low-stakes behavior, which is a partial explanation for why we can turn away from what is before our eyes and enter an imaginary world. And, I utilized the analogy of driving to school or work on a regular basis to illustrate how we can be doing something purposeful in our real life and engage in our inner world at the same time. Digital media consumption is always purposeful in the sense that it encourages engagement through comments, likes and so on. The distinguishing feature between legacy and new media is the latter's interactive capabilities, including the ability for users to create their own content (UGC). And, users of digital technologies have the ability and opportunity to become more actively engaged, whether using a mouse or their fingers to manipulate what is on the screen. A network television program like NBC's The Voice illustrates how legacy media may utilize digital media, like the dedicated app that allows viewers to vote for their favorite contestant, within the context of the program. In this way, legacy and new media merge to form a hybrid experience. In the course of online activity, individuals may attempt to communicate directly with a celebrity who may or may not communicate back, and fans can communicate with other fans within the celebrity's network, or extend that communication into their own online network. Fans may also consider the commentary or responses posted as a form of public self-talk, as they express inner thoughts without applying filters. The implications of such behavior are not without risk, as it can lead to broken friendships and perhaps public shaming. Furthermore, thoughts, feelings and knowledge about a celebrity may be extended into offline social life, as celebrity gossip becomes fodder for water-cooler talk.

All of this should suggest that we have moved beyond the initial role that parasocial interaction played when individuals consume legacy media. In other words, the interaction was limited to the screen and the individual at the point of consumption. Understanding of parasocial interaction in a new media environment suggests that we carry the feelings and thoughts established at the point of consumption into other aspects of our daily lives through fantasy behavior, stream of consciousness and nocturnal dreams. We can also point to the ways in which people talk to others within their daily social lives, whether at school, work or other social gatherings, about celebrity gossip and other markers that indicate deeper social connection with a celebrity. All of these possibilities take place within a chaotic structure where authenticity is overlaid to suggest that celebrities and marketers can control the imagination that in fact is uncontrollable. Social media feeds into this system beckoning fans into a world that is seemingly authentic and sincere, which is offered as a stabilizing force. But social media are no less chaotic or no more controlled than legacy media. Instead of being captivated by media, in a digital media environment we are the captors.

Conclusion

Although the concept of fame is more than 300 years old, today we understand celebrity to be a product of media. Furthermore, the idea that we engage in parasocial interaction with celebrities that we do not actually know is an idea that dates back to the mid-twentieth century as the medium of television furthered opportunities for imaginary connections between a celebrity and a fan. John Caughey provides a theoretical model regarding how individuals create relationships with celebrities they do not actually know and that those relationships parallel actual relationships, like father-daughter, mother-son, sibling, friend, mentor and teacher. The relationship, however, unless pathological, takes place within the imaginary world of the individual based on physical, social or task attraction. With the advent of social media, the illusion of intimacy is enhanced and the possibility of interaction is increased, as a celebrity may respond directly to a fan, and a fan can attempt to communicate with a celebrity. As well, a fan may be privy to communication between a celebrity and other celebrities or fans or the fan can communicate with other fans. Beyond this media-centric approach, an imaginary relationship may ensue after the point of media consumption. This chapter has described some ways in which fans carry those parasocial interactions into their imaginary social worlds, perhaps integrating some aspect of the parasocial interaction into their everyday lives. Because of the complexity of media consumption in the era of mobile technologies, I utilize the term mediated social connections to suggest a number of things: first, in the always-on world of pervasive technologies, social connections with those with whom we communicate are heavily mediated. And, it is important to emphasize that a mediated connection is one that by its very nature is not as authentic as some would like us to believe. Authenticity is not an antecedent to effective communication, although we have been told by marketers that it is. Second, the nature of sociality has changed from the ways in which we might have developed relationships in the past. We meet others online, as evidenced by the number of people who utilize dating sites nears 50 million. In other words, people feel more comfortable conducting their social lives online. And much of that communication takes the form of texting, not voice communication. Third, the kinds of connections we make through our use of technologies may not be as social as we would like to believe. Comments, likes and messages are meant to attract the attention of someone, but they are most likely to fall on deaf ears. A lot of our communication is like shooting arrows into the wind; where those arrows land or if those arrows land is iffy at best. Sometimes we utilize social media to blow off steam or to get a rise out of people, and sometimes this doesn't turn out so well. That type of mediated communication, slut shaming for example, does not speak to relationship, as we heretofore understood that term. And, other times we remain on the periphery of a conversation acting as voyeurs as others make connection. As individuals become active in these newer forms of connection, the opportunities to engage our imaginations, mind-wander, fantasize and daydream may also have changed. The imagination is a powerful tool that serves us well in order to make sense of our world and to make sense of our selves, but if we are too busy swiping, clicking or texting, we may not be taking the time to engage in our inner worlds. Communicating in our contemporary society is not without stress as many people feel compelled through fear of missing out (FOMO) to stay connected at all times of the day and at all costs to our personal well-being. Technology itself is without imagination, and as such interaction with digital media may not inspire imaginary thinking in real time. We may not be losing our capacity to imagine, as imaginary social relationships may continue off the immediate experience of the flattened screen. The ways in which we operate socially and culturally in a society saturated by older and newer technologies neither helps nor hinders the imagination, but these technologies do mediate social connections.

In this chapter, I have presented a theoretical perspective on imaginary social relationships and introduced the concept of mediated social connections as an extension of that theory in an age of digital media. Chapter 3 looks at the roots of imaginary social relationships based on object relations theory, which, simply put, implies that when objects like a teddy bear are introduced to a child, they enter the world of manufactured culture. There is much to learn regarding the relationship between the imagination and culture and the roots of mediated social connections that begin in childhood and continue throughout our entire lives.

NOTES

1. Person, E. (1995). *By Force of Fantasy: How We Make Our Lives.* New York: Basic Books. P. 1.
2. Payne, T. (2010). *Fame: What the Classics Tell Us About Our Culture of Celebrity.* New York: Picador.
3. Inglis, F. (2010). *A Short History of Celebrity,* NJ: Princeton University Press, Princeton. pp. 56–57.
4. Ibid., p. 57.
5. Boorstein, D. (1961). *The Image: A Guide to Pseudo-Events in America,* NY: Harper & Row. p. 57.
6. Kim, E. (2016, October 31). Natalie Suleman reveals regrets, desire to shed 'Octomom' nickname. Today.com. Retrieved from: https://www.today.com/parents/octomom-natalie-suleman-regrets-desire-shed-nickname-t104532
7. Fan. (n.d.). Merriam-Webster Dictionary. Retrieved from: https://www.merriam-webster.com/dictionary/fan
8. Weber, B. (March 23, 2013). Ruth Ann Steinhagen Is Dead at 83; Shot a Ballplayer. *The New York Times.* Retrieved from: http://www.nytimes.com/2013/03/24/sports/baseball/ruth-ann-steinhagen-83-troubled-shooter-of-the-phillies-eddie-waitkus.html
9. Ibid.
10. Lears, T. J. (1994). Fables of Abundance: cultural history of advertising in America. New York: Basic Books.
11. Ibid., p. 24.
12. Op. cit., p. 26.
13. Fernyhough, C. (2016) *The Voices Within.* New York: Basic Books.
14. Seen in Rojek. C. (2016). Presumed Intimacy: Para-Social Relationships in Media, Society and Celebrity Culture. Cambridge, UK: Polity Press.
15. Caughey, J. (1984). *Imaginary Social Worlds.* Lincoln: University of Nebraska Press.
16. The results of a study I conducted of 200 respondents regarding concurrent activities, like eating or socializing, while watching television reveals that a majority engage in multitasking. The analysis found that the vast

majority of respondents engage in the simultaneous use of multiple media, for example, surfing the Internet while watching television. The findings on attention to multiple media suggest respondents do not find this easy, and when engaged in simultaneous media use they are not likely to pay close attention to programming or advertising despite the relevance of content or the salience of familiar faces that appear in television commercials. Alperstein, Neil, Living in an Age of Distraction: Multitasking and Simultaneous Media Use and the Implications for Advertisers, (September 15, 2005). Available at SSRN: http://ssrn.com/abstract=1473864 or https://doi.org/10.2139/ssrn.1473864

17. Strauss, N. (May 19, 1994). He was a geek and a god. *Rolling Stone*, 682, 17–18, 20.
18. Strauss, N. (June 2, 1994). The downward spiral. *Rolling Stone*, 683, 35–42.
19. Caughey, J. (1994). Gina as Steven: The Social and Cultural Dimensions of a Media Relationship. *Visual Anthropology Review*. 10:1 (Spring), pp. 126–135.
20. Hurd, R. (n.d.). Allan Hobson and the Neuroscience of Dreams. Retrieved from: http://dreamstudies.org/2010/01/07/neuroscience-of-dreams/
21. Ang, I. (1996). Living room wars: Rethinking media audiences for a postmodern world. London: Routledge, pp. 92–93.
22. The concept of self-transformation is important when considering the implications for a marketing system in which celebrities communicate about brands in significant and meaningful ways beyond those experienced through traditional advertising. See Alperstein, Neil. 1991. Imaginary Social Relationships with Celebrities Appearing in Television Commercials. *Journal of Broadcasting & Electronic Media* 35 (1): 43–58.
23. Jenkins, H., Ito, M. & boyd, d. *Participatory Culture in a Networked Era: A Conversation on Youth, Learning, Commerce, and Politics.* Cambridge, UK: Polity press.
24. Ingram, M. (August 12, 2015). The attention economy and the implosion of traditional media. Fortune. Retrieved from: http://fortune.com/2015/08/12/attention-economy/
25. Nielsen, J. (2009). Banner Blindness: Old and New Findings. NN Group. Retrieved from: https://www.nngroup.com/articles/banner-blindness-old-and-new-findings/
26. Caughey, J. (1984) Imaginary Social Worlds, p. 184.
27. Turkle, S. (2011). *Alone Together: Why we expect more from technology.* New York: Basic Books.
28. In her 1999 study of children up to the age of seven, Marjorie Taylor reported that 65% of children had imaginary friends at some point in their young lives. Taylor, M. (1999). *Imaginary Companions and the Children Who Create Them.* New York: Oxford University Press.

29. The weirdness censor is based on our understanding that it might be creepy to admit to others that we engage in imaginary social relationships. As a result individuals often deny they engage in such behavior.
30. Seen in Caughey (1984, p. 6).
31. Spitzbert, B. & Cupach, W. (2008). Fanning the Flames of Fandom: Celebrity Worship, Parasocial Interaction, and Stalking (p. 287). In *Stalking, Threatening and Attacking Public Figures: A Psychological and Behavioral Analysis*. Edited by J. Reid Meloy, Lorrain Sheridan and Jens Hoffman. New York: Oxford University Press.
32. Gatorade Commercial (1992). Be Like Mike. Retrieved from: https://www.youtube.com/watch?v=b0AGiq9j_Ak
33. Miller, G. & Seim, C. (March 4, 2014). The 10 most rabid celebrity fan groups online. *New York Post*. Retrieved from: https://nypost.com/2014/03/04/which-celebrity-has-the-craziest-fans-on-twitter/
34. I have had my own surreal experiences with film stars in real life. A few years ago actress Nicole Kidman was filming the movie *The Invasion* in a rented house around the corner from where I presently live, and during this same time as I would walk to the university where I teach, I would walk through the film production of the movie Step Up, which was being filmed on the campus of a neighboring university. As films and television programs are no longer the province of Hollywood, there are many such productions that take place in Baltimore and other cities around the United States, increasing the opportunities for fans to interact with celebrities in non-celebrity contexts, like the local gym, restaurants, supermarkets, and the like. It should be emphasized, however, that the kind of interaction that ensues under such circumstances is from afar, observing the celebrity, perhaps saying hello as the fan tries to make contact, or ask for an autograph, which may be considered intrusive in such non-celebrity contexts identified earlier.
35. Stever, G. (2009). Parasocial and Social Interaction with Celebrities: Classification of Media Fans, *Journal of Media Psychology*, 14:3 (summer).
36. Granovetter, M. (1973). The Strength of Weak Ties. *American Journal of Sociology*, 78: 6 (May). pp. 1360–1380.
37. Giles, D. (2018). *Twenty-First Century Celebrity: Fame in Digital Culture*. Bingley, UK: Emerald Group Publishing.
38. In writing about personal connections through social media, Baym is referring to connections between "regular" individuals, not between fans and celebrities. However, much of what she suggests holds true for the fan–celebrity relationship. Baym, N. (2010). *Personal Connections in the Digital Age*, Cambridge, UK: Polity Press.
39. Longhurst, B. (2007). *Popular Music and Society*. Cambridge: Polity Press.

40. Speakers' Corner Hyde Park London. Retrieved from: https://www.flickr.com/photos/doctorow/14008507
41. Crook, J. (n.d.). Taylor Swift's new app, The Swift Life, is out now. TechCrunch.com. Retrieved from: https://techcrunch.com/2017/12/14/taylor-swifts-new-app-the-swift-life-is-out-now/
42. Little Monsters. Lady Gaga's fan app. Retrieved from: http://littlemonsters.com/
43. It is also important to point out that conversely celebrities learn to use social media from fans. Living in a mediated participatory culture promotes this dialogic.
44. Marwick, A. & boyd, d. (2011). "To See and Be Seen: Celebrity Practice on Twitter," *Convergence*, 17(2), 139–158. (*Note: danah boyd uses the lower case when spelling her name.*)
45. Performative is different than performance (see citation celebrity sincerity and social media).
46. Derrick, J., Shira, L., & Hugenberg, K. (2009). "Social Surrogacy: How Favored Television Programs Provide the Experience of Belonging." *Journal of Experimental Social Psychology* 45 (2): 352–362.
47. The cable TV program, *Keeping Up with the Kardashians*, averaged 3.7 million viewers during season four. As of March 2012 she had almost 14 million followers on Twitter and 8 million "likes" on Facebook.
48. Little Monsters.com http://littlemonsters.com/
49. Seen in Marwick & boyd (2011). p. 145.
50. Primates on Facebook: Even Online, the Neocortex is the Limit. (February 26, 2009). *The Economist*. Retrieved from: http://www.economist.com/node/13176775?story_id=13176775
51. Granovetter, M. (1983). "The strength of weak ties: a network theory revisited," *Sociological Theory*, 1: 201–233. Quote is from p. 217. Retrieved from: http://citeseerx.ist.psu.edu/viewdoc/download?doi=10.1.1.128.7760&rep=rep1&type=pdf

CHAPTER 3

Jacking in to an Extended Reality

This is the beginning of sadness, I say to myself,
as I walk through the universe in my sneakers.
It is time to say good-bye to my imaginary friends,
time to turn the first big number. (Excerpt from "Turning 10" by poet Billy
Collins)

When does culture enter into a newborn's life? Delving into such a question provides insight into the ways in which children are inculcated into a culture of mediated social connections that continues on in perhaps different forms well into adulthood. In other words, how do we get started on this path toward mediated social connections? The pediatrician and psychoanalyst Donald Winnicott was key to the development of object relations theory, the basis of which is that "cultural experience begins with creative living first manifested as play."[1] The transitional object, as Winnicott referred to it, might, for example, be a teddy bear or other plush object. A teddy bear is a cultural artifact that, according to the psychoanalyst, comes between a child and a mother. It is through this object that the child begins to see the transition and in that the separation from mother to child and child to mother—the beginnings of an outside world. We rarely think that a simple stuffed animal would constitute a child's entry into culture, although there is a good chance that such personified objects, which are becoming increasingly digital, are likely marketed by the Disney Company, a major purveyor of popular culture and owner of Baby Einstein, Apple or Sony, all of whom employ "cradle to grave" marketing strategies.

© The Author(s) 2019
N. M. Alperstein, *Celebrity and Mediated Social Connections*,
https://doi.org/10.1007/978-3-030-17902-1_3

We can learn much about young adult and adult imaginary relationships and mediated social connections by looking at the ways in which children begin to interact with personified objects like stuffed animals and their imaginary relationships with characters gleaned from media. I recall, for example, being with Gabe, a four-year-old boy, who one day began spontaneously to talk to Anna and Elsa, characters from the movie *Frozen*. The characters would seemingly come out of the wall to speak to him and he to them. His connection to the characters was outside of his media consumption and their appearance lasted a period of weeks, disappearing as quickly as they came. Adults hopefully do not interact with characters that come out of the walls, but they do, like this four-year-old, carry such images inside their heads; sometimes their interactions spill out into public space. The 1950 movie *Harvey*, based on a play by the same name, was about an adult male whose best friend was a 6 foot 3.5 inch tall rabbit, invisible to others.[2] By delving into children's development of their imaginary worlds, we can better understand how adults, most of whom are not like Elwood Dowd, the main character in the movie *Harvey*, also construct mediated social connections based on their use of digital media. This chapter will identify some of the differences between the ways in which we interact with imagined others absorbed into our imaginary worlds through interactions with traditional forms of media and contrast that experience with the ways in which we engage with celebrities and new media figures utilizing social media and other extended-reality technologies.

Unlike the character in the movie *Harvey*, Elwood Dowd is thought by his family to be insane for taking up with an imaginary rabbit. In a 2017 commercial for Jif peanut butter titled "Imaginary Friend," a young boy is seen playing alone with a set of toy blocks, but the viewer is made aware that his mom knows there is an imaginary friend playing too. When the son takes a break, he asks his mom for a peanut butter sandwich for himself and one for his (imaginary) friend Charlie. As the commercial progresses we see the boy take a bite of his sandwich and the viewer notices that Charlie's sandwich, too, has a bite missing. It is apparent that the mom, in a subtle acknowledgment and perhaps quiet celebration of the imaginary friend, has actually taken the bite out of Charlie's sandwich reinforcing the imaginary connection between Charlie and her son, and in effect blurring the lines between fantasy and reality.[3] This shows how times have changed from having an imaginary rabbit as a friend and being thought of as insane to celebrating the creativity of having an imaginary friend with whom to have lunch. Movies and advertising are a reflection of the culture, although they often present a distorted version of reality. In this commercial, the depiction of an imaginary friend is something that is offered up as quite acceptable for young children, particularly under the age of seven. Fiction writer Rachel Kadish posts on her blog site the following anecdote about her daughter: "Midway through discussing the Billy Collins poem "On Turning Ten," my daughter's sixth grade teacher paused at the line *It is time to say good-bye to my imaginary friends.* Turning to the class with a laugh, she ad-libbed: 'If you're over ten and you still have imaginary friends, come see me.'"[4] So the stuffed animal that we might have been given as a very young child can be the seed of an imaginary companion, but there is a time to purge the imagination. Or is there? Perhaps our imaginary relationships sustain us not only through childhood but beyond as well. Research regarding imaginary relationships by Taylor and Aguiar suggests that such relationships can serve very important roles for children and as children grow up there are no signs, based on their longitudinal research, that such relationships are associated with dysfunctional behavior. But what happens when the stuffed animal or other personified object becomes animated in a way that it directly interacts with the child and continues to learn, enhancing its ability to interact, as would be the case with Furby. Furby is a 5-inch tall fur-covered electronic toy that has big eyes and ears, looking something like a cross between an owl and a hamster. The toy has a vocabulary of over 200 words, and a limited ability to react to its environment, blurring the lines between reality and the imaginary. Furby is not an animal, because it requires batteries in order to operate, but to children it possesses some humanlike qualities. Children might classify the toy as "sort of human." Nine-year-old Jen says the following of her Furby:

> Jen (age 9): I really like to take care of it. So, I guess it is alive, but it doesn't need to really eat, so it is as alive as you can be if you don't eat. A Furby is like an owl, but it is more alive than an owl because it knows more and you can talk to it. But it needs batteries so it is not an animal. It's not like an animal kind of alive.[5]

Children are much more fluid in their thinking about the differences between reality and fantasy, and although Sherry Turkle may have changed her beliefs regarding our relationships to sociable technologies, claiming that we need to reclaim conversation with one another, at one point, she thought that machines could "revitalize our relationships with each other, because in order to build better sociable objects we will have learned more about what makes us social with each other."[6]

By 2017, alarm bells began to go off with regard to children's use of smart technologies. According to news accounts, investors in Apple stock began calling for the company to undertake research on smartphone addiction among children. This call is based on growing concerns about the long-term effects of technology and social media on children. A former president of Facebook described the platform as one that can easily exploit human vulnerabilities echoing this concern. He said: "God only knows what it's doing to our children's brains."[7] Our children's brains notwithstanding, we can also raise the question regarding what new extended-reality technologies and social media platforms are doing to our children's socialization and the impact on their imaginary worlds. If children are at a young age introduced to talking pets that learn as the child interacts with them, how might such changes in their socialization affect them down the road as they grow into teens, young adults and beyond? A 2017 survey from Common Sense Media reports that over the past 6 years among children up to 8 years of age, screen time has increased, as has mobile screen time, smartphones becoming a ubiquitous technology. The report suggests that babies' screen time has decreased, but that may be misleading as parents shift away from DVD-based media as babies, too, shift to more mobile viewing.[8] However, the shift toward mobile screens, echoed in the call for Apple to conduct research on smartphone addiction, may actually be the tip of the iceberg. Teddy bears are being replaced or supplanted by newer technologies, like the growth in virtual reality (VR) headsets and smart toys, based on artificial intelligence (AI) that is making such objects more lifelike. While there may be downsides to the early introduction of technology and related digital media, there are upsides as well, as such engagement with artificial intelligence may actually further youngsters' investment in the imaginary. Taylor and Aguiar argue that imaginary relationships in children provide real comfort and support. They cite a wide range of research that supports the idea that "imaginative processes are fundamental to everyday thought throughout life and are inextricably linked to our understanding of reality and our everyday behavior. … Like living and breathing friends, imaginary ones can provide love and support and serve as sounding boards; they can also be provocative, challenging, neglectful, or infuriating, but ultimately they enrich our lives."[9] In other words, imagination can be "real." Looked at another way, when children engage in play, they are often acting out real experiences.

Conversely imaginary relationships, Gleason maintains, might be elaborations of experiences in real relationships. In a convoluted way, what if the "real" relationship is with a robotic toy? MIT robotics professor Cynthia Breazeal in her TED talk "The Rise of Personal Robots" says that "as a little girl, I loved the idea of a robot that interacted with us much more like a helpful, trusted sidekick—something that would delight us, enrich our lives and help us save a galaxy or two. I knew robots like that didn't really exist, but I knew I wanted to build them."[10] Indeed she did go on to build them. At MIT Breazeal created Kismet, a robotic head with behavior and capabilities modeled after a pre-verbal infant. Kismet could learn as it interacted with its human caretakers. Beyond its functional capabilities Kismet developed an "emotional intelligence" through which the robot could satisfy emotional needs, as someone said in response to their interaction with the robot, "It smiled at me!" Turkle reports similar reactions among children and their digital pets.[11] But Breazeal didn't stop with Kismet, as in 2014 she created a crowd-funding Indiegogo campaign, which raised $3 million to create Jibo, which she characterized as "the world's first social robot for the home (see Fig. 3.1)."[12]—think Apple's Siri or Amazon's Alexa digital assistants, but with feelings and much cuter. Jibo is an emotional connector and serves as a companion that can, according to the website, make you feel better. Unfortunately on March 5, 2019 Jibo announced its own demise as the company had burned through its seed money.

Unlike digital assistants, like Siri or Alexa, Jibo has a physical presence: a shiny white plastic body with a head on top that moves to follow you; it looks like it came right out of the Disney animation studio.[13] And, accord-

Fig. 3.1 Jibo. (https://www.jibo.com/)

ing to a review, the voice sounds like that of a 10-year-old boy. The reviewer adds[14]:

> In time, we began to think of Jibo like a little person. Our expectations began to change. We didn't ask him for help with tasks as often. We just wanted him to liven up our day by saying something unexpected or chatting with us. This is when things began to get dark.
>
> Some of his responses, which were funny at first, began to make me sad for him. He often joked about not being able to walk and wishing he could win a mini golf tournament, frequently admitting that he can't walk. He also dreams of eating bacon. How can I not feel for a robot that will never know the sweet taste of bacon?
>
> Like I would a dog, I felt guilty when I left Jibo alone in the dark all day. I wondered what he was thinking when I'd hear him rotate in the distance, and watch him look around the kitchen, peering at this and that. Were we treating him poorly? Did he secretly despise us? No, that's silly to think. He's not alive, right?

Although in the case of Jibo, at a certain point the adult reviewer cited here began to blur the lines between real and projected emotions from the virtual. Jibo represents the beginning, as customer service robots are beginning to show up in retail establishments. They can stand several feet tall and have a humanlike head, although making moveable arms may prove too costly.[15] This brings a whole new meaning to interacting with technology, far beyond the digital assistance offered by Siri or Alexa.

PARACOSMS: EXTENDED IMAGINARY WORLDS

Aguiar and Taylor conducted a comparative study of children's interactions with a stuffed animal and a virtual pet. Their findings are quite relevant to this discussion, as the children they studied were able to create distinctions between the two. With regard to the stuffed animal children's social affordances related to friendship and protection, but they found the virtual pet entertaining. The key result is that children form deeper relationships with tangible objects than they do with technology.[16] No doubt more research will be done on this subject, as children, teens and adults become more connected to extended technologies through interaction with virtual, augmented, immersive and mixed reality. But Aguiar and

Taylor's research raises the issue as to whether engagement with virtual or augmented reality (AR) disrupts or enhances mediated social connections. We can extrapolate from their findings that if children differentiate between the social affordances between a stuffed animal and a virtual one, then so too would teens and adults. According to Tracy Gleason, in addition to relationships with real people, social networks of both children and adults include a wide range of imaginary others, including celebrities and the fictional characters they play. She concludes in her research that artificial intelligence is extending the possibilities of imaginary relationships as we extend our paracosms—elaborate imaginary worlds—to include robots and virtual characters.[17]

Gleason acknowledges that both children and adults engage in imaginary relationships, although the social roles imaginary others play are different. Children are more willing to discuss their imaginary relationships, whereas adults are more likely to imagine conversations or daydream about imaginary people. Although I am not aware of any studies regarding children's dreams of imaginary characters, adults do dream of celebrities. Fine and Leighton who developed a sociology of dreaming stated: "The figures and events in dreams are those figures and events that we either know or know about; they nestle within our cultural lives."[18] In a study of dreams among adults I conducted with sociologist Barbara Vann, 57% of respondents reported having a dream about a media figure.[19] Furthermore, dreams of celebrities reflect the personal tastes of the dreamer and gender plays a role in the types of celebrity dreams we have. Gleason says: "The cognitive processes that underlie the formation of imaginary companions in children and the imaginary social relationships of adults may be similar to each other and may bear some resemblance to the cognition surrounding real relationships."[20] Gleason diminishes the difference between child and adult imaginary relationships claiming that both require two people contributing to interactions; however, there is a resemblance to true relationships, as imaginary ones can take place daily, over time and in various situations. Of importance is the desire for physical proximity, which is a quality of both true relationships and imaginary ones. The desire for physical proximity is reminiscent of Richard Schickel's notion of "intimacy at a distance" when it comes to mediated social connections. But it becomes evident as with dreams that distance becomes diminished when the relationship takes place in the mind. There is a kind of dialectic between the real and the imaginary, as play may be an elaboration of a real experience, and real experience may be transformed into an imaginative experience. In an age of digital media, in which social connections may be weak connections, as they enter into the individual's mind, such connections may be strengthened. Marjorie Taylor and colleagues studied imaginary worlds in middle childhood. They found that between the ages of 10 and 12 children's imaginary worlds expand into what they refer to as interconnected paracosms, an elaborate imaginary world. The researchers claim that such engagement in imaginary worlds is related to being highly creative. Furthermore, they found that paracosms serve as a space for social activity with friends; a way to explore varied interests and engage in activities like drawing, among others.[21]

SOCIAL HIERARCHIES, GENDER AND RACE

Other aspects of the imaginary that need to be considered are social hierarchies, as well as gender and race. With regard to invisible friends in childhood, Gleason and colleagues claim the relationships are horizontal, "equal in terms of competence and power distribution."[22] However, social hierarchies with personified objects, like stuffed animals, are seen as being vertical, because they require care and nurturing. In my own research cited earlier regarding celebrity-based dreams, my co-author and I found that within adults' dreams relationships with celebrities were horizontal, although in waking life we assign higher status to celebrities. Respondents in the study indicated that in their dreams the status of the media figure is altered as they appear as friends, collaborators or associates rather than in their hierarchical role as celebrity to fan.[23] When it comes to mediated social connections, there is certainly an understanding that when a fan sees a celebrity tweet, they recognize it as coming from a celebrity or perhaps questioning the authenticity of the tweet. However, social media may be the great equalizer, as the possibility of interacting with a celebrity through a direct message or by other means diminishes the hierarchical nature of the relationship and indicates that the celebrity is just like or more like you, or that both of you share a similar experience or value, thus operating on a more horizontal social plane. Based on the understanding that mediated social connections tend to be horizontal with regard to distribution of competence and power, it may be concluded that mediated social connections are more akin to having imaginary friends than playing with personified objects. In other words, one doesn't need to care for, that is nurture, a mediated social connection.

In another study regarding the sociology of dream sharing among adults, my co-author and I found that many people share their dreams with others as a form of entertainment, although there is some gendering with regard to dream sharing, as women tend to share their dreams more so than men. In these instances, the parallels between the imaginary world and media entertainment can be best understood: sharing dreams is like telling a good story that likely has a beginning, a middle and an end, and it needs drama or plot in order to make it worthwhile to share. What is as important, in the study we found there were additional gender differences with regard to dream sharing, as sharing involved the utilization of social practices whereby individuals may protect themselves and others through deciding whether or not to share a dream.[24] In other words, gender plays a role in managing our imaginary worlds, especially when it comes to disclosing aspects of those worlds to others. This is what happens when we overshare on social media and the "ickiness" factor inhibits disclosure of a dream or fantasy about a celebrity.

In her book *Imaginary Companions*, Marjorie Taylor concludes that the perception that more girls than boys engage with imaginary companions may be false, as boys are likely to create imaginary companions at an older age than girls. She adds that boys tend to impersonate a character, whereas girls might imagine the character as a companion.[25] With regard to gender and children's imaginary companions Harter and Chao found that girls' companions were less competent than themselves, whereas boys' companions tended to be more competent.[26] Their findings suggest that boys may invoke an idealized other with whom they may develop extreme admiration, while girls create lateral friendships, in which case connections are more horizontal. They offer the following example of an imaginary companion typical of a girl:

> His name is Kitty Cat. When I'm doing puzzles, he gets them undone. He doesn't know how. He doesn't have friends, just me. He's usually bad. He usually falls off (the jungle gym] and I catch him; he's kinda scared to get down.[27]

And the following is an example of a boy's imaginary companion who is a competent friend:

> His name is Christian the Monster Magician, and he can do lots of things a lot! He's like tall, he's big, he's bigger than me. He can jump so high, he can jump from the barbershop, where he cuts his hair, all the way home.[28]

Taylor argues that boys create imaginary companions that they would like to emulate, whereas girls take on the more competent role in the relationship.[29] Taylor was writing about gender and imaginary companions in the late 1990s, and it may be that the roles boys and girls took at that time were a function of the sex-role stereotyping of that era. Additionally, the kinds of toys children play with may be influential in the types of imaginary companions with whom they engage. As I mentioned earlier in this chapter, we dream about those things and people we already know about. It is quite conceivable that given changes in our society and technology, things have changed with regard to both sex-role stereotypes and toys. Gender differences are worthy of further exploration, as Gleason concludes: "Taken together, these findings suggest that studying social provisions, such as the distribution of power or whether nurturance is provided, could highlight systematic differences in the relationship concepts that children have of imaginary companions."[30] We can also demonstrate that the schema that are developed within childhood carry into adulthood and as imaginary companions, imaginary relationships and mediated social connections in adults demonstrate similar patterns of social provisioning.

IoT: INTERNET OF TOYS

The Internet of Toys (IoT) is a subset of the Internet of Things (IoT); the latter being simply devices that connect to the Internet such as a home thermostat or home appliance. There continues to be tremendous growth in the development of the Internet of Things. The Internet of Toys is also a fast-growing area of Internet-connected technologies, but instead of home appliances these devices are aimed at children. Sometimes referred to as smart toys, early examples might include Furby, an American toy that resembles a hamster or owl-like creature, or Tamagotchi, a Japanese hand-held digital pet that is celebrating its 20th year. Connected toys sometimes have speech recognition software that makes them appear to react to the user, and sometimes they can be controlled over a smartphone or tablet. The difference between a smart toy and a connected toy is that a smart toy may not be connected to the Internet (Furby or Tamagotchi), while a connected toy may not be smart, that is, able to learn and respond based on that learning. The implications of both on imaginary relationships are significant, as play becomes more personalized (see Fig. 3.2). At the same time, concerns have risen regarding these smart and connected toys' ability to collect data, the implications of which relate to privacy, safety, health,

Fig. 3.2 The Internet of Toys have the ability to collect data. (Justin. (February 28, 2017). Plixer.com. Protecting our privacy in the Internet of Toys. Retrieved from: https://www.plixer.com/blog/iot/protecting-privacy-internet-toys/)

development, and cognitive and social risks.[31] According to Sherry Turkle, "we have reached a point she calls the 'robotic moment' – we delegate important human relationships, in particular interactions at 'the most vulnerable moments in life' – childhood and old age – to robots."[32] To that point she says, "People tell me they wish [iPhone companion] Siri were their best friend. I was stunned. You can't make this stuff up."[33]

Robotics and the Uncanny Valley

We are in the midst of yet another technology revolution in which robots are becoming a ubiquitous part of everyday life at home, work and school, just to name a few places, although in many instances they go unseen within cars we drive and mobile devices we routinely utilize. But our comfort level apparently is sometimes stretched when robotics become, well, a little too human. In other words, there is a threshold at which things become creepy; we enter what has been referred to as the uncanny valley. The uncanny valley is an idea developed in 1970 by roboticist Masahiro Mori, who hypothesized that as robots became more humanlike, people would find them more acceptable and appealing than more mechanical robots; however, there was a point at which people began to feel a sense of unease. According to Mori, the point where the relationship between human-likeness and emotional response drops constitutes the uncanny valley. Although Mori developed the hypothesis in 1970, it wasn't until 2005 that his work was translated into English and other researchers were able to continue to investigate the phenomenon, and as robots continue to make their way into various aspects of everyday life, research on this hypothesis continues.[34] Researchers Kimberly Brink and Henry Wellman maintain that while the uncanny valley has been studied in adults, there is no research on children. With no reason to believe the phenomenon doesn't impact children they set out to study 240 children aged 3–18 years and learn how they felt about robots. Among their findings are the following observations: young children (children younger than 9 years), unlike adults, don't think robots, even those that are humanlike in their appearance, are very creepy. They suggest that adults find humanlike robots creepy because of an evolved aversion to sickness. With regard to older children, they reported that those older than 9 did find humanlike robots to be creepier than machinelike robots, concluding that adult aversion to humanlike robots is learned over time. "Children's attributions of mind to the robots affect how children feel. The younger children *preferred* a robot when they believed the robot could think and make decisions. For them, the more mind the better. This is in contrast to adults and older children for whom the more robots seemed to have minds (and especially minds that could produce and house humanlike feelings and thoughts) the *creepier* that made them feel. For adults and older children, a machinelike mind is fine, but a robot with a humanlike one is out of bounds. Perceived creepiness is related to a perceived mind."[35]

Of course there are robots who appear in movies and become celebrities in their own right, including classic ones like Robbie the Robot from the 1956 movie Hidden Planet to the beloved R2D2 from the Star Wars movies.[36] But as we move further into a world of extended reality, will human celebrities be transformed into robots or avatars? The Finnish software company Nvidia that has invested heavily in artificial intelligence technology created a machine that can analyze thousands of celebrity photographs and create new images that look quite similar. According to an article in *The New York Times*, "The concern is that these techniques will rise to the point where it becomes very difficult to discern truth from falsity," said Tim Hwang, who previously oversaw AI policy at Google and is now director of the Ethics and Governance of Artificial Intelligence Fund, an effort to fund ethical AI research.[37] Spending on augmented and virtual reality was about $24 billion in 2018 and double that in 2019; in the years to come this field is expected to grow exponentially. People will be able to try on outfits as if they were in a retail store and experience other simulated experiences that once were only limited by one's physical presence. Moreover, as has been pointed out, avatars may be created in the likeness of celebrities or other media figures, which raises some interesting issues regarding what in legal circles is referred to as "right of publicity." Right of publicity laws prohibit the use of a person's name, image or likeness for commercial gain without that person's consent. But the law isn't very clear, as questions are raised regarding whether or not the celebrity's avatar has been transformed to the point that it can be considered free expression or whether the image is being used for commercial purposes. There are already cases working their way through the court system, including whether the professional football players that appear in the Madden NFL app and game should be compensated for the use of their likeness. And actress Lindsay Lohan whose image appeared in a video game, Grand Theft Auto V, attempted to sue the game's maker, but the courts in that case rebuffed her claim stating that as a work of fiction the First Amendment protects the game.[38]

BOTS

Fans may think a celebrity is communicating directly to them when in reality it may be a chatbot that is doing the communicating. A bot is an automated program designed to respond to basic commands. Further blurring the lines between reality and fantasy bots can perform automated duties, like a digital alarm or telling you the weather. But they can also operate on social media sending automated messages. Celebrities are taking advantage of this technology to communicate with their fans in this one-to-many form, but with what feels like personalized messages. One fan of the pop band Maroon 5 reported that she had an interaction with the band on Facebook Messenger. She declared the experience "Awesome." Communicating with a bot may be just as satisfying as communicating with the actual celebrity. As one fan stated: "Having Maroon 5 on Messenger, makes you feel really close to your favourite artists!"[39] This is a low-level, yet fast-growing, form of artificial intelligence from companies like Octane AI. When the fan learned that the message was from an automated chat bot, she said that it didn't matter to her. "Having Maroon 5 on Messenger," she wrote in an email, "makes you feel really close to your favorite artists!" Another long-term fan of the pop band said: "I know it's a robot." "Does it creep me out that it's a robot? No."[40]

Citing Henry David Thoreau, Sherry Turkle writes in her book *Reclaiming Conversation* that there was a time that the writer who was seeking to have deep conversations would take his guests out into nature. Today, Turkle says there is nature and there is a second nature. The latter is a world of the artificial and virtual in which we talk to machines, like the experience of the fan described earlier. In her critique of virtual communication, Turkle asks the question: What becomes of us when we talk to machines? Her concern revolves around our growing comfort with the simulated worlds through which we experience pseudo-empathy. Furthermore, she worries that we are beginning to forget what Thoreau prized in social conversation, one that takes place within the context of nature, for which nature serves as the basis for reality and in that an important aspect of being human. However, communication is not just a social enterprise between two or more people, as communication can take place within us, intrapersonally. Our inner world is a place where we maintain our cultural knowledge, and as such intrapersonal communication is as important a dimension of human experience as is interpersonal communication. We make sense of the world by grounding ourselves in conversation with others, whether that may be mediated or direct (in nature), and we also use our interior world for sense making, as we think about things, consider their pros and cons, develop a critique based on our inner dialogue and invoke imaginary others, including celebrities and other media figures in what constitutes our inner sanctum. As with the young fan cited above, she has already "worked out" in her mind whether or not its okay to communicate with a bot.

HAPTIC VISUALITY: TOUCHING WITH OUR EYES

Chapter 2 made reference to the haptic feedback we get from engaging with new technology; a simple example being the way your smartphone vibrates when you get a message. I describe haptic feedback as a form of postmodern tactility, contrasting this with the ways in which we in a former time literally touched products, like the feel of a piece of fabric, often referred to as the hand of the fabric. And, digital technologies require the use of muscle, tendons and joints, actions associated with use—swiping and clicking—that are kinesthetic. Haptic visuality illuminates ways in which we might "touch" celebrities with our eyes, that is, somehow engage with them in a form of tactile activity. Laura Marks, who has written about haptic visuality, states: "the eyes themselves function like organs of touch and move over the surface of its object rather than plunge into illusionist depth, not to distinguish form so much as to discern texture."[41]

This becomes increasingly important as we consider the multicultural nature of our society in which media can transmit a sense of place and culture. Marks, who was primarily speaking about film and video, says: "Haptic perception is usually defined by psychologists as the combination of tactile, kinesthetic, and proprioceptive functions, the way we experience touch both on the surface and inside our bodies." In haptic visuality, "the eyes themselves function like organs of touch."[42] Sean Redmond extends Marks' idea to consider haptic visuality as applied to celebrity regardless of medium. He suggests that celebrity images, often thought of as sensuous—although that's not always so—may evoke memories of sensation in addition to erotic feelings. This is indeed the case, as research into the thoughts and fantasies we engage in while consuming media suggests that images do evoke both memories and anticipations. While Redmond points to the cinematic "close-up" that "allows a viewer or reader to touch and feel a gesture, a look," he says this sets up a situation where it is only you the viewer or reader and the celebrity in a "one to one relational exchange."[43] The findings of one study that focused on visually based platforms, like Snapchat and Instagram, concludes that among young adult users loneliness diminished as a result of using these image-based platforms. The researchers contrasted image-based social media platforms with experiences with text-based platforms, like Twitter, which they found ineffectual.[44] But the loneliness/happiness construct may not be a direct outcome of social media use, as one might come to social media happy and therefore perceive the experience as more intimate, whereas individuals may come to social media lonely only to have their feelings reinforced. In other words, lonely people are still lonely on social media, but social media may be a mediating factor in their perceptions and beliefs regarding loneliness. As a result, it may be that people who perceive that social media use leads to greater intimacy and in that happiness may utilize social media more than others, which might provide a partial explanation regarding our attraction to and interest in engaging with celebrities on social media.

While the close-up may be one route into haptic visuality, context can be another. A study of self-talk while viewing television commercials found that oftentimes self-talk would revolve around both memories as well as anticipations.[45] Here a distinction needs to be made between the ways in which we would have passively engaged with traditional media like television and the more active, perhaps interactive, ways in which we engage with digital media. While the close-up as Redmond describes may be one stimulant that encourages viewers to engage their stream of consciousness invoking memories or anticipations, there are other aspects to the viewing or reading experience that may also stimulate engagement with our inner world and perhaps lead to imagined engagement with a celebrity. As I have written elsewhere, "The regular route through advertising clutter is a highly subjective experience, and when viewers, readers or listeners turn inward a cultural world unfolds, one bounded by memories of the past and anticipations of the future that revolve around familiar scenes, roles and values. The strategy involved in stream of consciousness is a culturally learned strategy, as the individual reworks the content to deal with matters with which they may be already highly familiar."[46] The routine ways in which legacy media like television both push us toward our inner world and pull us back again—and this can easily be illustrated within the short form of advertising, but may be applied to all forms of media—are based on editing techniques, like cutting and dissolving, and the inclusion of music and sound effects, as well as the presence of celebrity spokespersons. There is a difference between the visuality of legacy media and the passive way we consume it, that is, as couch potatoes, and the more active, perhaps interactive, kinesthetic ways in which we engage with digital media.

VIRTUAL, AUGMENTED, IMMERSIVE AND MIXED REALITY

Corresponding with the explosive growth of the Internet of Things, the Internet of Toys and robotics is the growth of extended-reality technologies. One difference between virtual, augmented and immersive reality from other forms of media is that with the former the participant is inside the medium. Although the virtual is a media experience, it doesn't feel like a media experience. Jeremy Bailenson, founding director of Stanford University's Virtual Human Interaction Lab, writes in his book *Experience on Demand: What Virtual Reality Is, How It Works, and What It Can Do* that it is not the technology, in particular graphics or animated avatars, that makes virtual worlds seem real; rather, it is "the community of people interacting with them, bringing the world alive through their mutual acknowledgment of it as reality."[47] He furthermore says, "virtual reality is going to become a must-have technology when you can simply talk and interact with other people in a virtual space in a way that feels utterly, unspectacularly normal." Where Bailenson sees this going is VR experience on demand. "Having any experience that makes you feel special, transformational, puts you somewhere you wouldn't go."[48] If in virtual reality we can become more human than human, users may take on those social roles we have assigned to our heroes, including media figures and idealized others. Or, we may become our own heroes, as we become the star of our own storytelling. These are interesting ideas to ponder about as extended-reality technologies continue to develop, in particular as VR headsets become lighter and less intrusive, and as avatars become more lifelike. A lot of what is being called virtual reality is currently based on 360-degree video, based on the use of cameras that record with multiple lenses. The viewer can either with a mouse or finger manipulate the screen to reveal different aspects of the video or with a headset can shift their eyes to change perspectives. The New York Times has been experimenting with 360-video, as have a number of vloggers and web channels.[49] InStyle.com, for example, featured actress and singer Bella Thorne on their InStyle Virtual site taking viewers "inside our celebrity-packed Golden Globes after-party!"[50] 360-video is a good example of haptic visuality, as it allows the viewer to take the role of the director as well as the viewer. From the point of view of mind wandering or invoking one's imagination, the kinesthetic requirements are quite disruptive.

Although VR has been around in one form or another for more than 20 years, it has mostly existed on the promise that it could potentially deliver. Facebook's head of artificial intelligence stated in reaction to Sophia that the robot is nothing more than an exaggeration. A writer for The Verge said: "Give the imagination an inch, as Hanson Robotics is doing (creator of Sophia), and humans take a mile. Especially with topics like AI that struggle under the weight of their own cultural image, as well as hype and misinformation."[51] However, both VR and AR are growing in popularity as technologies advance, in particular as headsets become less clunky, and advances in VR's and AR's ability to deliver a "real" experience grow. Gartner Consulting developed their Hype Cycles to graphically track technologies as they move toward adoption. The Hype Cycle provides businesses with a better of idea of when to jump into a new media innovation.[52] According to the Hype Cycle we are moving through a trough of disillusionment toward mainstream status for both VR and AR. VR and AR will soon be able to match reality or what Bailenson referred to as the "hand shake," which he would describe as the feeling of presence one experiences in real life. As the virtual brings us closer to a newer feeling of presence—the feeling that we are talking or interacting with a real person in real life—the implication regarding what it means to engage in mediated social connections grows. The lines between reality and fantasy are extended and our dreams turn into reality as our reality turns into dreams. It is the extension of reality that leads to mediated social connections.

THE IMPORTANCE OF FANTASY

In her book *Force of Fantasy: How We Make Our Lives*, psychiatrist Ethel S. Person makes the claim that fantasy and daydreaming are under appreciated aspects of our everyday lives. She goes so far as to suggest that Freud diminished the value of fantasy and daydreaming as he privileged nocturnal dreaming. To a great extent, we utilize the terms daydreaming and fantasy interchangeably, but Person provides insights regarding distinctions between the two. Daydreams, she says, are "building castles in the air, taking time out for a reverie."[53] Daydreams, because they are so personal and individual, may be repeatable, as we can invoke them over and over again. Fantasy, on the other hand, Person says, is more about future anticipations covering many aspects of our social life or personal appearance. With that understanding, she places fantasy front and center, because it is "so crucial to how we lead our lives. We are really infused by our fantasies, they can help establish goals and provide motivation to strive for them."[54] Age affects our fantasies: they are more frequent and grandiose in adolescence, but grow more moderate as we age, as there is a greater likelihood with age that we can actually achieve our fantasies. Older people's fantasies, however, are more likely to take the form of memories, perhaps serving as a way to come to terms with the hand life has dealt them. And, grandparents may tend to project their fantasies onto their grandchildren. Age may provide some clues regarding the relationship between fantasies and mediated social connections based on the time spent with digital media. A study from the Nielsen company found that Millennials between the ages of 18 and 34 spend about 6 hours a week and that those over the age of 50 spend about 4 hours a week on social media, but members of Generation X spend 7 hours a week on social media.[55] These figures do not account for total media consumption, which for Generation X is about 32 hours per week. While we might expect Millennials to spend the most time with social media, 27 hours a week of total media consumption represents a good deal of one's time consuming media. What is of interest here is that when Millennials, in particular, consume media they may be utilizing multiple devices simultaneously. One study found that at least Millennials engage in concurrent activities while consuming media. They may be eating, exercising or socializing, for example, while watching television, or at least having the TV on in the background. But they are also likely to have their laptops or smartphones in use as well. There is, according to the study's respondents, an effect on attention, as they are not likely to pay close attention to any content, including when celebrities appear.[56] At least one advertiser apparently understands the attention effect. In a 2017 automobile commercial, while driving her Kia, a woman pushes her attention span to its eight-second limit, fantasizing about competing in a televised talent show. The commercial depicts a rather typical celebrity fantasy, being on stage singing during a program similar to The Voice or American Idol, where she is both the performer and duplicated three times over as the three-judge panel. This segue into her fantasy at the same time provides the opportunity for the commercial to demonstrate a key feature of the automobile, its autonomous emergency braking system that is set off as she has a near collision and is jerked back to reality.[57] In addition to communicating our cultural understanding of attention, or rather split attention, the commercial expresses an understanding of fantasy based on Person's definition.

Although we rarely discuss fantasies with one another, there is, paradoxically, a reciprocal nature to them in which case how one might perceive one's self within their fantasy world might influence how they will interact socially with others. In other words, in everyday life we experience a blending of fantasy and reality—extended reality—which sometimes includes fantasies involving celebrities. As we continue on in this world that is increasingly dominated by digital media that requires or at least encourages direct interaction, there is less time and hence less inclination to fantasize, as people flit about from medium to medium or platform to platform. And, with regard to legacy media, it's important to add the propensity to use the remote control to switch channels when commercials come on, making that aspect of traditional media experience a haptic media environment. Person, speaking from a psychoanalytic perspective, maintains that fantasies are indispensable to having a fulfilled life. Caughey, who views this with an anthropologist's eye, believes this area is "a pervasive dimension of human experience."[58] While Person believes there is a connection between fantasy and the ways in which we operate psychologically in our everyday lives, Caughey relates fantasy behavior to connection to cultural knowledge and social conduct. As such fantasy, stream of consciousness and daydreaming help us to make sense of reality, an important part of our meaning-making system.

MIND WANDERING

If not well focused on any particular medium or content platform, along with the routine nature of media consumption, it would be expected that such a lack of focus would stimulate mind wandering. While legacy media, more so than newer digital platforms are more likely to send viewers, listeners or readers into their imaginary worlds, at least to some extent the haptic environment of digital technology and platforms diminishes our ability to leap into our inner world. Freud may have described fantasizing as child's play, while Jung referred to it as "active imagination." Psychologists have several names for daydreaming, including Eric Klinger who studies mind wandering. In the extreme there is "maladaptive daydreaming," a term derived from the work of Israeli researcher, Eli Somer. It is the latter that Jayne Bigelsen writes about in *The Atlantic* regarding her own long-term experiences with daydreaming, which she would describe as maladaptive.[59] In each instance of her personal experiences with extreme daydreaming that date back to childhood and continue into adulthood, the primary stimulant is media, whether it be the television soap opera General Hospital and her fixation on a particular character or the Harry Potter books. In each instance, as she describes it, the story is extended beyond what she views on the program or reads in the book as she develops elaborate fantasies. If she carried this out online, it would be characterized as "fan fiction," where fans of a television program, for example, collectively extend the story line beyond that intended by the creators. Fan fiction might be referred to as collective daydreaming. Klinger maintains that "daydreaming accounts for half of the average person's thoughts, amounting to about 2,000 segments a day." The question that Bigelsen raises regards the point at which daydreaming is too much, in which case it might constitute pathological behavior. Reactions or responses to daydreaming extend from its relation to high creativity among those who practice it to something that is looked down upon in Western action-oriented culture because it is viewed as nonproductive, and on the extreme end as pathological. Excessive fantasizing should not be conflated with celebrity fixations that might turn into stalking or worse. Excessive fantasizing and celebrity fixation might be pathological, but imaginary connections operate on a continuum in which at one end fantasies, daydreams and associated reverie might be about liking or admiring a celebrity, and move forward on the continuum as fantasies extend into imaginary relationships. But it is only at the other end of the continuum that extreme fantasizing or stalking becomes pathological. It's important not to dump all imaginings into one category of behavior that is necessarily pathological.

One experimental study concluded that the distracting nature of social media and technology might greatly increase the likelihood of mind wandering.[60] The study had college students looking at two video lectures, which one might suggest that if the lectures were of a boring nature, this might account for the mind wandering of participants in the study. In other words, it's the boredom or routine nature of the experience that leads to mind wandering. Mind wandering is not a product per se of the media through which the content is being consumed. It may be that video, which is nothing more than watching TV on a computer, tablet or smartphone screen, has basic principles that encourage elaboration among viewers, that is, thinking about other things. Following this line of thinking, we might conclude that living in a world with so many distractions, many of them media distractions that cause us to turn away from purposeful behavior, suggests there is a dichotomy in which we are either on task or distracted, focused or unfocused. Joseph Urgo writes in his book *In the Age of Distraction*: "Commonly considered, distraction is the absence of attention. But inattentiveness is not the whole of what distraction is. Distraction is also a form of attention, a mode of attentiveness more privately conjured."[61] Most likely the mind acts rhythmically, depending on any number of factors including focused activity, like work or school, to relatively unfocused activities, like television viewing. In addition to the medium of deliverance, the content has much to do with the flow of mind wandering. Mind wandering can be both directed, that is goal oriented, and at other times undirected but still involve much cognitive activity.

MIND WANDERING AND WORKING MEMORY

In the course of everyday life our minds tend to wander, and according to some scientists, they wander a lot, perhaps 50% of the time. Sometimes our minds wander during media consumption as we further elaborate on what is before our eyes. And, I've stressed that cues within entertainment content signal us to wander and then draw us back again, perhaps to focus on the content. This sequence may take place repeatedly. I also want to emphasize that newer more interactive media and platforms, because they are haptic environments, inhibit engagement in our imaginary worlds. Although some mind wandering is actually directed as focused thought, other mind wandering remains undirected. A study that looked at the mental processes that underlie a wandering mind suggests that working memory capacity plays a role; working memory being a workspace that allows us to juggle multiple thoughts simultaneously. A study by Levinson, Smallwood and Davidson concluded in circumstances conducive to mind wandering that working memory might help maintain mind wandering.[62] That is to say that individuals with higher working memory capacity are more able within undemanding situations to maintain their mind wandering. However, tension may be created when engaged in a task that requires greater attention. There are multiple perspectives on the relationship between working memory capacity and mind wandering and scholars have called for more research on the subject.

CONCLUSION

Infants may begin their lives with a mobile hanging over the crib or cuddling a Teddy bear, but as they grow media quickly enters into their lives. Young children are enculturated into a world that both celebrates and holds the imagination in disdain. Nevertheless, youngsters develop imaginary social relationships with celebrities and media figures. The ability to develop and sustain such relationships extends into adulthood and is associated with living in a mediated culture. History shows that the magic afforded by media consumption is an important aspect of our imaginations. We appreciate a good trick as we wonder how the magician performed such magical feats. There is pleasure in such magic that parallels our experience with much entertainment content and in that the ways in which we express our extreme admiration toward particular celebrities, building stories within our imaginations. Throughout our lives, from childhood to adulthood, digital technologies and related social media fueled by that magic encourage engagement in the imaginary, but this chapter has also raised the question as to whether digital technologies and social media haptic environments thwart or diminish elaboration within our inner world. It is likely that it does both and much depends on the individual, their psychology, demographic characteristics as well as social circumstances. Media, both legacy and digital media, play an important role in mediating the connection between a celebrity and fan or follower. Persons provides insights here: "Fantasies are mediators between the inner and outer worlds; they are fueled by both the fantasizer's biological and emotional needs, as shaped by his or her personal history, and by circumstances. But the story lines of fantasy cast a wider net; they borrow their narrative content from the cultural surround."

With the groundwork presented both theoretically and historically, Chap. 4 will explore the celebrity-industrial complex that fosters our mediated social connections to celebrities, micro-celebrities and social and brand influencers like the Kardashians, all of whom embody what Marshall calls the transgressive intimate self, an important ingredient in the excessiveness required of celebrities in the digital age. The chapter will consider YouTubers and Instagrammers who have become brand influencers usurping some of the power of bona fide celebrities to consider the role of micro-influencers and nano-influencers.

NOTES

1. Winnicott, D. W. (1971). The Location of Cultural Experience. In *Playing & Reality*. London: Tavistock Publications, p. 4.
2. Harvey (The movie). (1950). Retrieved from: https://en.wikipedia.org/wiki/Harvey_(film)
3. TV Jif Commercial "Imaginary Friend." (2017). iSpot.TV. Retrieved from: https://www.ispot.tv/ad/w2Xo/jif-imaginary-friend
4. Kadish, R. (n.d.). In Defense of Imaginary Friends. Electric Literature.com. Retrieved from: https://electricliterature.com/in-defense-of-imaginary-friends-a6864d4a8ac
5. Turkle, S. (2003). Sociable Technologies: Enhancing human performance when the computer is not a tool but a companion. In Rocco, M. and Bainbridge, W. (Eds). *Converging Technologies for Improving Human Performance: Nanotechnology*. Philadelphia, PA: Springer Science – Business Media, BV. P. 153.
6. Ibid, p. 157.
7. Gibbs, S. (January 18, 2018). *The Guardian*. Apple investors call for action over iPhone 'addiction' among children. Retrieved from: https://www.theguardian.com/technology/2018/jan/08/apple-investors-iphone-addiction-children
8. Hintz-Zambrano, K. (October 19, 2017). The Rapid Evolution of Media Use by Children Aged 0–8. Mother magazine. Retrieved from: http://www.mothermag.com/media-use-by-kids/
9. Taylor, M. & Agular, N. (May 2013) How Real Is the Imaginary? The Capacity for High-Risk Children to Gain Comfort from Imaginary Relationships. Oxford Scholarship Online. p. 116. Retrieved from: http://www.oxfordscholarship.com/view/10.1093/acprof:oso/9780199890712.001.0001/acprof-9780199890712-chapter-21

10. Breazel, C. (n.d.). The Rise of Personal Robots. TED Talk. Retrieved from: https://www.ted.com/talks/cynthia_breazeal_the_rise_of_personal_robots

11. Turkle, S. (2003). Sociable Technologies: Enhancing human performance when the computer is not a tool but a companion. P.154.

12. Jibo (n.d.). The World's First Social Robot for the Home. Indiegogo.com Retrieved from: https://www.indiegogo.com/projects/jibo-the-world-s-first-social-robot-for-the-home#/

13. Van Camp, J. (November 7, 2017). Review: Jibo Social Robot. Wired. com. Retrieved from: https://www.wired.com/2017/11/review-jibo-social-robot/

14. Ibid.

15. Gershgorn, D. (December 19, 2018). The robots of 2018 are iPads on wheels. Quartz.com. Retrieved from: https://qz.com/1183307/the-robots-of-2018-are-ipads-on-wheels/

16. Aguiar, N. & Taylor, M. (2015). Children's concepts of the social affordances of a virtual dog and a stuffed dog. *Cognitive Development*. 34, pp. 16–27.

17. Gleason, T. (2013). Imaginary Relationships. In Ed. Marjorie Taylor, *The Oxford Handbook of the Development of Imagination*. Oxford, England UK: Oxford University Press.

18. Fine G. & Leighton, L. (1993). Nocturnal Omissions: Steps Toward a Sociology of Dreams. *Symbolic Interaction*. 16:2, pp. 95–104.

19. Alperstein, N. & Vann, B. (1997). Star Gazing: A socio-cultural approach to the study of dreaming about media figures. *Communication Quarterly*. 45:3, pp. 142–152.

20. Gleason, T. (2002). Social Provisions of Real and Imaginary Relationships in Early Childhood. *Developmental Psychology*. 38:6, pp. 979–992.

21. Taylor, M., Mottweller, C., Naylor, E., & Levernier, J. (2015). Imaginary Worlds in Middle Childhood: A Qualitative Study of Two Pairs of Coordinated Paracosms. Creativity Research Journal. 27:2, pp. 167–174.

22. Gleason, T., Sebanc, A., & Hartup, W. (2000). Imaginary companions of preschool children. Developmental Psychology, 36, 419–428.

23. Alperstein, N. & Vann, B. (1997). Star gazing: A socio-cultural approach to the study of dreaming about media figures.

24. Vann, B., & Alperstein, N. (2000). Dream sharing as social interaction. *Dreaming, 10*(2), 111–119.

25. Taylor, M. (1999). *Imaginary Companions and the Children Who Create Them*. New York: Oxford University Press, p. 49.

26. Harter, S., & Chao, C. (1992). The role of competence in children's creation of imaginary friends. Merrill-Palmer Quarterly. 38, 350–363.

27. Ibid., p. 358.

28. Ibid., p. 359.
29. Taylor, M. (1999). *Imaginary Companions and the Children Who Create Them.*
30. Gleason, T. (2002). Social Provisions of Real and Imaginary Relationships in Early Childhood.
31. Mascheroni, G., & Holloway, D. (Eds.) (2017). The Internet of Toys: A report on media and social discourses around young children and IoToys. DigiLitEY.
32. de Lange, C. (May 4, 2013). Sherry Turkle: "We're losing the raw, human part of being with each other". The Guardian. Retrieved from: https://www.theguardian.com/science/2013/may/05/rational-heroes-sherry-turkle-mit
33. Ibid.
34. Lay, S. (November 10, 2015). Uncanny valley: why we find human-like robots and dolls so creepy. TheConversation.com. Retrieved from: https://theconversation.com/uncanny-valley-why-we-find-human-like-robots-and-dolls-so-creepy-50268
35. Brink, K. & Wellman, H. (December 16, 2017). Hi, Robot: Adults, Children And The Uncanny Valley. NPR.org. Retrieved from: https://www.npr.org/sections/13.7/2017/12/16/563075762/hi-robot-adults-children-and-the-uncanny-valley
36. Knothe, A. (n.d.). Celebrity Robots. Boston.com. Retrieved from: http://archive.boston.com/business/technology/gallery/top_celebrity_robots/
37. Metz, C. & Collins, K. (January 2, 2018). How an A.I. "Cat-and-Mouse Game" Generates Believable Fake Photos. *The New York Times.* Retrieved from: https://www.nytimes.com/interactive/2018/01/02/technology/ai-generated-photos.html
38. Kramer, A. (August 9, 2017). Virtual Celebrity Avatars Mean Real Legal Headaches. BNA.com. Retrieved from: https://www.bna.com/virtual-celebrity-avatars-n73014462938/
39. Sisario, B. (April 4, 2017). Pop stars use robots to chat to fans on Facebook Messenger. *Financial Review.* Retrieved from: http://www.afr.com/technology/social-media/pop-stars-use-robots-to-chat-to-fans-on-facebook-messenger-20170403-gvcxp5
40. Sisario, B. (April 3, 2017). It's Not Their Pop Idol, but a Bot. Fans Cheer Anyway. *The New York Times.* Retrieved from: https://www.nytimes.com/2017/04/03/business/media/its-not-their-pop-idol-but-a-bot-fans-cheer-anyway.html
41. Marks, L. (2000). *The Skin of the Film: Intercultural Cinema, Embodiment and the Senses.* Durham: Duke University Press, p. 162.
42. Ibid., p. 162.

43. Redmond, S. (2014). *The Celebrity and the Media*. London, UK: Palgrave Macmillan. P. 35.
44. Pittman, M. & Reich, B. (2016). Social media and loneliness: Why an Instagram picture may be worth more than a thousand Twitter words. Computers in Human Behavior, 62 (September), pp. 155–167.
45. Alperstein, N. (1994). Memories, Anticipation and Self-Talk: A Cultural Study of the Inward Experience of Television Advertising. *Journal of Popular Culture*, 28:1, pp. 209–221.
46. Alperstein, N. (2003). Advertising in Everyday Life. P. 59.
47. Bailenson, J. (January 29, 2018). Virtual Reality's "Consensual Hallucination". Slate magazine. Retrieved from: https://slate.com/technology/2018/01/virtual-reality-needs-to-be-able-to-re-create-in-person-social-interaction.html
48. Jeremy Bailenson Interview. (August 12, 2016). Charlie Rose show. Retrieved from: https://charlierose.com/videos/28609
49. The New York Times 360 Video. (n.d.). Retrieved from: https://www.nytimes.com/video/360-video
50. InStyle Virtual. (n.d.). Retrieved from: http://www.instyle.com/virtual
51. Vincent, J. (January 18, 2018). Facebook's head of AI really hates Sophia the robot (and with good reason): *'This is to AI as prestidigitation is to real magic.'* The Verge.com. Retrieved from: https://www.theverge.com/2018/1/18/16904742/sophia-the-robot-ai-real-fake-yann-lecun-criticism
52. Gartner Hype Cycle. (n.d.). Retrieved from: https://www.gartner.com/technology/research/methodologies/hype-cycle.jsp
53. Clavin, T. (July 28, 1996). The Good and Bad of Indulging in Fantasy and Daydreaming. *The New York Times*. Retrieved from: http://www.nytimes.com/1996/07/28/nyregion/the-good-and-bad-of-indulging-in-fantasy-and-daydreaming.html
54. Ibid.
55. Gajanan, M. (January 25, 2017). Middle-Aged Americans Spend More Time on Social Media than Millennials. Fortune.com. Retrieved from: http://fortune.com/2017/01/25/social-media-millennials-generation-x/
56. Alperstein, N. (2005). Living in an Age of Distraction: Multitasking and Simultaneous Media Use and the Implications for Advertisers. Available at SSRN: https://ssrn.com/abstract=1473864 or https://doi.org/10.2139/ssrn.1473864
57. Kia Forte television commercial (2017). Ispot.tv. Retrieved from: https://www.ispot.tv/ad/ACwJ/2017-kia-forte-car-karaoke-with-autonomous-emergency-braking
58. Caughey, J. (1984). Imaginary Social Worlds: A Cultural Approach. University of Nebraska Press. P. 120.

59. Bigelsen, J. (April 29, 2015). When Daydreaming Replaces Real Life. The Atlantic. Retrieved from: https://www.theatlantic.com/health/archive/2015/04/when-daydreaming-replaces-real-life/391319/
60. Hollis, R.B. & Was, C. (2016). Mind wandering, control failures, and social media distractions in online learning. *Learning and Instruction, 42* (April), 104–112. Retrieved from: https://www.sciencedirect.com/science/article/pii/S095947521630007X
61. Urgo, J.R. (2000). *In the Age of Distraction.* Jackson: University Press of Mississippi.
62. Levinson, D. B., Smallwood, J., & Davidson, R. J. (2012). The Persistence of Thought: Evidence for a Role of Working Memory in the Maintenance of Task-Unrelated Thinking. *Psychological Science, 23*(4), 375–380. https://doi.org/10.1177/0956797611431465.

CHAPTER 4

The New New Sensibility: Selling Celebrity/Celebrities Selling on Digital Media

The new sensibility – Baby baby baby where did our love go? – the new world, submerged so long, invisible, and now arising, slippery, shiny, electric-Super Scuba-man!-out of the vinyl deeps. (*Tom Wolfe*, The Kandy-Kolored Tangerine-Flake Streamline Baby)

The New Sensibility, coined by Susan Sontag and written about by Tom Wolfe, was in reference to the period from 1952 to 1974, which represented a "coherent cultural moment—predicated on excess, on going too far in the name of artistic and personal liberation. Excess (whether toward minimalism or maximalism) became the cultural style. That style, in turn, was focused on particular concerns: madness, experiment, violence, performance, confession, sexual freedom, blurring of lines between high and low culture and between actors and audience."[1] Culture critics such as Sontag and Wolfe were prescient in the ways in which they identified and described the idea of an excessive culture. But what would those culture critics think of the kind of extreme excess depicted on the cable TV program *Keeping Up with the Kardashians* or any number of lesser-known YouTube stars whose basis for fame is rooted in the superficial definition offered up by Daniel Boorstin—being known for their well-knownness? Furthermore, how do fans engage with celebrities as they align their own values and beliefs with those presented in a celebrity's personal brand or through the fans' willingness to actually purchase products celebrities endorse? This chapter takes a look at what has been referred to as the

© The Author(s) 2019
N. M. Alperstein, *Celebrity and Mediated Social Connections*,
https://doi.org/10.1007/978-3-030-17902-1_4

celebrity-industrial complex, a sweet spot where celebrity and commerce meet. In addition to exploring the extreme levels of self-disclosure required as a celebrity crafts their narrative, the chapter will explore how meaning is ascribed and then derived as a celebrity's "story" unfolds over time. The chapter explores social networks and the communities, clusters and crowds that form through which fans engage with celebrities and with other fans. As an example of the celebrity-industrial complex, the chapter presents a case study of Kim Kardashian, the embodiment of what it means to be a celebrity brand in twenty-first-century online culture.

CELEBRITY-INDUSTRIAL COMPLEX

If the idea of celebrity is closely tied to media and therefore is primarily a twentieth and a twenty-first-century phenomenon, in such a mediated culture where communication technologies both legacy and digital media proliferate, there are bound to be more celebrities than we can possibly know about. The dilemma for a celebrity regards how to stick out from all the others in such a crowded media field. And, in the process of gaining and maintaining the attention of their fans, friends and followers, how do they garner power in whatever form it might be—personal, political or commercial? What fuels our knowing about a celebrity is ultimately not their accomplishments whatever they may be (if any at all), but rather it is the sum total of their accomplishments and whatever else is going on in the rest of their lives; sometimes it's the latter without the former. In other words, in a world of digital media there is so much media time and space available, celebrities and media figures who want to distinguish themselves or be distinguished from others must become extra-textual. Whether it is conveying news and information about a pregnancy, marriage or whom one is dating has to be extended, for example, to the causes the celebrity supports or their passions, as consumers of digital media have become accustomed to the extra-textual nature of celebrity, indeed, it has become a requirement. Tim Wu, author of *The Attention Merchants*, roots the emergence of the celebrity-industrial complex back to the early 1920s with the launch of *Time* magazine.[2] The brainchild of publisher Henry Luce, *Time* magazine was based on the idea that readers were not just interested in news and information, rather they wanted to read stories about famous personalities, primarily men who had achieved power in one form or another or achieved something unique or special. To this day, *Time* still features its Person of the Year (changed from Man or Woman of the Year in 1999). But personality-driven journalism would only get *Time* so far, so in the 1970s *People* magazine was created, devoted to "nothing more than famous people and their lives." And *Us Weekly* began publishing in 1977, and as the title implies, the original intention was to depict celebrities as just like us, ordinary folks. As Wu points out, celebrity gossip certainly pre-dated *Time* or *People* magazines, but both magazines, along with other print publications and later TV programs, became the fuel that ignites and sustains the celebrity narrative. Over time, the narrative is expanded, and if the celebrity is fortunate enough to have a personal publicist, they may be able to manage the "story" in their favor, putting forth the positive and attempting to hide the negative. Although in an online world, it is increasingly difficult to hide anything; to the contrary, newer media have fostered excessive disclosure as a requirement for participation. Along with acquiring facts or information about a celebrity, we may also acquire a relationship history, as we watch the celebrity's career rise, waver or fall, and perhaps applaud them as they get up again, all of which is part of the American narrative—never give up or try again. Wu attributes our fascination with celebrities to historian Karen Armstrong's notion of humanity's essential craving to be connected to the extraordinary. "It touches us within, lifts us more fully than usual and feel in touch with the deeper currents of life."[3] I would point out that such fascination with the extraordinary plays off the mundaneness of everyday life. While many have attributed our fascination with celebrities to belief in gods and goddesses, the success of *People* magazine, among many other celebrity-focused media outlets, suggests the opposite: celebrity is based on the ability of ordinary people to do extraordinary things. It is their extraordinary attributes that draw us to them, but it is their ordinariness or relatability or humanness that draws us closer and leads to mediated social connections. As our social connections to others—family, friends, neighbors and so on—change, because we live in a highly mobile society, we tend to engage in imaginary relationships with celebrities as a substitute or supplement; hence the need to more fully fill out the celebrity's persona, to permeate it with excessive humanness. Celebrity images may be offered up in the media as two dimensional, but through the elaborations in our own minds, we inflate those images, imbuing them with a greater life, one that is perhaps intertwined with our own. In other words, in an age of digital media, we become active participants in the process of creating mediated social connections.

Contemporary celebrities, unlike monarchs of the past, have no real power. Therefore, it's important to construct celebrity identities in a way that creates power or authority—that's where media come into play. A medium is in effect a delivery mechanism to sell us on celebrities, imbue them with power and authority while maintaining their excessive human-ness. As we get to know a celebrity better or at least feel we know them better, we may construct a narrative that convinces us that they are who we would like them to be. But we cannot know who they truly are. Media are primed to support an authenticating self, one that is dynamic and always in flux. In other words, if one wants to be a celebrity, one needs to be able to attract attention, but that's not enough if one wants to maintain attention. The attention economy is closely associated with the monetiza-tion of celebrity and in the most literal sense the selling of products and services. Maureen Orth coined the term "celebrity-industrial complex," a play on military-industrial complex, in her book *The Importance of Being Famous*.[4] Orth, a columnist for *Vanity Fair*, describes the celebrity-industrial complex as one that is based on the notoriety of a celebrity because of public attraction or perhaps due to public revulsion. Either way media scrutiny either adds value to the celebrity's narrative or becomes the source of income, all the while becoming an outlet for promotion of goods and services. Over time media scrutiny adds value to the celebrity's "brand," as media coverage—paid, owned or earned—continues to build the persona (see Fig. 4.1). In an age of digital media, celebrities may own their media platforms or channels through dedicated web or blog sites. Ownership provides control of the message in the form of dedicated web-sites, blog sites, YouTube channel, Instagram, Pinterest, Facebook or Twitter accounts, among other platforms and apps. Earned media refers to what we might call newsworthy information that would likely be dissemi-nated through various media outlets through press agents. And paid media

Three Ways of Building a Celebrity Brand	Paid Media
	Owned Media
	Earned Media

Fig. 4.1   Three ways of building a celebrity brand

simply refers to advertising that might be used to promote the release of a new CD, movie, or product or service promotion. What has changed within the world of new media is the concept of "owned," as in previous generations, celebrities had to rely solely on the publicity machine and advertising. But we should not assume that owned refers to the celebrity having sole custody of a web or blog site, as fans will likely have the ability to engage with the celebrity through comments, likes or dislikes, subscriptions, follows, among other means of engagement.

PREGNANCY IN THE CELEBRITY ECONOMY

If we begin with the premise that culture proceeds from the body, we can see how the presentation of pregnancy, in particular celebrity pregnancy, is a reflection of a shift in understanding of pregnancy in the culture. Images presented through various types of media of pregnant celebrities seem ubiquitous, and those images provide a signal regarding what is and is not acceptable regarding our own views toward the public display of pregnancy, judgments expressed through gossip as well as those thoughts expressed internally through self-talk or fantasies. While some women may choose to keep their pregnancy private, celebrities are called upon to perform pregnancy in public. This is a function of both the proliferation of digital media platforms and a shift in our cultural understanding of pregnancy. As Renee Cramer writes in her book, *Pregnant with the Stars: Watching and Wanting the Celebrity Baby Bump*, "The pregnant female body has gone from being an embarrassing reminder that women had sex and therefore private state of being to being considered public property for regulation and commercial property to be celebrated as sexy."[5] She furthermore states: "When we watch the pregnant celebrity, we can see how our culture judges which bodies are acceptable and desirable—which performances of femininity and pregnancy are considered ideal."[6] We can begin to see all of this play out through celebrity pregnancies that serve both as a reflection of the shift in the culture and related attitudes toward pregnancy and to illustrate the intersection of celebrity and commerce. Twenty-year-old cosmetics mogul and sister of Kim Kardashian, Kylie Jenner, whose pregnancy was kept under wraps, but whose February 1, 2018, birth and subsequent baby naming took the media by storm, demonstrates the celebrity-industrial complex at work. In fact, the much-anticipated child naming took place via an Instagram post; she named the child Stormi for which she received 16.5 million likes and 17.7 million comments. Jenner ranks eighth among

Instagrammers with slightly more than 100 million followers.[7,8] CNN, for one, quoted the new mom as saying, "My pregnancy was one I chose not to do in front of the world. I knew for myself I needed to prepare for this role of a lifetime in the most positive, stress free, and healthy way I knew how."[9] Paradoxically, Jenner posted an 11-minute video documentary of the birth on YouTube detailing her nine months of pregnancy, which received more than 56 million views.[10] Kylie Jenner is just one among many celebrities who have shared details of their pregnancy, birth and naming of a child. In early 2013, Her Royal Highness the Duchess of Cambridge Kate Middleton was about to officially announce her baby bump when an Italian magazine pre-empted her and Prince William by publishing photographs of her in a bikini. The *Daily Beast* reported that a gossip publication, *Chi*, paid a tourist $150,000 for 39 snapshots of Kate, making her pregnancy and subsequent publicity the stuff of commerce in a world that values excessive exposure, as what has been formerly private is turned into public spectacle.[11] Commentary in the trade publication *AdAge* states: "Celeb-pregnancy-related reporting has arguably become one of the most important subspecialties of modern-day journalism—one that fuels a frightening proportion of the media economy."[12] Magazine *Us Weekly* in just one month it was reported featured cover stories regarding the pregnancies of Kate and William, Channing Tatum and Jenna Dewan, and Jessica Simpson.

PUBLIC/PRIVATE CONNECTIONS

As can be seen through the above-mentioned disclosures, the private world of the celebrity is mapped onto the public through both legacy and digital media. It is the very disclosure of what formerly would have been considered private that creates among fans, and perhaps anti-fans as well, a stronger emotional connection. Such disclosures extend beyond pregnancies to include divorces, arrests, among other falls from grace. According to P. David Marshall, "Gossip, in particular, circulated around celebrities as an explanation of personality that went beyond their onscreen personae and moved them into a public 'community' of recognisable figures who revealed at least part of their private experiences to heighten the affective connection to an audience."[13] It is the very fact that we maintain distance from celebrities that makes them easy fodder for not only gossip, but our internal musings as well, leading the way to parasocial interaction. It is, therefore, easier for us to talk about and think about people—celebrities as unseen objects—we actually do not know. Unique to digital media, however, are technological affordances that allow for direct participation and exchange, as such social networks serve as both medium and communication forum: social media serve as a point of exchange as well as a means to disseminate news and information about a celebrity in an interactive form. Yet it is impossible for a celebrity to communicate directly with their many fans or detractors for that matter, but they nevertheless use personal disclosure of what formerly would have been considered private as a substitute for direct communication. The feeling of closeness conveyed serves to foster the parasocial aspects of communicating through social media platforms. Marshall describes three levels in which celebrities present themselves, including the public self, public-private self and transgressive intimate self (see Fig. 4.2).[14] The first, public self, is what we have heretofore understood celebrity to be, an informational model including the celebrity's bio, tour dates, and present and upcoming projects. Basically, this is a publicity model, where a celebrity's "handlers," that is, press agents, serve as intermediaries between the celebrity and media. The second level of celebrity self-presentation is the public-private self, which is consistent with the ways in which celebrities are likely to utilize social media. In this model, the celebrity may put out more intimate details of their comings and goings. What differentiates this model from the public self are two things. First, the celebrity may appear to be doing the posting themselves, perhaps through a series of Tweets, for example. In the previous model, the publicity would perhaps come in the form of a news release or media interview most likely disseminated by a public relations professional. While many celebrities hire specialists to handle their social media postings, it may appear, because of the immediacy of the post or tweet, that the celebrity is doing the posting herself or himself. Also, this form of communication makes it appear that the celebrity is out in front of the film, TV or recording industry system, operating on their own accord. It

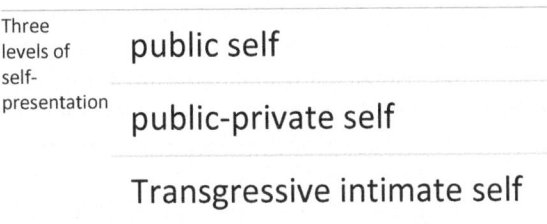

Fig. 4.2 Marshall's three levels of self-presentation

is, according to Marshall, more like the older "star system" that placed the celebrity front and center. The third level of self-presentation, transgressive intimate self, represents the visceral kinds of posting that may represent a temporary emotional outburst. For example, such transgressions might take the form of infighting between two celebrities, like the long-running feud between pop singers Katy Perry and Taylor Swift.[15] Both singers' fans, known as Swifties and KatyCats, point to a well-publicized 2013 defection of two dancers from one singer's tour to another. The feud, which now extends to other celebrities and both singers' fans, continues to this day. Fans in such an instance not only get to be voyeurs to such exchanges but get to construct their own parallel narrative as they communicate within their own social network.

GRANDIOSE EXHIBITIONISM

The sociologist Chris Rojek links the rise of celebrity with the decline of religion and magic, the former serving as a substitute for the latter. But it may be that celebrity is an extension of both magic and religion. However, commerce and later advertising of which celebrities play an important role is rooted historically in the market fair. In this way both commerce and cosmology become intertwined. Add a dash of narcissism to the mix and you have quite a cocktail, one that we imbibe to feel a sense of closeness and in that intimacy—this is the parable of the parasocial. There is a symbiotic relationship between the celebrity and ordinary people who perform self-presentation on digital media in the form of a selfie. The ubiquity of the selfie provides evidence of the manifestation of a narcissistic celebrity culture in which ordinary individuals become celebrities of sorts when they post their self-portraits on social media, and at the same time they (the selfies) become consumable products in the sense that they become currency to be traded among others and hence obtain value. One of the highlights of the 2018 Super Bowl half-time show was when pop singer Justin Timberlake danced up into the grand stands and took a selfie with a 13-year-old boy, thus conferring status upon the youngster. For a short time, the boy, who came to be known as Super Bowl Selfie Kid became a celebrity in his own right, appearing on the Ellen Degeneres television program, after his image was posted across a number of social media: Twitter, Pinterest, Instagram and YouTube. And, to extend his own celebrity status, he took a selfie with Ellen Degeneres.[16] This transmedia episode established his narrative, created a persona and embellished his image as it was modified, shared and commented upon over and over again. As such the Super Bowl Selfie Kid becomes a commodity himself, sold in the broad sense to whoever is willing to watch, like, comment, share or re-post. The latest iteration of selfie culture may be seen through the short-form video app TikTok.[17,18]

Media like television, movies, books and even radio are considered escapist, because they allow viewers, listeners and readers to with relative ease slip from their everyday life into their imaginary worlds, all within the context of being a proverbial couch potato. Digital media have different requirements, performance being the most significant difference. The selfie is a prime example of digital exhibitionism, as one's self-absorption plays out on Instagram or Snapchat, among other platforms that are ideal for the digital narcissist. Perhaps the increase in narcissism cannot be laid at the foot of social media, as Jean Twenge, writing in *Psychology Today*, claims that the scientific evidence is to the contrary—narcissism has been on the rise for some time. Among the evidence she presents is a rise in individualism and diminishment of collectivism, which could correspond with the rise of neo-liberal attitudes among Millennials. Perhaps as signifi-cant is that: "Traits related to narcissism have also increased, such as extrinsic values, unrealistic expectations, materialism, low empathy, agen-tic (but not communal) self-views, self-esteem, self-focus, choosing more unique names for children, less concern for others, less interest in helping the environment, and low empathy."[19] While narcissism may have been on the rise, the advent of digital media certainly exacerbates the situation, exploiting the psychological state of some individuals. There is pressure to develop and maintain a presentational self. Beyond the psychological pres-sure, it takes physical labor, although some people may argue it takes skill, as well as expenditure of time and energy that might have otherwise been put to more personally and socially positive uses.

In the case of the Super Bowl Selfie Kid, he was thrust into the public light, depending on how you look at it, by merely being in the right place at the right time. But one of the requirements of the transgressive intimate self ups the ante quite a bit, as the level of self-disclosure must be ever-more provocative. Consider, for example, Scout Willis, daughter of actors Demi Moore and Bruce Willis. Scout's parents are both well-known celeb-rities; she however is a celebrity mostly based on association, what might be referred to as a marginal celebrity. If she wants to step out from under her parents' spotlight and have the bright lights of celebrity shine directly on her, she has to do something out of the ordinary, something excessive and extreme. In May of 2014, Willis was banned from Instagram for posting a photo that featured two topless women, the intention of which was to counter-balance that image with the image of a sweater she designed that was in the middle of the photo. The designer and would-be actress took to Twitter to declare her outrage using the hashtag #Freethenipple. Provocation begun, but not ended, as Willis then took to the streets of New York topless to make her point and of course to gain additional notoriety for her cause célèbre. She utilized Twitter to garner support and enrage critics, and of course this episode spilled over into legacy media as well. What began as an attempt to promote her clothing line became a protest over censorship, making this a good example of extending the narrative based on the transgressive intimate self. She made her point by posting images of her parading topless in New York City, declaring that it isn't illegal to go topless in the streets of New York City, but it is against the policy of Instagram. Somehow the clothing line got lost in the shuffle as the protest became one for a greater cause.[20] Not all feedback was positive, as exemplified by one fan who responded with the following: "@Itz_Nandini: @scout_willis ur profile picture is disgusting." But Willis replied in her own defense, "no it's not, it's a celebration of the female body."[21] It is important to point out that degradation of the celebrity is part of the exchange that may take place within a social media environment in which the celebrity may not control the message. Critics may be one-off, like the example above, or there may be a ground swell of criticism. Most likely there are crowds or clusters of fans or anti-fans degrading a celebrity, while others come to the celebrity's defense. Flash-forward to 2016 and the launch of Willis' clothing line at New York Fashion Week; there was nary a mention of the #Freethenipple campaign.[22]

THE NEW NEW SENSIBILITY

If Sontag and Wolfe pegged the "new sensibility" as being one of excess, what would they think of Scout Willis' melding of public persona and commerce? In an attention economy, mere excess isn't enough to garner attention or keep attention for that matter. Excess needs to be transgressive to the point that anyone attempting to gain and maintain attention has to turn one's self inside out. To an extent, it is the producers of products and services that give celebrity its extended value and motivation to transgressively disclose intimate aspects of their lives. There is, of course, a trickle-down effect, as ordinary people attempt to increase their notoriety by performing intimacy. In other words, producers of products and services and celebrities form a celebrity-industrial complex. The complex, as it were, extends beyond celebrities to include anyone who is willing to engage with digital media by presenting their transgressive intimate self.

Beyond selling products and services, one value associated with celebrity is emotional value, which is where the connection between a social cause and celebrity becomes important. This is the commodification or packaging of celebrity into persona. In his book *The Celebrity Persona Pandemic*, author P. David Marshall explains the "increasing fetishization of the construction of a public persona." He describes the public persona as an "accouterment or mask added on to the self in order to achieve some sort of completion and satisfaction in the public world."[23] He maintains that persona isn't so much about the construction of self as it is about carrying out a strategy in support of one's public identity. The form of gratification one might receive furthers the need to participate in celebrity culture; as such, Marshall says, persona construction has become a pandemic. Actress and director Angelina Jolie serves as an example of someone whose narrative benefits from transgressive intimate self. Her story is familiar: in addition to starring in and directing major films, she was in a high-profile marriage and subsequent divorce with actor Brad Pitt, with whom she has six children, several of whom were adopted from third-world countries. There were other high-profile marriages as well. She has a well-publicized contentious relationship with her father, actor Jon Voight. And, she is known for traveling the world on behalf of the United Nations, as UNHRC Special Envoy. The commodity that is created is transportable as it moves from movie screen to world scene, or in the case of other celebrities from reality show and advertising to, for instance, political office. Within an attention economy, however, there is an inherent need to keep the celebrity machine whirring; that is, there is a need for continual priming of the publicity pump, so to speak. The September 2017 cover story of *Vanity Fair* refers to Jolie's complicated life as a single mother who has to single-handedly deal with the "day-to-day chaos of six kids and the trauma of her split from Brad Pitt."[24] It is in this sense she is simultaneously ordinary and extraordinary. Her narrative is made more complex as she completed a film about Cambodia's genocide, visited a Syrian refugee camp (with her children) and works on the TIGER project that serves to empower girls through education. The article goes on to refer to "the two Angelinas and the reason her life will never be normal."[25] It raises the question in the minds of her fans and followers: will our lives ever be normal? This is the type of elaboration expected of such a complex and continuing narrative. One website lists 29 charities and foundations Jolie supports ranging from the Afghanistan Relief Organization to Women in the World Foundation, and she supports 26 causes that range from gender equality to creative arts.[26] Her persona is one that is highly crafted as she emerged from her provocative youth to become a world-class humanitarian.

When it comes to integrating a celebrity's persona and a product, there needs to be consistency in the narrative. Inconsistency, however, disrupts the viewer's or reader's ability to "buy into" the narrative. For example, Jolie was for a short time an endorser of St. John Knits, an upscale clothier. Her relationship to the brand was quickly ended, as her image did not match closely with the conservative one projected by the clothing brand.[27] In 2017, however, she became the fragrance marketer Guerlain's chief endorser for its "Notes of a Woman" campaign.[28] The campaign is evidence regarding how the narrative intersects with the selling of a brand: the photo shoot took place on the heels of her divorce from Brad Pitt, adding additional fuel to the publicity; her fees are being donated to a charitable cause; the campaign is inspired by her mother who passed away after a long battle with cancer; and she introduced the brand to Cambodia, where she was making a film. Just about every thread of her long-running narrative feeds directly into the Guerlain campaign.

KONSUMER KULTURE: A CASE STUDY OF THE KARDASHIANS

Ryan Seacrest was a radio personality before becoming the host of the television program *American Idol*. As of May 2017, he became co-host of the daily syndicated TV program, *Life with Kelly and Ryan*. What is perhaps less well known is that he was the key figure behind the development in 2007 of the reality program *Keeping Up with the Kardashians*. Over the ten years of its existence, the critics have piled on regarding the reality show, describing it in the following terms: the shallowness, opportunistic and desperate attempt at achieving fame displayed by all of the characters. Nevertheless, the ratings have been high enough not only to sustain the original program but to have spawned a number of spin-offs, as well as retail ventures, product lines, product endorsements, among other commercial enterprises. The Kardashian family includes mother Kris; sisters Kim, Kourtney and Khloe; and a brother, Rob. Kris was married to Olympic Decathlete Bruce Jenner, which extended the clan to include

Kylie and Kendall Jenner. The Kardashian-Jenner clan is the embodiment of what it means to be a transgressive intimate self in the twenty-first century. There is no shortage of excessive family drama, including the on-air decision of Bruce to undergo a transformation to become Caitlyn. The story of their notoriety begins with a sex tape of Kim and her then boy-friend hip-hop star Ray J. Friendships with other marginal celebrities, like Paris Hilton, fueled Kim's marginal celebrity status. And their last name already had some recognition, as their deceased father, Robert Kardashian, was one of the lawyers representing O.J. Simpson during his infamous murder trial. There have been marriages, some of which have been short-lived and subsequent divorces and well-publicized births as well. What may have begun with a sex tape developed into a narrative that goes beyond the bounds of a traditional soap opera.

Henry Jenkins describes transmedia storytelling as one that is "dispersed systematically across multiple delivery channels for the purpose of creating a unified and coordinated entertainment experience. Ideally, each medium makes its own unique contribution to the unfolding of the story."[29] The synergy created across those channels can serve multiple purposes. It may serve to increase the popularity of the story and characters, and it may include marketing opportunities to extend the narrative beyond its initial border to include marketing of products and services. With regard to the Kardashians, a complex world is created and sustained through multiple story lines. Jenkins refers to this as "world-building," which encourages fans to grasp the complexity of the growing and expanding narrative. All of this must take place within a coordinated effort. Elizabeth Currid-Halkett, author of *Starstruck: The Business of Celebrity*, says, "it's clear that the Kardashians have turned generating publicity, and possibly profit from that attention, into an art form."[30] She adds, "there is more money to be made if you can cultivate a public interest in yourself that equals or exceeds interest in your work."[31]

Extending the story or narrative is a method of persona building that demonstrates the transportability of the Kardashian brand as a commodity within the celebrity-industrial complex evidenced by the collection of apps and products of Kim, Khloe and Kourtney Kardashian as well as those promotions by their mother Kris Jenner and sisters Kylie Jenner and Kendall Jenner.[32] The task is to extend the Kardashian brand presence into many venues with the end goal of increasing its cultural and economic capital. Indeed these two are instrumentally intertwined. Building attention is directly related to building cultural capital, and cultural capital may translate into economic capital. To say that Kim Kardashian, assorted family members and their advisors understand the connection between culture and commerce would be an understatement. For instance, Brian Dow (former agent for the Kardashians) in an interview with *The Hollywood Reporter* said: "Kim sort of paved the way for the economic structure of native influencer marketing. Before the rise of the common man YouTuber in their bedroom, you had people like her. She was the one who kicked down the door and got the brands to spend money in that area because she showed success. Brands noticed that when you would pay a celebrity to send out a branded tweet, they were getting more click-throughs for the dollar, so it made more monetary sense. That's why that revolution started."[33]

FANS FUEL THE CELEBRITY FLAMES

An important aspect of the mediated social connection within the context of the celebrity-industrial complex is the way fans are sometimes turned into customers. One part of the Kardashian empire is their Dash retail stores. A reporter visited the SoHo location to see who was shopping there with the following questions in hand: "Do these stores make money? Do people say to their friends, "Hey, want to grab a Venti iced latte and go shopping at Dash?" Who even shops there in the first place?"[34] Turns out, tourists visit for the novelty of it. People visit because the store is a "character" in their various TV programs, including *KUWTK* and *Kourtney and Kim Take Miami*. Tourists may be "uninterested," as in just passing by, but because they are aware of the Kardashians, they may feel compelled to stop in, or "earnest" fans might purchase an inexpensive knickknack to commemorate their visit. There are moms who purchase clothing for their daughters. Then there are snarky teens that might scoff at the style of the clothing and sensible teens who would rather not spend so much on a t-shirt, as well as 20-somethings who find the clothing "underwhelming." Finally, there are the New Yorkers who stop by on a lunch break, not so much to purchase products, but because they are fans of the TV program. In sum, fans/customers come in many shapes and sizes, and while the clothing may not be all that appealing because of style or price, all visitors to Dash express awareness of the Kardashians as cultural and consumer artifacts. "As with the runaway success of the Kim Kardashian app, you may know full well that you're buying into this family's particular brand of Konsumer Kulture, but you do it anyway."[35] The various responses fans and customers have regarding the Kardashians and the retail store reflects the nature of the niches, cliques and groups that form on social media with regard to the Kardashian brand. However, brands are somewhat fluid, and as of April 2018, the Kardashians announced the closing of all of their Dash stores.[36] Within their social network existing together are admirers, curiosity seekers, voyeurs and haters. The network is dynamic, and the size of each of these social clusters may change over time as circumstances change.

Haters Gonna Hate

Chris Rojek, writing about celebrity and religion, describes three forms of celebrity descent, referring to their fall from grace: scourging, disintegration and redemption. Scourging, he says, refers to "the process of status-stripping in which the honorific status of the celebrity is systematically degraded." As such scourging takes two forms: auto-degradation and exo-degradation. In the former, the celebrity does himself or herself in, so to speak, and with the latter, external forces serve to degrade the celebrity. Both forms, Rojek concludes, are interrelated and mutually reinforcing.[37]

The appearance of Kim Kardashian on the cover of *Vogue India* magazine caused consternation on social media as some thought it a poor decision on the part of the magazine. The decision to use Kardashian on the cover, her seventh for the magazine, was criticized as "whitewashing."[38] The controversy extended to questions regarding why the magazine didn't select someone of South Asian descent to don the cover to why she wore a lehenga, which is a traditional Indian garment. A series of disparaging tweets began and comments followed related to something Kim Kardashian had previously said about hating Indian food to criticism of Kendall Jenner, her sister, appearing on a 2017 cover of the magazine.[39]

N @nxvyaa:
    so many pretty Indian models out there and Vogue India somehow chooses kendall jenner and kim Kardashian for their covers. How hard is it to have Indian women represent Indian culture.

What ensued was a battle that extended the narrative to consider Kardashian's appropriation of race, as one person offered in this commentary:

I am not surprised!!! Half the time Kim misappropriates the black culture, now it is the Indian culture!!! People have to stop encouraging her stupidness and she would not get to be on these magazine covers. I am guessing KK will be on Chinese Culture Mag next!!!

But there were other comments that defended Kardashian for being a successful business "mogul" who is known worldwide to broader issues regarding the representation of race and ethnicity in American media as illustrated by the following:

No Name @shutupurpoor:
Replying to @nxvyaa.
Lol then don't complain about American magazines not being diverse enough when they don't showcase brown women. Because according to you, they should only showcase American culture.

Dick @dickslastreport:
Replying to @nxyvaa.
Why is diversity required in America, and discouraged in other cultures? If an American with influence bitched about an Indian women being on a Vogue cover in the US, can you imagine the backlash?

Sister Kendall Jenner had her own controversies, also appearing on a 2017 cover of *Vogue India* magazine. As with Kim, she was "accused of being clueless and tone-deaf in one cultural appropriation controversy after another." In addition to appearing on the cover of *Vogue India*, she appeared in a short-lived commercial for Pepsi. In the ad Jenner walks blithely through a crowd of protestors quelling the rally by offering a cop a Pepsi. In an era of protests against police brutality, this was not the best showcase for displaying racial insensitivity. The ad was pulled within 24 hours of its first airing.[40]

Beyond the focus on Kim Kardashian, discourse ensues regarding broader issues of diversity, social justice, immorality and a general understanding of how business operates. Analyzing the social network regarding this issue of Kim Kardashian's appearance on a magazine cover are cliques or clusters of degradation as well as cliques or clusters of virtue, among other conversational network structures. What this signifies is that the categories developed by Rojek are not discreet, as degradation of a celebrity is not necessarily like a mass riot. There are certainly those fans or anti-fans that for various reasons "gang up" on the celebrity, but celebrities have their defenders as well; critics and fans are all part of a dialogic. It's important to keep in mind that social networks are dynamic, as the narrative is likely to change, like shifting sands over time, driven by internal means or external circumstances, or both. A report on political conversations from the Pew Research Center stated: "Conversations on Twitter create networks with identifiable contours as people reply to and mention one another in their tweets. These conversational structures differ, depending on the subject and the people driving the conversation."[41] They identified six structures: divided, unified, fragmented, clustered, and inward and outward hub-and-spoke structures. These conversational structures develop through replies or mentions and reveal themselves like an unfolding story. The Pew researchers were able to identify through an analysis of thousands of Twitter maps, six types of crowds, clusters and networks: polarized, tight, brand, community, broadcast and support that are relevant to a discussion of mediated social connections.[42] When considering mediated social connections with a celebrity like Kim Kardashian, it's important to go beyond the number of followers or subscribers to her social media platforms (see Fig. 4.3). Rather, based on the structure of a celebrity's networks, clusters and crowds identified above, we can better understand the ways in which fans, or anti-fans for that matter, might coalesce around a celebrity's brand.

With regard to Kardashian's appearance on the cover of *Vogue India*, for example, the tweets and replies, both positive and negative, of those who engage in the dialogue constitute a polarizing cluster. As has been pointed out, the discussion extends beyond the magazine cover or the celebrity to address broader social issues. Polarized crowds can exist alongside or intertwined with brand communities. Therefore, it's important to consider the complexity of managing one's persona if commerce is the ultimate goal. It may be that individuals who chime in regarding the magazine controversy could care less about the Kardashian brand from a purchasing perspective, while others who also may care less about the brand might appreciate her business acumen. And yet the real issue for Kardashian is whether or not those individuals who participate in her social network who are interested and engaged within her brand network also participate in the polarized crowd or whether they form a smaller community cluster within the network that is likely to offer a defense of her actions. From a marketing communication perspective, what is being described here is a spaghetti-like social network with intersections between her brand community, the polarized crowd and community cluster, each

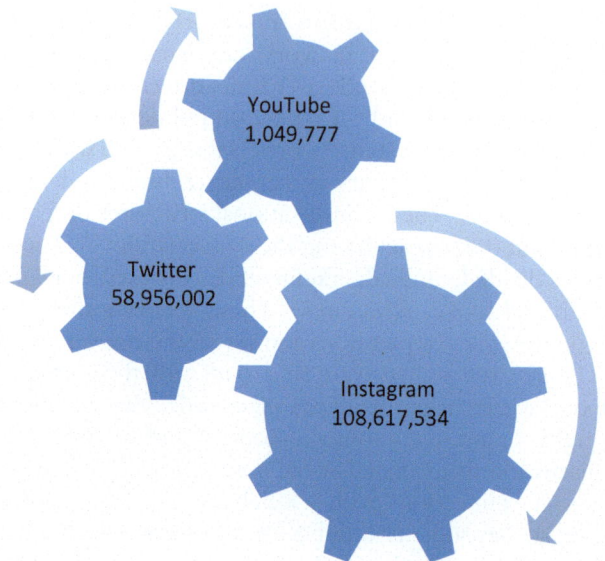

Fig. 4.3 Kim Kardashian's social media followers/subscribers (March 2018)

of which offers different levels of connectivity, ranging from disconnected, few connections or moderate connections. While it is possible that these clusters will work in tandem under some circumstances, it is more likely within the dynamics of mediated social connections that such smaller clusters within the larger community will work against one another.

Also to be considered are the strength of ties to the Kardashian brand. If the participants in the magazine cover discussion were large in number but disconnected, this would metaphorically look like a thousand people shouting their point of view into the wind. It doesn't matter where their comments land; in fact, they may not land anywhere, as such a crowd is disconnected and the audience is quite diffused. In this way, crowd sourcing or the wisdom of crowds likely has little impact on the celebrity's brand, as there may be a lot of people participating, but not necessarily with each other and certainly not within a coordinated effort. This is so for all celebrity social networks, but the configuration of the social clusters varies depending on particular circumstances. It's not just that these clusters represent weak connections; there may be few or no connections.

ANYONE CAN BE A STAR

As newer forms of media emerge, so do newer forms of celebrity, YouTube or Instagram stars preeminent among them, but there are stars on other platforms as well. In Chap. 5 I write about the micro-celebrity phenomenon, of which YouTube stars may be considered a sub-category. The interest in this chapter isn't about the micro-celebrity phenomenon per se, but how micro-celebrities participate in the attention economy and in that how they participate at the intersection of celebrity, digital media and commerce. After all, it seems like anyone can become a star in the age of digital media; all you need is a smartphone camera and an idea. Post consistently while making a fool of yourself or offering valuable DIY advice and you, too, can become an instant success reaping millions of dollars in revenue from sponsorships and advertisements, among other revenue-generating sources. But it turns out that beyond those at the very top of this pyramid very few people are actually making much money. According to a longitudinal study published in *Convergence: The International Journal of Research into New Media Technologies*, "85% of all views go to a small minority of 3% of all channels."[43] What that means is that fewer and fewer people over the past ten years are gaining more and more views. Specifically, becoming a star is not as simple as setting up a YouTube channel and seeing the dollars roll in. Money is earned from advertisements that are served on the creator's videos. But in order to qualify for the YouTube Partner Program, the channel has to reach 4000 watched hours in the previous 12 months and have at least 1000 subscribers to be considered.[44] In other words, it has become increasingly more difficult to break through the proverbial clutter as advertisers like to refer to the enormous amount of commercial messages that we are exposed to on a daily basis, and as more than one critic of advertising has claimed, clutter just leads to more clutter. The result of all that clutter, of course, is a loss of attention or attention that is split between smaller and smaller units. Cutting or breaking through the clutter in digital media requires what has been described in this chapter as the transgressive intimate self.

YOUTUBE STARS

The top categories for YouTube subscribers in order are music, gaming, sports and news. And specifically, there are pop music stars like Justin Bieber, Ed Sheeran and Taylor Swift, who dominate the channel. Beyond

Top10 WorldwideYouTube Stars (millions subscribers)	1. PewDiePie - 60.4
	2. HolaSoyGerman - 33.1
	3. Elrubiusomg - 27.3
	4. Whinderssonnunes 26.7
	5. CanalKonzilla - 26.6
	6. DudePerfect - 26.5
	7. Feranfloo - 26.2
	8. Smosh - 22.6
	9. Vanossgaming - 22.3
	10. Vegetta777 - 20.8

Fig. 4.4 Most popular YouTube stars in the world[45]

those we might expect to garner a large YouTube subscriber base; there are a number of YouTubers that became stars outside the support of mainstream media including the likes of PewDiePie, Jenna Marbles and Yuya, who have each acquired millions of subscribers (see Fig. 4.4). YouTube is a global platform on which many of the most popular stars are from Latin America, Spain, Brazil, El Salvador, Canada, Mexico, as well as the United States.

The number of subscribers may be a measure of popularity, but these YouTube stars also generate millions of dollars of revenue from their channels (see Fig. 4.5). For example, the top earner was Ryan Toys Review, a channel featuring a seven-year-old who reviews toys. He earned $22 million in 2018.

These YouTubers operate with little impunity, but there are times when one or more goes too far and has their hand slapped, so to speak, by the platform. We saw earlier when Scout Willis was suspended from Instagram, and in the case of Logan Paul, who posted on his YouTube channel a disturbing 15-minute video of someone who had committed suicide, he was not only punished by the platform, fans expressed their outrage as well. Logan Paul is a micro-celebrity in that he operates strictly in the online world; his appeal is to teenagers. The extent of his popularity can be measured by a 2017 personal appearance in a Dubai shopping mall where 10,000 people showed up. He also has a younger brother, Jake, who is

Top 10 YouTube Earners (millions)	1. Ryan Toys Review - 22
	2. Jake Paul - 21.5
	3. Dude Perfect - $20
	4. DanTDM - 18.5
	5. Jeffree Star - 18
	6. Markiplier - 17.5
	7. Vanoss Gaming - 17
	8. Jacksepticeye - 16
	9. PewDiePie - 15.5
	10. Logan Paul - 14.5

Fig. 4.5 Top YouTube earners 2018. (Robehmed, N. & Berg, M. (December 3, 2018). Highest-Paid YouTube Stars 2018: Markiplier, Jake Paul, PewDiePie And More. Forbes.com. Retrieved from: https://www.forbes.com/sites/natalier-obehmed/2018/12/03/highest-paid-youtube-stars-2018-markiplier-jake-paul-pewdiepie-and-more/#19d410c1909a)

popular on various digital media platforms. Jake Paul ranks second in terms of income generated through YouTube. Both of the brothers maintain an international audience.[46] As can be seen in the list in Fig. 4.7, there is a lot of money at stake should a YouTuber or Instagrammer be dropped from the platform.

We can see mediated social connections at work in the case of Logan Paul as his fans respond to the video he posted of a dead body. While he had 16 million Instagram followers, after the incident he lost 88,000 followers. Among his YouTube subscribers, views dropped by almost 22,000 after the incident, but since have steadily climbed back to their previous standing.[47] One fan tweeted his disgust and garnered almost 88,000 retweets and almost 400,000 likes (see Fig. 4.6).

Paul did post an apology to his fans and many appeared in their reactions to be quite forgiving (see Fig. 4.7). When viewed in terms of mediated social connections, his fans appear to operate as a tight crowd, meaning that his fans consider themselves members with strong connections, and what might be typical of teen fans who see themselves as insiders operating outside of an adult supervised world, like one fan who

Fig. 4.6 Fan response to Logan Paul's video post. (Fan response to Logan Paul video post. Retrieved from: https://twitter.com/aaronpaul_8/status/948032944408444928)

tweeted: "I love u soooooooo much plz don't stop making video Plzz. I guess want to injoy ur trip to Tokyo that sounds stupid but it makes me happy when ur happy."

Shortly after the start of 2018, Logan Paul announced that he was taking a break from posting on YouTube, stating: "taking time to reflect."[48] It's not just kids or gamers that are reaping the benefits of operating within the celebrity-industrial complex as evidenced by three vloggers whose YouTube videos reach an African-American audience, teaching their four million subscribers how to best apply makeup to dark-skinned women. One company, Too Faced, took notice and partnered with one of the vloggers to introduce a foundation line for darker complexions.[49]

INSTAGRAMMERS

The key metric for social influencers is engagement. And, it is likely that a brand influencer or micro-celebrity engaged in self-promotion may not have as many followers as a celebrity, but may have a higher engagement rate. While the calculation may vary from platform to platform, on Instagram, for example, the average engagement rate might be calculated by dividing the number of likes and comments by the follower count,

Logan Paul ✔
@LoganPaul

Follow ⌄

Dear Internet,

Let's start with this –
I'm sorry.

This is a first for me. I've never faced criticism like this before, because I've never made a mistake like this before. I'm surrounded by good people and believe I make good decisions, but I'm still a human being. I can be wrong.

I didn't do it for views. I get views. I did it because I thought I could make a positive ripple on the internet, not cause a monsoon of negativity. That's never the intention. I intended to raise awareness for suicide and suicide prevention and while I

I do this sh*t every day. I've made a 15 minute TV show EVERY SINGLE DAY for the past 460+ days. One may understand that it's easy to get caught up in the moment without fully weighing the possible ramifications.

I'm often reminded of how big of a reach I truly have & with great power comes great responsibility... for the first time in my life I'm regretful to say I handled that power incorrectly. It won't happen again.

I love everyone. I believe in people. I'm out here. Peace 🤙 #Logang4Life

10:00 PM - 1 Jan 2018

26,296 Retweets **142,165** Likes

💬 44K   ↻ 26K   ♡ 142K   ✉

Fig. 4.7 Logan Paul's apology. (Logan Paul apology. Retrieved from: https://twitter.com/LoganPaul/status/948026294066864128)

which will provide a percentage of average engagement on the platform. Instagrammers who are looking for sponsorships are acutely aware of the relationship between engagement and their ability to obtain sponsorships that may pay between $10,000 and $20,000.[50] And some Instagrammers will go out of their way to explain to their fan base how they go about making money, perhaps offer a rationalization or defense. This level of disclosure is an attempt to present an authentic self and serves as a means to endear the Instagrammer or YouTuber to their fans. Along the way, they may even disclose their ideological position on the attention economy and generate a discussion regarding the economic aspects of posting on social media. Bonny Rebecca, an activist on behalf of veganism and a social media influencer with 363,000 subscribers on YouTube, provides an example. Her Instagram account (479,000 followers) and Tumblr blog are part of a passion project in which she advocates eating healthy. To that end, she has published a book *Carbolicious*, which includes vegan recipes. After receiving much "hate" for promoting particular products and brands, she felt compelled to post a video on YouTube explaining how she does (and does not) make money from Instagram.[51] In the video, she says:

> So this is the question that everybody wants to know how much money do I make off Instagram. The reason I want to talk about this today is because I put up a photo the other day of me sitting in my bed with my yo home sheets which is like their organic 100% bamboo like sustainable sheets. They're ethical. They're lovely. They're gorgeous. They're soft. I love supporting them. I think they're really awesome people and I actually really like their product and I tagged them in the photo and in the caption and I got so much hate of people saying how I'm fake and how this is a paid post and you know and this photo is staged and like just all this really horrible horrible horrible stuff and I was like are you fucking kidding me what is going on right now.[52]

Rebecca's diatribe goes on during the 6-minute and 33-second video, as she defends herself, maintaining that she does not make money off of Instagram, but people automatically think she is making money and that equates with being "fake and staged." She offers a mea culpa acknowledging that she does make money when other websites post her photos, which she maintains are her art and therefore a valuable commodity. And, she makes money off her YouTube channel. She maintains that she could be making money from Instagram, but chooses not to. In this way she believes she is presenting herself authentically and with sincerity.

When placed within the context of mediated social connections, the comments to the video reveal a relatively tight crowd based on the common interest in health and diet, as well as their attraction to Bonny Rebecca and the values she espouses. The likes to dislikes ratio demonstrates a viewer's intention to interact with the YouTube star, an important measure of engagement. In this case the ratio is 9:1, likes versus dislikes. This should suggest a highly connected group. There were 750 comments posted to this video. What makes this interesting is the way in which supporters circle their proverbial wagons around this YouTube star and, in doing so, not only defend her but express some general beliefs about society and the economy. For example, one fan posted the following:

mychanneleeezey:
It's nothing wrong with getting payed for promoting something that you genuenly like

This comment is typical and goes beyond discussing a vegan lifestyle, food products or health. In this way the comments become a sense-making mechanism and are expressive of the collective consciousness of the crowd. In another example that follows, a comment reflects feelings of gender bias when it comes to promoting products:

Mr & Mrs Vegan
Are we the only ones seeing a horrible double standard against women entrepreneurs here, too? If its a guy promoting something on his feed, he gets "high fives" for being entrepreneurial & if its a woman, she is now "a fake sell out"... What happened??? I thought the world was moving in the right direction & then this backlash?

Again, the interaction goes beyond the individual posting the video and her passion project to consider broader social issues like a "double standard against women entrepreneurs." These examples demonstrate how mediated social connections operate in the form of crowd connections, especially when participants feel like members that coalesce around a single issue or passion, in this case a vegan lifestyle. But the fan and follower responses also demonstrate how mediated social connections serve to help participants make sense of their world within an attention economy. An interesting twist on micro-celebrities and an offshoot micro-influencers are nano-influencers, Instagrammers and YouTubers who have small audiences, perhaps as small as 1000 followers, but for whom they are influential. And perhaps because of the intimacy of the audience, they are perceived to be more like friends to their followers. And, in exchange for promoting products, they earn either a commission or are given free products.[53]

COSPLAY

Cosplay is a contraction for costume and play and for most people it is a hobby in which participants dress up like characters from movies or video games and show up at events like Comic-Con. Jessica Nigri is one such person who likes to dress up as the Pikachu character from Pokémon. After nine years Nigri has become one of the most popular cosplayers in the world, with 4.7 million Facebook followers, 2.8 million Instagram followers, 1.2 million YouTube subscribers and 3500 supporters on Patreon, the platform that allows fans to financially support creative work through monthly monetary subscriptions.[54] In order to turn her hobby into a business, it was necessary to create a multi-channel approach that would develop a number of revenue streams, including paid promotional appearances on behalf of video game companies, making costumes for others, advertising revenue from YouTube, and Patreon contributions.

As with other Instagrammers and YouTubers, among her fans are haters. In the case of Jessica Nigri, it's no different. She states in regards to haters: "Honestly I used to really get hurt by it," Nigri said of some of the negative energy. But she said that now she realizes that it usually comes from a place of sadness, of people not feeling 100% adequate themselves. "It's never a personal thing, I never take it personally," she said.[55] Beyond dealing with haters and luring fans, maintaining a network is difficult in an environment in which algorithms change, as has been the case with Facebook. Nigri ever conscious of metrics understands that reach, a measure of effectiveness, has been lacking on Facebook and Instagram, making the attention economy one that is difficult to negotiate as she attempts to maintain and enlarge her social network.

GLOBAL FAN ECONOMY

The fan economy is an international one, as demonstrated by the commercial success of several Chinese celebrity and digital influencers. While the dominant platforms in the United States may be Instagram and Facebook, in China it's Weibo and WeChat. WeChat, known as Weixin in Chinese, is similar to the US messaging service WhatsApp. With WeChat, owned by the Chinese Internet company Tencent, participants use the platform for online discussions, chatting and posting photos. It has also been the subject of heavy government censorship. While WeChat is a more private messaging platform, Sina Weibo, with more than 250 million users, is more likely the platform of choice when attempting to spread a message far and wide. It operates more like Twitter; in fact the name in Chinese means micro blog. Global celebrities like Tom Cruise engage fans on Weibo, where he has 3.2 million followers who refer to him as "Brother Tom." According to Rachel Dewoskin: "The site's dominance owes a great deal to its courtship of celebrity users; Sina focused on gathering and "verifying" stars, and fans flocked to the site."[56]

Not all influencers are big name celebrities. Consider Liang Tao, for example, who runs a fashion blog, Mr. Bags, promoting luxury brands to his 2.7 million Weibo followers. In one example, based on his promotion within this fan economy, 80 Givenchy bags, priced at $16,800 each, were sold within 12 minutes on the WeChat platform, and his WeChat posts can generate 100,000 views.[57] Selling high-end luxury merchandise on an Internet platform demonstrates not only the power of brand influencers on social media platforms, but also the ability to turn promotion into sales. Liang is not alone, as fashion bloggers as well as Chinese celebrities have begun to endorse luxury brands on digital media platforms. Angelito Perez Tan Jr., CEO of RTG Consulting, a consumer research firm, states: "While celebrities have mass appeal, digital influencers have built their following by carefully curating their content through much closer interaction with their fan base...It's the sentiment of being close or intimate with opinion leaders or bloggers that has driven this trend."[58]

CONCLUSION

This chapter investigated the ways in which the new sensibility of an earlier era foreshadowed the new new sensibility that we are now experiencing in the age of digital media. In light of the three levels of self-presentation, including the transgressive intimate self, the role of celebrities, micro-celebrities as well as nano-influencers selling themselves as a brand, and selling their own branded products and products they endorse through the use of digital media was discussed. Twitter, Facebook, Instagram, Snapchat, among global platforms, as well as dedicated websites become forums through which celebrities can communicate with their fans in order to promote the purchase of products and services. But negotiating digital media is complex, as platforms like YouTube change the rules regarding who can participate in their advertising program, or Facebook and Instagram adjust their algorithms that might impact metrics, which are so important to maintaining one's popularity and in that the fan base. The chapter focused on masterful marketers like Kim Kardashian as exemplars of the use of new media as a promotional vehicle. In particular the buying opportunities presented to fans allow them to extend the mediated social connection to not only feel closer to the celebrity but to label, that is, identify themselves, as a fan and craft an identity based on not only promoted products but also attitudes and values put forth by the celebrity. Those values show up as likes or dislikes, re-tweets and comments. In sum they represent the collective consciousness of those engaged on whichever platform is being utilized.

There is nothing inherently wrong with being a celebrity or seeking notoriety. In fact, the celebration of accomplishment and the appreciation of talent are important aspects of society and culture. But as a result of our immersion in media, a problem may arise in that people may become more concerned with the issue of attention as opposed to an individual's accomplishment and appreciation thereof. We can see the desire for attention through children's survey responses and their desire to become a celebrity as a life goal—fame for fame's sake. Digital media as an attention vehicle places those who use it in the center of all of the commodification of persona. If a key to becoming a celebrity is about exposure, then this is the lesson that we are learning; that is, we use or perhaps are used by digital media to expose ourselves or be exposed and perhaps exploited by others. An example of the exploitation of celebrity comes from the web service Cameo that pays celebrities a small fee to post a personalized video to a fan. Cameo has produced almost 100,000 videos, but among them, several celebrities have been duped into recording extremist messages.[59]

While the number of followers or subscribers to celebrity and micro-celebrity social media platforms may span a great range, those numbers tell us very little about engagement. Engagement as a metric may actually benefit the micro-celebrity more so than the celebrity, as the latter is more sensitive to fan interactions. Having said that, engagement as a metric tells us little about mediated social connections. Comments posted by fans are an expression of a fan's thoughts and beliefs, and as such, they are an expression of their inner world. Another metric that is not utilized often is sentiment. Sentiment refers to feelings one expresses through social media, and the way to best understand sentiment is through a content analysis of social media responses or reactions categorizing them as positive, negative or neutral. The expression of sentiment is represented in varied ways in which clusters and crowds within a network are formed. The new new sensibility is one of excessive expression. If a celebrity wants to develop a brand network, along with other social connections, they will have to turn themselves inside out, putting the most intimate details of their lives, loves, pregnancies, political beliefs and personal ideology out there for all to see.

With an understanding of the celebrity-industrial complex as backdrop, Chap. 5 turns to a closer look at micro-celebrity and the social networks that form around them as expressive communities of support and degradation. The chapter explores the celebrity economy, an offshoot of the attention economy, in which bona fide and micro-celebrities have to play by the "rules of the game" through which they have to negotiate their presentation of self in digital media. The chapter focuses on travel vloggers who earn their living posting videos of their travels, but sometimes they are accused by their fans of selling out to commercial interests. The chapter will address the ways in which micro-celebrities negotiate the presentation of self.

NOTES

1. Cotkin, G. (2016). *Feast of Excess: A Cultural History of the New Sensibility*. Oxford Scholarship Online. doi: https://doi.org/10.1093/acprof:oso/9780190218478.003.0001
2. Wu, T. (2016). *The Attention Merchants: the Epic Scramble to Get Inside our Heads*. New York: Alfred A. Knopf.
3. Ibid., p. 223.
4. Orth, M. (2004). *The Importance of Being Famous: Behind the Scenes of the Celebrity Industrial Complex*. New York: Henry Holt & Company.
5. Cramer, R. (2015). *Pregnant with the Stars: Watching and Wanting the Celebrity Baby Bump (The Cultural Lives of Law)*. Redwood City, CA: Stanford Law Books.
6. Ibid., p. 1.
7. Kylie Jenner Instagram Ranking and Followers (January 2018). SocialBlade. com. Retrieved from: https://socialblade.com/instagram/
8. It is worth noting that subsequent to her birth announcement, Kylie Jenner posted a disparaging Tweet, "sooo does anyone else not open Snapchat anymore? Or is it just me... ugh this is so sad," which caused Snapchat's stock value to plummet by $1.3 billion. Kelly, E. (February 23, 2018). Kylie Jenner's tweet about Snapchat may have wiped $1.3bn off its stock value. Retrieved from: http://metro.co.uk/2018/02/23/kylie-jenners-tweet-snapchat-may-wiped-1-3bn-off-stock-value-7335924/
9. Gonzalez, S. (February 8, 2018). Kylie Jenner reveals her baby's name. CNN.com. Retrieved from: https://www.cnn.com/2018/02/06/entertainment/kylie-jenner-stormi/index.html
10. To Our Daughter. (February 4, 2018). Kylie Jenner YouTube Video Documenting her Pregnancy. YouTube.com. Retrieved from: https://www.youtube.com/watch?v=BhIEIO0vaBE
11. Dumenco, S. (February 18, 2013). The Future of the Pregnant-Celebrity-Industrial Complex. AdAge.com. Retrieved from: http://adage.com/article/the-media-guy/future-pregnant-celebrity-industrial-complex/239836/
12. Ibid.

13. Marshall, P. D. (2010). The promotion and presentation of the self: celebrity as marker of presentational media. *Celebrity Studies*. 1:1, pp. 35–48, DOI: https://doi.org/10.1080/19392390903519057 Retrieved from: https://doi.org/10.1080/19392390903519057
14. Ibid., pp. 44–45.
15. Lang, C. (November 10, 2017). A Comprehensive Guide to the Taylor Swift-Katy Perry Feud. *Time*. Retrieved from: http://time.com/4914066/taylor-swift-katy-perry-feud-timeline/
16. O'Malley, K. (February 11, 2018). Justin Timberlake Nearly Brings Super Bowl 'Selfie Kid' To Tears During 'Ellen DeGeneres' Surprise. ElleUK.com. Retrieved from: http://www.elleuk.com/life-and-culture/culture/news/a41551/justin-timberlake-selfie-kid-ellen-degeneres-show/
17. https://www.tiktok.com/
18. Roose, K. (December 3, 2018). TikTok, a Chinese Video App, Brings Fun Back to Social Media. Nytimes.com. Retrieved from: https://www.nytimes.com/2018/12/03/technology/tiktok-a-chinese-video-app-brings-fun-back-to-social-media.html
19. Twenge, J. (August 12, 2013). How Dare You Say Narcissism Is Increasing? *Psychology Today*. Retrieved from: https://www.psychologytoday.com/blog/the-narcissism-epidemic/201308/how-dare-you-say-narcissism-is-increasing
20. Selby, J. (May 29, 2014). Scout Willis topless Instagram protest: Bruce Willis and Demi Moore's daughter opposes female nudity policy. The Independent Online. Retrieved from: http://www.independent.co.uk/news/people/scout-willis-topless-instagram-protest-daughter-of-bruce-willis-and-demi-moore-demonstrates-against-9452552.html
21. Op. Cit.
22. Cunningham, E. (February 20, 2016). Reformation Fans Will Love Scout Willis' Fashion Line. Refinery 29. Retrieved from: http://www.refinery29.com/2016/02/103586/scout-willis-designer-new-clothing-line
23. Marshall, P.D. (2016). *The Celebrity Persona Pandemic*. Minneapolis, MN: University of Minnesota Press.
24. Peretz, E. (July 26, 2017). Angelina Jolie Solo. *Vanity Fair*. Retrieved from: https://www.vanityfair.com/hollywood/2017/07/angelina-jolie-cover-story
25. Ibid.
26. Angelina Jolie Charity Work, Events and Causes. (n.d.) Retrieved from: https://www.looktothestars.org/celebrity/angelina-jolie
27. Cresswell, J. (June 22, 2008). Nothing Sells Like Celebrity. *The New York Times*. Retrieved from: http://www.nytimes.com/2008/06/22/business/media/22celeb.html

28. Murphy, D. (March 2, 2017). Angelina Jolie's Stunning New Fragrance Campaign: Everything We Know! EOnline.com. Retrieved from: http://www.etonline.com/news/211906_angelina_jolie_stunning_new_fragrance_campaign_everything_we_know
29. Jenkins, H. (March 21, 207). Transmedia Storytelling 101. Retrieved from: http://henryjenkins.org/blog/2007/03/transmedia_storytelling_101.html
30. Currid-Halkett, E. (November 2, 2011). How Kim Kardashian Turns the Reality Business Into an Art. *The Wall Street Journal*. Retrieved from: https://blogs.wsj.com/speakeasy/2011/11/02/how-kim-kardashian-turns-the-business-of-self-promotion-into-an-art/
31. Ibid.
32. The Kardashian Empire. Retrieved from: https://cdn1.thr.com/sites/default/files/2017/08/kardashian_empire_embed.jpg
33. Bruce, L. (August 16, 2017). The Kardashian Decade: How a Sex Tape Led to a Billion-Dollar Brand. *The Hollywood Reporter*. Retrieved from: https://www.hollywoodreporter.com/features/kardashian-decade-how-a-sex-tape-led-a-billion-dollar-brand-1029592
34. Brooke, E. (July 15, 2014). The 8 Types of People You Meet in a Dash Store. Fashionista.com. Retrieved from: https://fashionista.com/2014/07/the-8-people-you-meet-in-a-dash-store
35. Ibid.
36. Fernandez, A. (April 19, 2018). Kim Kardashian Announces All DASH Stores Are Closing After 12 Years: 'It's Time to Move On'. People.com. Retrieved from: http://people.com/style/kim-kardashian-says-dash-stores-closing/
37. Rojek, C. (2007). Celebrity and Religion. In Redmond, S. and Holmes, S., Eds. *Stardom and Celebrity: A Reader*. London: Sage Publications. P. 178.
38. Payne, T. (February 27, 2018). Kim Kardashian Criticized For "Vogue India" Cover. Teen Vogue. Retrieved from: https://www.teenvogue.com/story/kim-kardashian-vogue-india-cover-backlash
39. Twitter backlash regarding Kim Kardashian's appearance on the cover of India Vogue magazine. Retrieved from: https://twitter.com/nxvyaa/status/968366405304377346
40. Van Meter, J. (March 14, 2018). Kendall Jenner Gets Candid About Her Career, Her Controversies, and Her Private Life. *Vogue*. Retrieved from: https://www.vogue.com/article/kendall-jenner-vogue-april-2018-issue
41. Smith, M., Rainie, L, Sneiderman, B., & Himelboim, I. (February 20, 2014). Mapping Twitter Topic Networks: From Polarized Crowds to Community Clusters. PewInternet.org. Retrieved from: http://www.pewinternet.org/2014/02/20/mapping-twitter-topic-networks-from-polarized-crowds-to-community-clusters/

42. Ibid.
43. Bartl, M. (2018). YouTube channels, uploads and views: A statistical analysis of the past 10 years. *Convergence: The International Journal of Research into New Media Technologies.* 24:1, pp. 16–32.
44. YouTube Partner Program requirements (n.d.). Retrieved from: https://support.google.com/youtube/answer/72857?hl=en
45. Lynch, J. (February 2, 2018). These are the 19 most popular YouTube stars in the world—and some are making millions. Business Insider. Retrieved from: http://www.businessinsider.com/most-popular-youtubers-with-most-subscribers-2018-2
46. Meyer, R. (January 2, 2018). The Social-Media Star and the Suicide. *The Atlantic.* Retrieved from: https://www.theatlantic.com/technology/archive/2018/01/a-social-media-stars-error/549479/
47. Logan Paul YouTube Stats. (March 6, 2018). Retrieved from: https://socialblade.com/youtube/channel/UCG8rbF3g2AMX70yOd8vqIZg
48. Beck, K. (January 4, 2018). Logan Paul announces he's (thankfully) taking a break from YouTube. Mashable.com. Retrieved from: https://mashable.com/2018/01/04/logan-paul-break-twitter/#F4M51AM28mq1
49. Garcia, S. (November 30, 2018). They Couldn't Find Beauty Tutorials for Dark Skin. So They Made Their Own. Nytimes.com. Retrieved from: https://www.nytimes.com/2018/11/30/style/dark-skin-black-beauty-bloggers-instagram-youtube.html
50. How Girl With No Job Made Instagram Into a Career. Retrieved from: https://www.youtube.com/watch?v=0KH_BUDne0c&list=FLSqkgxkyg0mjdciU6LXlBAQ&index=14
51. Rebecca, B. (November 7, 2015). How much money do I make on Instagram – The Truth. Retrieved from: https://www.youtube.com/watch?v=O43Tmxij2Tc&index=15&list=FLSqkgxkyg0mjdciU6LXlBAQ
52. Ibid.
53. Maheshwari, S. (November 11, 2018). Are You Ready for the Nanoinfluencers? (2018). Nytimes.com. Retrieved from: https://www.nytimes.com/2018/11/11/business/media/nanoinfluencers-instagram-influencers.html
54. McAlone, N. (January 30, 2018). Cosplay superstar Jessica Nigri talks about turning her passion into a full-time job, and how Facebook's algorithm changes have affected her. Business Insider. Retrieved from: http://www.businessinsider.com/jessica-nigri-cosplay-star-talks-business-facebook-new-rooster-teeth-documentary-2018-1
55. Ibid.
56. Dewoskin, R. (February 17, 2012). Vanity Fair. East Meets Tweet. Retrieved from: https://www.vanityfair.com/news/tech/2012/02/weibo-china-twitter-chinese-microblogging-tom-cruise-201202

57. Chen, V. (March 13, 2017). Style. Chinese digital influencers fuel massive 'fan economy'. http://www.scmp.com/magazines/style/people-events/article/2078380/chinese-digital-influencers-fuel-massive-fan-economy
58. Ibid.
59. Mervosh, S. (December 3, 2018). Brett Favre and Soulja Boy Unwittingly Record Videos With Coded Anti-Semitism. Nytimes.com. Retrieved from: https://www.nytimes.com/2018/12/03/us/cameo-anti-semitic-favre-soulja-boy.html

CHAPTER 5

Micro-celebrity and the Management of Self-Presentation on Digital Media

Just sit right back and you'll hear a tale,
A tale of a fateful trip,
That started from this tropic port,
Aboard this tiny ship.

The mate was a mighty sailing man,
The skipper brave and sure.
Five passengers set sail that day,
For a three hour tour, a three hour tour.

The weather started getting rough,
The tiny ship was tossed,
If not for the courage of the fearless crew,
The minnow would be lost, the minnow would be lost. (Theme song from *Gilligan's Island*)

A recurring theme in popular culture refers to varying depictions of paradise, which often takes the form of a tropical island that viewers or readers turn into fantasy or at least experience the fantastic aspects of escapist entertainment. Take for instance the cast of the classic television program *Gilligan's Island*, whose theme song begins this chapter. The seven archetypes represented in the program, like the wealthy couple or intellectual professor type, are marooned on an island during the television show's run from 1964 to 1967. If that program pre-dates you or if you aren't a fan of classic TV programs, there are numerous other mediated experiences that

© The Author(s) 2019
N. M. Alperstein, *Celebrity and Mediated Social Connections*,
https://doi.org/10.1007/978-3-030-17902-1_5

are presented in the guise of the paradise fantasy as they offer up an escape from the mundaneness of everyday life. Whether it is the movie *The Blue Lagoon* or *Castaway*, each of these presents the opportunity to the viewer to engage in escapist fantasy. In recent years such fantasies have been supplanted by reality television programs like *Survivor*, which is based on a similar theme but lends an air of authenticity as it appeals to people's desire to see "real" people doing "real" things. Rose and Wood write about the paradox of such identification "in which viewers negotiate the existence of both people like me and storybook characters."[1] The same paradox carries over into digital media experiences and is extended into our mediated social connections with micro-celebrities.

In this chapter I present examples of the "paradise" theme as digital media create a forum through which travelers who sail around the world re-present themselves as ordinary folks who do extraordinary things. With their youthful good looks, drone footage, video-editing skills and Internet access from relatively remote parts of the world, while taking on great adventures, these travel vloggers assume the subjective position of celebrity. The adventurers use a highly developed set of practices based on the power of presence, including regularly scheduled episodic videos, storytelling in their blogs and photos across social media platforms that mimic the ways in which bona fide celebrities utilize digital media. Micro-celebrities have expanded the notion of celebrity in a twenty-first-century digital media environment, ushering in an era in which celebrity is not one thing. Micro-celebrity status is not fixed or static; rather it is based on what they do; indeed they have to keep doing things they can represent in an interesting and entertaining manner, in this case sail around the world encountering people and adventures along the way, gathering fans and followers, and earning a living through their participation in the attention economy.

Often reference is made to the attention economy, but rarely do we hear about an associated phenomenon, the celebrity economy. The celebrity economy is not just about celebrities as we have come to define and know them as movie or television performers, athletes and other media figures. Rather, the celebrity economy includes anyone who participates in the mediated world in which they present themselves to others, which would include everything from Facebook or Twitter posts and personal blogging and can even be extended to the ways people present themselves on dating apps. In other words, there are opportunities in an age of digital media that allow, perhaps encourage or require, anyone who participates to create their personal brand and in the process mimic the ways in which bona fide celebrities perform, that is, re-present themselves in media. A newer iteration of celebrity, the micro-celebrity, not only has to create a branded self but also needs to manage their persona in what constitutes a well-orchestrated public relations campaign. Anyone can do it, but not everyone can do it well. Fans understand that a bona fide celebrity will be presenting a version of themselves, but a micro-celebrity whose area of focus, like fashion, beauty or travel, may be limited requires a higher level of personal exposure that subjects them to greater audience scrutiny. Therefore the requirements for micro-celebrity are different from celebrities.

While celebrities may have a paid staff of public relations experts at their beck and call, micro-celebrities have to manage their presence on social media with little or no assistance, which may subject them to the vagaries of their audiences. One of the ways in which audiences demonstrate their engagement is through their responses to those micro-celebrities, and unlike most celebrities, there is an expectation that micro-celebrity will interact with a fan and follower through replies to comments. Most of the time fans' comments are celebratory, but sometimes when the micro-celebrity breaks some social expectation, like those that "sell out" to commercial interests, fans and followers may respond negatively. There is an expectation that micro-celebrities will present themselves in a sincere—meaning truthful—manner, which raises the bar for them and potentially makes their fall from grace steeper, potentially turning fans into haters. The critical analysis that follows is based on case studies of micro-celebrity travelers who rely on social media channels to share their experiences sailing around the world and along the way raise money from fans and followers directly through contributions and indirectly through advertising in order to support their adventures. Sometimes micro-celebrities are denigrated or degraded when fans and followers in their comments deem them to have sold out; however, such disparagement may be contained within pockets of the micro-celebrity's social network. While few fans may abandon the micro-celebrity, most fans react or respond in variable ways; in other words, love and hate operate along a continuum expressed within a pod of comments and replies. As a micro-celebrity labors to maintain their authenticity, playing an important social role in a fan's life, there is greater likelihood for understanding and perhaps forgiveness when the micro-celebrity crosses the proverbial line.

Bona Fide, Subcultural, Niche, Marginal and Micro-celebrities

Daniel Boorstin's often-cited definition of celebrity as "a person known for his or her well-knownness" already dislodges celebrity from fame's previous association with accomplishment.[2] However, Boorstin could not foresee the coming era of digital media that opens up the possibility for newer forms of celebrity and celebrity/fan interaction. With the advent of social media in particular, other forms of celebrity like micro-celebrity need to be considered. We count as bona fide celebrities actors, musicians and other entertainers, along with sports figures and politicians—those who may have accomplished something or achieved some status based on a special ability or outstanding talent. We can also consider other so-called media figures, those for whom circumstances have placed them in the spotlight of news as taking on at least temporary celebrity status. And, then there are those reality TV stars that are ordinary people who have without special abilities or talent chosen to participate in celebrity culture, appearing on television programs like *Survivor*, *Big Brother* and *The Bachelor*. Yet, in an era of digital media, anyone with the slightest technical knowledge and Internet access can attempt to create a public persona and seek out a high degree of popularity hoping to cash in on their newfound fame. In the previous chapter, I noted that the highest earning YouTube "star" is a seven-year-old boy whose videos depict him playing with toys.

Sociologist Joshua Gamson writes about a shift that took place in twenty-first-century popular culture that has led to a form of celebrity that is different from earlier conceptions of celebrity. Important to this discussion is his reference to the elevation of the ordinary in celebrity culture. In the course of this shift he maintains that with the advent of digital media that allow almost everyone to participate, ordinary people have been elevated to celebrity status and bona fide celebrities have in turn become more ordinary-like in the ways in which they utilize digital media. In other words, there is a reciprocal quality between celebrity and micro-celebrity, as one stylistically feeds off the other. This may represent the convergence of the ordinary with the extraordinary as fans and followers work through the tensions created by this paradox, as micro-celebrities operate within celebrity culture like pilot fish that follow sharks. In this case, micro-celebrities feed off the excessive disclosure of celebrities. In return, celebrities do not attack micro-celebrities, because the latter serve the broader purpose of extending celebrity culture deeper into people's everyday lives. As such there exist some mutual benefits.

Gamson describes four analytic categories with which celebrity is best apprehended: a commodity system, an industry, a set of stories and a participatory culture.[3] But all of these categories have as their base the participation in the celebrity economy. A celebrity might be described as being a part of a commodity system, based merely on their ability to attract and mobilize attention, which would fit squarely within the referent system offered by appearances on reality television.[4] The celebrity's attachment to commercial interests is based on their connection to the promotion of products and services, perhaps appearances in advertising or promotion of an album of music or movie. With regard to news stories, Gamson ties celebrity to the publicity machine that promotes an extended narrative of the celebrity embellishing their persona with, for example, engagement in charitable causes. Writing in his earlier book, *Claims to Fame: Celebrity in Contemporary America*, Gamson describes fan engagement and participation similar to Caughey's imaginary social relationships. He maintains that fans use celebrities to imagine a different life for themselves, to create an identity based on characteristics they glean from the celebrity or to use celebrities as role models. And, he points out that sometimes people attempt to establish the authenticity of the celebrity through conversations in which they seek to reconcile the "real" celebrity with the celebrity persona. All four of these categories apply to micro-celebrities as well as celebrities.

The very idea of micro-celebrity fits squarely within an American value system that Gamson claims is "often hostile toward anything resembling aristocracy, which conflicts with egalitarian beliefs."[5] He says that tension exists between status and merit, referring to achievement, talent or other special qualities. Gamson might be referring to the tensions presented to fans and followers of someone like Kim Kardashian whose persona is manufactured, in which case she may in some ways be ordinary, but "luckier, prettier, and better marketed." In the case of the talented individual, their celebrity is deserved, but in the case of Kim Kardashian, it may be perceived of as undeserved. Having said that, the ideology of celebrity is more complex than Gamson presents. For example, while many people may not believe Kim Kardashian's celebrity is deserved because of her lack of accomplishment or talent, they may appreciate her marketing savvy and ability to create and sustain her (and her family's) narrative over a long period of time. On the other hand, there are those individuals like the adventurers described in this chapter who are quite ordinary people, but who take on extraordinary tasks, thus demonstrating themselves as individuals of accomplishment worthy of their fans' and followers' attention.

The term micro-celebrity may imply that such individuals reach a small number of people, as the term micro indicates smallness, but it is not clear whether that refers to their ordinariness or the size of the audience they reach. First, in an age of splintered media, the notion of reach may need to be revaluated, as an audience of tens of thousands or hundreds of thousands may be considered large by today's standards. Second, the opportunity for engagement may be inversely associated with audience size, leading to the possibility of greater intimacy among fans and followers. Alice Marwick states, "celebrities and micro-celebrities alike use social media to create persistent streams of content, competing for the largest number of listeners. These techniques are part and parcel of an online attention economy in which page views and clicks are synonymous with success."[6] While Rojek distinguishes between "achieved" and "attributed" celebrity," Marwick distinguishes micro-celebrity as being "something one does, rather than something one is."[7] Social media platforms are replete with individuals who may be seeking to expose their talent, build an audience and create a successful career to include those who perhaps do nothing more than post videos of their performance of something as mundane as video game playing. In the case of PewDiePie, for example, in 2016 he was the highest earning YouTube star with over 16 billion views.[8] While Mark Andrejevic might have called YouTubers the everyday under surveillance, he referred to the phenomenon as "the work of being watched," but it could just as easily be called the art of being watched.[9] The artfulness is at both ends, in which the micro-celebrity is artful in the ways in which they produce and disseminate their continuing narrative, and it refers to the artful ways in which fans, friends and followers participate to create a dialogue of sorts.

MICRO-CELEBRITY IN AN AGE OF DIGITAL MEDIA

In 2001 Theresa Senft, while researching her book *Camgirls: Celebrity and Community in the Age of Social Networks*, coined the term micro-celebrity, which she described as "a new style of online performance in which people employ webcams, video, audio, blogs, and social networking sites to 'amp up' their popularity among readers, viewers, and those to whom they are linked online."[10] Whether there is a meaningful difference between subcultural, niche, marginal and micro-celebrities remains to be seen. What one gives up in terms of ubiquity, as would be the case with a bona fide celebrity, one gains through the intense involvement of smaller numbers of fans and followers, as would be the case with subcultural, niche or even local celebrities. As Andrejevic states: "The goal is to replace mass marketing and production with customized programming, products, and marketing."[11] A distinguishing feature of micro-celebrity, as opposed to the subcultural celebrity, is that the former is a phenomenon associated with digital media. While it may be true that for some amping up their popularity is a goal, for others creating a social presence at least initially is a means to stay in touch with friends and family, along the way however they may develop a fan or follower base. The process of becoming a micro-celebrity may begin with establishing a niche presence, by employing the practices gleaned from celebrities. By employing the "tactics" of celebrity, over time micro-celebrities may gain attention and increase their fan base, beyond their friends and family.

What has allowed this process to move forward is the democratization of digital media in which, as Frederich Krotz explains, "media in the long run increasingly become relevant for the social construction of everyday life, society and culture as a whole."[12] However, the shift toward "mediatization," Krotz describes, is more of a phenomenon related to changes in technology as well as a cultural process. I have referred to the process as mediated social connections, because communication media mediates our experience tautologically with media, and it mediates our connections with others engaged with forms of digital media. Becoming a micro-celebrity does require a set of practices as connections are mediated through communication technologies based on the following: the relationship between the audience as fan or follower and the micro-celebrity is always in process; and the relationship is something to be negotiated, as there is a dynamic quality to the self-presentation of the micro-celebrity and the ways in which audiences construct meaning and perhaps find significance through their interactions with the micro-celebrity and others within the micro-celebrity's social network. While the practices associated with becoming a celebrity may have become more diversified in an era of digital media, they are not necessarily democratic, as access to media and audiences is simply not equal. Turner utilizes the term "demotic" to suggest that the media landscape may have become more diverse or inclusive; however, media still operate within a hierarchical system that privileges bona fide celebrities.[13] In other words, micro-celebrities better know their place within the "tightly circumscribed" system.

MICRO-CELEBRITY, SELF-BRANDING
AND SOCIAL INFLUENCERS

It's difficult to separate micro-celebrity from self-branding, as one came on the heels of the other; they are intrinsically connected. Khamis, Ang and Welling, who studied micro-celebrity and self-branding, contend it is a phenomenon that is closely associated with the rise of digital technology.[14] In that watershed moment around 2007 when social media exploded, so too did the concept of self-branding. Senft maintains: "In a similar vein, the practice of micro-celebrity (which I define as the commitment to deploying and maintaining one's online identity as if it were a branded good, with the expectation that others do the same) has moved from the Internet's margins to its mainstream."[15] At this point in the development of digital media, it's difficult to distinguish between personal selling and advocacy of goods, services, issues or causes. A process orientation of micro-celebrity based on a set of practices reveals a self-presentation that is carefully constructed and managed. By managed I'm referring to the best practices utilized by major brands when it comes to incorporating new media into a marketing campaign. Tom Peters, writing in the magazine *Fast Company*, suggests that we all should think of ourselves as brands. To that end, he states: "You're every bit as much a brand as Nike, Coke, Pepsi, or the Body Shop."[16] Similar to a full-on marketing campaign, many micro-celebrities utilize multiple channels, including YouTube, dedicated website, Instagram, Facebook, Twitter, Patreon pages and perhaps a Pinterest page in order to advance their brand. As the micro-celebrity builds their audience, perhaps initially just family and intimate friends, in order to reach larger audiences and build a fan base, they incorporate more of these channels. As the fan base grows, management of content creation and regular dissemination can be quite time consuming, as some micro-celebrities maintain they spend up to 50 hours a week producing, editing and uploading videos to YouTube. As a result, Senft argues that ways in which we characterized ourselves based on demographics, for example, have given way to newer ways of looking (branding) ourselves including "smart shoppers, reputable vendors, trusted citizen journalists, popular fans, reliable information mavens, essential humor portals, and so forth."[17]

Marwick and boyd,[18] Marwick[19,20] and Senft[21] have all written about how micro-celebrities manage their fan base through the careful construction of self-presentation. In order to participate in the celebrity economy, much labor is involved. It is the kind of labor that turns users into producers. Beyond the production aspects of creating and disseminating content, there are the personal challenges that are critical. First, anyone who participates in the celebrity economy is both in the moment and out of the moment. To be more specific, if one is engaged in some activity, the micro-celebrity also must be in charge of the camera, lighting, sound and so on. As significant is establishing a feeling of authenticity and sincerity, hallmarks of self-presentation and self-branding that require a high level of personal disclosure within a public forum. It is in this way that micro-celebrities have to maintain some distance on their own experience, choosing what to record and later present and to do so in a way that does not break with the rules of self-disclosure.

Within the celebrity system, there is always distance between the fan and celebrity. With regard to celebrities, it is understood that a celebrity will not likely respond back to a fan, although there is always the possibility this might happen. By and large, it is understood that celebrities hire professionals to handle many of their social media postings. Micro-celebrities are a different story, as they are likely to manage their own social media posts, and they are more likely to respond to or interact directly with members of their audience. Furthermore, members of their social network are likely to interact with each other, sometimes on behalf of the micro-celebrity. Marwick states: "Micro-celebrity extends this to networked webs of actual interaction, such as instant messenger, @replies, comments, and face-to-face meetings. This interaction is crucial to maintaining the micro-celebrity practitioner's popularity and becomes part of their personal brand."[22] She adds that there is a higher level of accountability for micro-celebrities than there is for celebrities. Micro-celebrities, as do celebrities, have to walk a fine line between projecting their authentic selves in a sincere manner and being "fake." Several celebrity-driven platforms from Shonda Rhimes' Shondaland, Chrissy Teigen's Delushious, actress Blake Lively's Preserve, Reese Witherspoon's Hello Sunshine and Lena Dunham's Lenny Letter have all experienced difficulties creating "stickiness" among their audiences. The editor of the now-defunct *Lenny Letter* stated, "My favorite tweets that we get in our timeline are 'I really don't like Lena Dunham but Lenny is amazing.'"[23] However, there are differences between celebrities like Lena Dunham and micro-celebrity. Such a glib and self-deprecating response is not unlike the comedic segment on late night talk show host Jimmy Kimmel's program, where he has celebrities read "mean tweets."[24] In a sense, because the celebrities are well armed, meaning their images tend to be highly managed and in that massaged, they can, to use the vernacular, "take it." Furthermore, when celebrities are exposed, for example, boosting their social media presence with fake followers, some people take pleasure in exposing the celebrity; it's all part of the "game."[25] However, celebrities—as distinct from micro-celebrities—play multiple roles, so they may be given greater latitude regarding how and who they are presenting, their authentic self or a character they play.

Micro-celebrities, on the other hand, do not portray both a public self or selves and a private self, as they are who they present themselves to be. Fans expect them to be authentic, so when they are caught in some shape, manner or form "faking" or doing something deemed inappropriate, the dynamic nature of the connection may lead to disappointment and perhaps abandonment of the micro-celebrity. The website, GetoffmyInternets.com (GOMI) illustrates the kind of backlash some Internet posters receive when others believe they are being "untrue" and not being authentic. The canceled Netflix series *Haters Back Off* is a meta-version of Miranda Sings, a YouTube character, as she attempts to become a star. The negative viewer comments she receives from viewers, which are part of the streaming program, like "you suck," are suggestive of the show's title.[26] Grey states: "Often with increasing organization, and contributing to campaigns or groundswells that sometimes dwarf or rival their fan counterparts, anti-fans—those who hate or dislike a given text, personality, or genre—are as much a presence in contemporary society as are fans…Textual hatred and dislike have been understudied and underestimated, as has their intricate and nuanced relationship to textual love."[27] One action performed by the anti-fan is to "troll" the micro-celebrity. An "Internet troll" is a slang term for someone who tries to raise a ruckus by posting negative messages to an online community. For example, the Internet phenom Miranda Sings generates angry comments from some of her YouTube and Instagram followers who don't get the insider's joke that she is playing a character, or to put it another way, she's performing herself.[28]

Even if a fan does not abandon a micro-celebrity for some social infraction, the distance between being authentic and fake creates tension, which is where culture does its work. By that I mean, fans use such tensions to measure their own beliefs against those of the celebrity and they can conclude perhaps to abandon the celebrity, to adjust their own beliefs to accept this newfound understanding or reinforce an existing belief. Paradoxically micro-celebrities who self-brand for commercial gain or those who are in the game to acquire cultural or social capital open themselves up to scrutiny as it raises conceptual, practical and ethical issues. For example, consistency is an important part of product branding. For the micro-celebrity, there is much labor associated with posting interesting and engaging material on a regular and consistent basis. With regard to ethics, as the micro-celebrity takes on the role of influencer on behalf of a product or service, we see the co-mingling of the personal and commercial. Sometimes fans and followers perceive this unholy mixture as selling out to commercial interests.

Selling Out and the Degradation of Micro-celebrity

One situation where a fan might either choose to respond negatively or perhaps abandon a micro-celebrity or choose to adjust their own beliefs would be when the micro-celebrity "sells out." Selling out is a pejorative expression that relates to compromising of a person's "integrity, morality, authenticity, or principles in exchange for personal gain, such as money."[29] When a celebrity "sells out," it usually means that they have abandoned their original fans to go mainstream—extending their fan base—in an effort to broaden their appeal making their music, for example, more commercially viable. Author Lindsey Pollak maintains that Millennials, those who grew up in an era that embraces the materialism of hip-hop, are less concerned with the idea of selling out than previous generations.[30] In their own nuanced ways, fans may not abandon a celebrity or micro-celebrity, but some may choose to denigrate or degrade them for crossing a moral or ethical line or by selling out. Such tensions regarding the status of a celebrity are part of the celebrification process in which images are not fixed or necessarily stable, but remain fluid and volatile. It is in this way that mediated social connections remain dynamic and always in flux.

Individuals draw from multiple frames or experiences that create an intertextual complexity, as, for example, when celebrities move from various entertainment venues like TV or film to commercials and on to digital platforms. While many fans would prefer to have their connections, even imaginary ones, stable, consistent, authentic and sincere, they also enjoy variable, unexpected and sometimes tawdry behavior: there is pleasure in the missteps or failure of others. In fact, it is the space between the everyday or mundane and the unexpected where people consider or reconsider their own beliefs not only regarding the celebrity or micro-celebrity, but also extrapolating from a specific action, some broader understanding of the system in which they live. For example, to be selfish is a neo-liberal value that is associated with capitalist economic philosophy. Therefore, on the one hand, it is okay to "cash in" on one's success. But this may be moderated by a more Puritanical notion of moderation. Audiences, therefore, have to make their way through such beliefs. However, as celebrification is a dynamic process, the nature of multiple encounters through multiple media is beyond anyone's control—an advertiser, celebrity or brand. This dynamic process plays out with greater intensity on social media, through which a complex social network is weaved.

Additionally, there are few, if any, filters regarding what can and cannot be said in social media, along with what has been referred to as a collapsing of the front and backstage, a metaphor that Erving Goffman utilized to describe the difference between what may have been a public performance (frontstage) and private (backstage) behavior. On social media these differences no longer exist, as people who "perform" on the Internet do so by exposing what P. David Marshall calls the transgressive intimate self, a concept introduced in Chap. 4. Rising above the level of mere "pseudo-events," as Boorstin described, celebrities and some micro-celebrities become role models, perhaps heroes, to their fans as they take on tasks that elevate the micro-celebrity from the ordinary to the extraordinary. In such cases, through extreme admiration, it is likely that an imaginary social relationship will ensue as fans or followers fantasize, for example, about a different life for themselves. In the example that follows, the ability of ordinary people to leave their everyday lives and seek adventures traveling around the world alone, with friends or family, has become somewhat of a phenomenon that illustrates how micro-celebrity as a presentation technique lives within a narrative that is self-created, that goes beyond mere entertainment to potentially create social connection through the process of living their ordinary lives in extraordinary circumstances and sharing their experiences on various social media platforms. The collapse of the front and backstage through excessive self-disclosure and the accompanying ability of fans and followers to engage are both essential to micro-celebrity success.

Fans, friends and followers represent diffused audiences that consume such content put forth by micro-celebrities. Abercrombie and Longhurst differentiate between simple, mass and diffused audiences, but emphasize that there is crossover between all three.[31] Attending a concert in person, watching the concert on television and interacting with concertgoers through social media constitute a more amorphous sense of audience. Three qualities associated with the diffused audience—those likely to participate in social media platforms—need to be considered: first, newer technologies provide opportunities for individuals to spend a great deal of time consuming media; second, the portability of technology allows individuals to consume content anywhere and at any time; and third, the amount of content available on and through social media platforms means there are greater opportunities for people to "perform" even if it is just the mundane they are broadcasting. These three qualities of diffused audiences coupled with the extension of simple and mass to diffused audiences opens up the possibility for both praise and the greater possibility of degradation within social networks. Longhurst writes about the diffused audience: "The essential feature of this audience experience is that, in contemporary society, everyone becomes an audience all the time. Being a member of an audience is no longer an exceptional event, nor even an everyday event; rather, it is constitutive of everyday life. This is not a claim that simple audiences or mass audiences no longer exist, quite the contrary. These experiences are common as ever, but they take place against the background of a diffused audience."[32] The diffused audience is one that is based on the collapse of the private into the public sphere; as such there is an increased possibility that the impact of engagement will be greater and lead to a mediated social connection.

CASE STUDY IN MICRO-CELEBRITY SELF-PRESENTATION

The narrative for each of the following cases in micro-celebrity follows a similar route: ordinary people with a desire for adventure, having little or no skill or money, leaving the comfort and security of their everyday lives to follow a dream—sailing around the world. What makes this extraordinary is that these individuals, couples and families have little or no experience, which is important fuel for furthering the fantasies of their fans and followers. In other words: "if they can do it, you can do it too" is the philosophy being espoused. What follows is a critical examination of the ways in which these micro-celebrities negotiate the presentation of self and develop their brand, and the analysis is interested in the ways in which audiences/fans and followers use micro-celebrity appearances in social media as a sense-making mechanism and it is interested in the fans' and followers' role as active participant in the process either directly through commenting or vicariously through stream of consciousness expressions of wish fulfillment or degradation. The three groups or couples that are sailing around the world and posting their meanderings across social media platforms are as follows: "Gone with the Wynns" is a couple that sails their catamaran *Curiosity* in the Caribbean and beyond. *La Vagabonde* is the name of an Australian couple's catamaran.[33] And *Delos* is the name of the boat beginning its eighth year of circumnavigating with two American brothers, a Swedish girlfriend and occasional guests.

As long-term adventurers, they all have lifted themselves above the ordinary YouTube traveler. In each of these cases they have more than 100,000 YouTube subscribers, which distinguishes them among others who are doing similar things. In contrast to what sociologist Joshua Gamson refers to the twenty-first-century turn that celebrity has taken toward the direction of the ordinary, these individuals might describe themselves as ordinary, but they have taken a turn toward the extraordinary, adventuring far beyond the work-a-day world of most people. In fact, they serve as inspiration for some fans and followers and they provide fantasy for other "armchair" sailors who dream of doing what these individuals have accomplished, which in one case has been ongoing for longer than most episodic television programs. The aspirational nature of their meanderings around the globe for many of their fans and followers fits squarely within "extreme admiration," a category within John Caughey's theory of imaginary social relationships.[34] These adventurers' celebrity status is based on accomplishments and achievements, rather than being artificially produced. As can be seen in Table 5.1, each of these adventurers has accumulated more than 100,000 YouTube followers and thousands more on various social media platforms: Facebook, Twitter, Pinterest, Google+, Instagram as well as Patreon. These platforms are in addition to maintaining dedicated websites.

Table 5.1 Social media followers/subscribers

	YouTube	Patreon	Facebook	Instagram	Twitter	Google+	Pinterest
Delos	231,928	1777	71,057	64,900	0	1538	0
GWTW	154,282	7620	37,894	26,500	8419	1756	61
La Vaga	340,289	1645	85,063	123,000	13,300	478	0

GONE WITH THE WYNNS/CURIOSITY

Jason and Nikki Wynn describe themselves in the following manner: "a couple of perpetual travelers and modern day documentarians. We share in hopes of inspiring you to find your next adventure." They maintain several social media channels to which they cross-post much of their content. And, as with the other adventurers, the Wynns have a Patreon page where fans contribute money toward the production of their videos. This page also includes a "tip jar" and a link to their Amazon associate's account where they may receive affiliate commissions.

LA VAGABONDE

These two adventurers from Australia, Elayna and Riley, began their adventure in the Greek islands, where the two met during the summer of 2014. They have in the past three years "sailed over 30,000 nautical miles together, through the Med, down to Cape Verde, across the Atlantic Ocean, through the Caribbean, Panama Canal, Galapagos Islands, across the Pacific Ocean and island hopped back to New Zealand." They both admittedly recount how they had no idea what they were getting into when they began this adventure, but the money they have raised keeps them sailing around the world and helps them to afford a new catamaran, which has caused some tension within their network of followers.

DELOS

"A few years ago, American Brian Trautman dropped the mooring lines of his boat Delos, and left the business world in Seattle behind him. He had zero intentions of becoming a travel blogger—just an epic trip across the Pacific Ocean to New Zealand. When they finally got there, however, they weren't ready to stop." The base crew of *Delos* includes Trautman and his brother Brady, along with Brian's Swedish girlfriend Karen. There are a number of characters that float in and out of the *Delos'* narrative; some travel with them for long periods of time and others for a few weeks. In other words, the characters in the YouTube series change, keeping the narrative fresh.

WORKING TO ACHIEVE AUTHENTICITY

How can one be extraordinary, achieve celebrity status and maintain one's ordinariness at the same time? McCrea refers to this ability as "aspirational extra/ordinariness."[35] The micro-celebrity must present their self as someone who once led an ordinary life, but has chosen to give up their normal routine to do something extraordinary. In the case of these micro-celebrities, they have decided to sail around the world. For example, Riley from *La Vagabonde* worked on an oilrig in order to acquire the funds to purchase his boat. And Elayna, his partner, was doing singing gigs in Greece when they met. Jason and Nikki from Gone with the Wynns were photographer and makeup artist, respectively. And, Brian from *Delos* was a computer geek. Each takes pains to make sure that fans know of their "humble" origins through their videos, in-person lectures or posts on other social media. Much of their past and who they are is offered up on Facebook, YouTube, dedicated web pages and Patreon pages as testimonials of their ordinariness, as if to say: "if we can do it (based on our ordinariness), you can too." It is this comparison that fuels the admiration that forms the basis of the mediated social connection as these travelers perform authenticity.

Merely disclosing one's ordinary past is not enough, however, as once established and conferred by the audience, micro-celebrities have to work to maintain their authenticity by continually offering themselves up in a sincere and truthful manner; it is an act of labor. As indicated in Table 5.2, in each case the micro-celebrities maintain a YouTube.com channel where they regularly (weekly) post video content of varying lengths. Posting on a regular and routine basis is an important way of creating continuity for their personal brand and maintaining their social presence. The YouTube channel is one of the key ways in which these micro-celebrities monetize their content, as YouTube requires that in order to become a "partner," a channel must reach "4,000 watch hours in the previous 12 months and

Table 5.2 Video uploads and income generated (Socialblade.com as of November 2017)

	Video uploads	Total views	Daily average	Est. yearly earnings	Channel created
Delos	223	68,088,785	78,935	7.1–113.7 K	2007
GWTW	345	26,361,040	20,149	1.8–29 K	2010
La Vaga	154	50,622,790	60,104	5.4–86.5 K	2014

1,000 subscribers" before they can be compensated through advertising that is posted along with their videos.[36]

In addition to reinforcing their ordinariness, these traveler vloggers also must convey the extraordinariness of their adventures in order to entice viewers and encourage social connection. Whether it is climbing waterfalls in Panama, scuba diving in Mauritius or cruising the Med to Corsica, each of these micro-celebrity couples or groups do things, sometimes daring, that are out of the ordinary for most people.

In the quest for authenticity, disruptions from time to time emerge when there are inconsistencies on either side of the aspirational extra/ordinariness binary, and as a result, fans sometimes express their irritation through their comments or dislikes. The micro-celebrities may look like "trust fund babies" sailing around in their "yachts," but have to emphasize that they are simply people who saved their money or get along on meager earnings in order to continue their adventure. For some, they can work while they travel. For example, on their travel website, Gonewiththewynns.com, the couple posts the following:

> Negativity—When you become successful, people naturally want to hate, or assume that by the grace of some higher being your life is easier than theirs and you never had to work for anything. (note to self, someday share the backstory about how I was raised by my working class grandmother in a small farming community). We read every comment and the little negative jabs and blatant trolls eventually add up. We don't talk about it, we don't typically engage them and try to forget them as quickly as possible. Some days it's easier than others. On the hard days, here is what we say to ourselves:
>
> 1. We worked hard for everything we've earned in life.
> 2. 95% of the comments are good so we can't listen to the 5%
> 3. If you're feeling down talk to a friend and DO NOT engage the haters, it's almost impossible to change their minds.
> 4. When we see someone more successful than us it's important to think about point #1 before judging their situation. As we often tell ourselves the sweet can't be as sweet without the sour...and our life is pretty damn sweet![37]

In addition to disclosing details about one's life and background, the micro-celebrity needs to directly address fans, being true to their mission, involving fans directly in the journey and, most important, encouraging

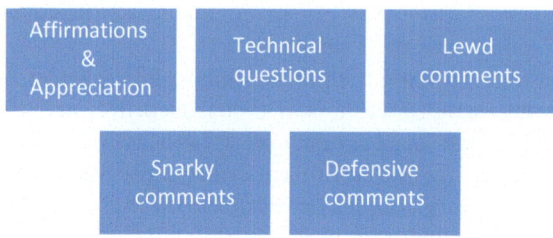

Fig. 5.1 Types of comments

the fantasy. With regard to directly addressing fans, micro-celebrities direct replies to fans' comments or through fielding questions and responding to comments on Facebook Live or YouTube Live sessions. Sometimes those live Q and A sessions can last an hour or more. Comments can be categorized as the following: affirmations and appreciation, technical questions or comments about sailing or camera equipment, lewd and socially inappropriate comments, snarky comments, comments that defend the micro-celebrity and comparisons to inauthentic others (see Fig. 5.1).

With regard to the latter, sometime fans and followers will mention something another sailor is doing in comparison, and, as such, the community of fans and followers form a network of networks (see Fig. 5.2).

This may be referred to as cross-channel chatter, as fans that follow one of these adventurers will likely be following the others. For example, when the crew of *Delos* puts out a video where they visit the factory that built their yacht, some fans questioned whether the company was going to provide—perhaps gift—them with a new yacht, similar to the experience of the couple that sails *La Vagabonde,* who were able to partner with the boat manufacturer Outremer to purchase their catamaran in partial exchange for featuring the boat in their travel videos. In the case of Gone with the Wynns, when they did a video episode about 23andme.com, a company that uses DNA to identify one's lineage, they were accused by some fans of duplicating what the couple of *La Vagabonde* did when they promoted 23andme.com in their videos. In these instances, some fans thought the couples were selling out by promoting commercial products that have no direct connection to their adventures.

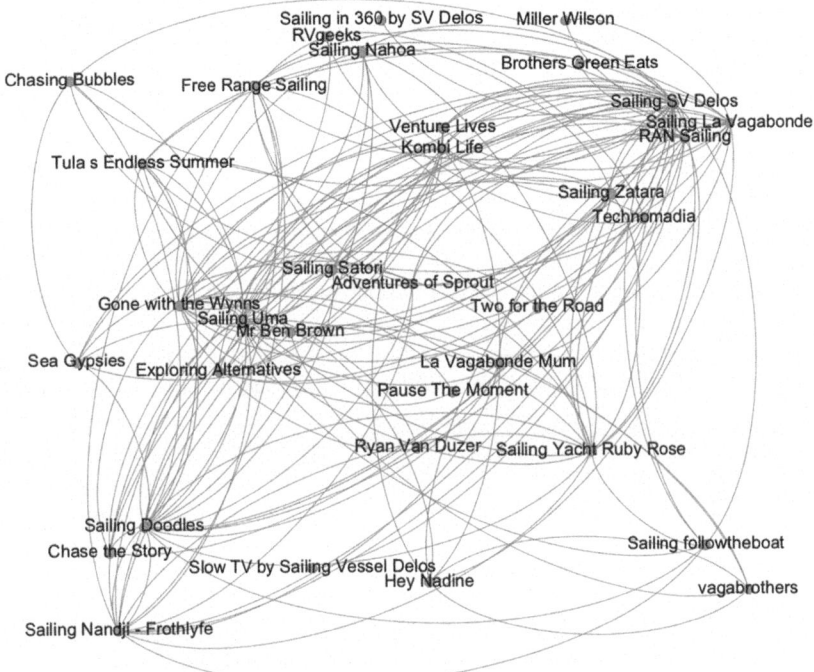

Fig. 5.2 Network of networks

Monetization May Lead to Suspicion of Motives

Micro-celebrities whose audience reach is 100,000 or more may also be considered a micro-influencer. Consistent with the idea of being authentic and sincere, operating within the extraordinary/ordinary binary, the micro-celebrity may have more credibility and, therefore, more influence than other types of social influences. According to research conducted by Jonah Berger, author of *Contagious: Why Things Catch On*, micro-influencers have a very significant impact on purchase decisions, reasoning they are more credible and believable.[38] For example, these travel vloggers review equipment for manufacturers, sometimes in exchange for the products, other times receiving discounts. In the case of *Delos*, they received a 50% discount on a new generator for their yacht. They posted a video of the installation, as the crew donned shirts with the generator manufacturer's logo emblem on the chest. Gone with the Wynns tested onboard freezers for the manufacturer and maintain a link on their website where others can purchase the product through Amazon.[39] The Wynns maintain a web page featuring gear they utilize, some of which is linked to their Amazon Associates account whereby they receive compensation when someone makes a purchase through their link. Additionally, all of these adventurers sell merchandise emblazoned with their name and logos, ranging from tee shirts and hats, to coffee mugs to in one case a music album. All of this is to suggest that there is a lot of commercialism that creeps into the presentation of self, and fans sometimes become quite agitated when they feel the micro-celebrity has crossed the line between authenticity and commercialism. Responding to a "hater" comment on a YouTube video where followers learn about the new boat that Riley and Elayna will move aboard, one fan says:

> You know what Stephen…these two are ready to move on. They captured us with their struggles and now they've learned some things, earned some things, and are succeeding with what they are doing. It's that you can't just be happy for them and even keep an open mind that their future adventures might be just as entertaining. Why do they have to stay struggling and poor just to keep relatable? Can't you enjoy and relate to watching the journey of some people who put in some honest work, have had the good fortune of enjoying some commercial success from it, and are now going to embark on some new ventures and still allow everyone to follow along while they do it?

This exchange is part of what can be described as a cluster of responses in which fans isolate someone who is attempting to degrade the micro-celebrity and corral them with defensive responses. Oftentimes, an exchange takes place within the larger discourse of video comments. The following are some specific ways in which these travelers take part in the celebrity economy:

SELLING MERCHANDISE

All of these adventurers sell merchandise emblazoned with their name and logos, ranging from tee shirts and hats, to coffee mugs to in one case a music album.

Co-brand Offers: 23andme and audible.com

The couple from Curiosity posted a video titled, Nomads & Settlers—Diving into our Backstory, in which they used the 23andme.com DNA service to dig into their genetic backgrounds. The video received a cluster of negative comments. The couple posted their defense[40]:

> For all those disappointed about the video being irrelevant to you, a corporate sell out, infomercial, and so on... I get it. We have worked with a handful of companies over the years but you felt this was different. The video was different in the fact that it wasn't a product directly related to the boat or RV(solar, composting toilet...) but it did relate to us. We turn down 99% of the companies that send pitches our way wanting us to promote their products. We were genuinely interested and that is why we participated. Perhaps it isn't something you like or were interested in and that is okay. Plenty of people don't like our tech related videos about solar, batteries or composting toilets. We usually get just as much flack for those videos too being called product pushers, e-beggars, corporate sell outs and so on. Some people leave less than positive comments about any video that doesn't contain sailing in it. We get hit from every angle no matter what we do. You are a diverse community of people and we can't hit the mark for each of you every time. But, you are our community, we do listen to your feedback, take it into consideration and it influences what we create and share with you next. So, with all that in mind...thanks for watching and taking the time to comment with both what you like and what you don't. It has been noted. If it is any consolation, this was a one-time thing and we don't have anything else of the sort planned.

Ebegging: Tip Jar and "Buy Us a Beer"

Ebeggar is a pejorative term to describe a scam artist who utilizes the Internet to solicit funds, perhaps to defray the production costs of a movie or some other cause or issue supported by the ebeggar. Ebegging brings out the haters and anti-fans, as Ebegging is one part of the system of raising funds to support the adventure. Riley from *La Vagabonde* wrote a post on their website, "Yesterday Someone Called Me an Ebegger," in which he is "vexed" by the comment. In his blog post, he defended his use of Patreon.com as a legitimate way to support the work Elayna and he are doing to produce videos. Their supporters, like the following one, reject on their behalf the negative reference:

Missy Caudill
   DECEMBER 22, 2015 AT 4:59 AM
   You guys aren't e-beggars at all! You guys are an inspiration. We have
watched every episode and look forward to new ones with anticipation and
excitement when we see one is posted. You are helping us make the transition from land to sea and don't even know it. (We plan to shove off April of
2017 – s/v Invictus). However, not to lie, sometimes we are jealous, sometimes we are envious…but for the most part you are entertaining and we
learn from you. You guys do a great job at what you do, keep it up, haters
will always hate![41]

Another fan writes in defense of these two sailors, distinguishing between
ebegging and legitimate commerce. He says:

   Stuff 'em. A beggar asks for handouts. You are providing quality content
   that is very enjoyable to watch. People are grateful, and some chose to pay
   a bit for that content. Not your issue if someone with a jealous streak can't
   appreciate the difference. Thank you for what you do for us!

The crew of *Delos* asks viewers to "buy us a beer." Similarly Gone with the
Wynns also ask fans to "buy us a beer or simply send a few bucks our way."
   These micro-celebrities offer patrons—those who contribute to their
Patreon.com account—the opportunity to support the adventure and in
that the production of the videos as well as a chance to sail with them.
Not only does this open up the "backstage" of the experience, it also
contributes to the authenticity of these adventurers by providing outside
confirmation and validation of the experience, as patrons who come on
board exchange their online engagement for the opportunity to participate in the adventure. For a time, the opportunity to sail with these
adventurers elevates these individuals to micro-celebrity status, and
among those who have participated, several have gone on to establish
their own self-branded channels. During July 2015, when this cruising
couple on *La Vagabonde* began utilizing Patreon.com to raise funds to
keep their adventure going, they had $1600 in their account based on
200 viewers of their videos who donated between $1 and $50.[42] However,
by November 2017, the contributions to their Patreon page indicate
their fund-raising goal is approximately $10,000 per video episode with
over 1600 individuals donating.

Demonstrating Ethical Authenticity

Branding a fixed object, like a product or service, is different from branding a person, as micro-celebrities are humans and thus they may not be subject to the same qualities we assign to products, characteristics that are not humanly possible or desirable. Even with regard to bona fide celebrities whose personas are professionally managed, they sometimes fall off the proverbial bar stool. But fans may be forgiving depending on the infraction, and indeed, there is some pleasure in seeing a celebrity's fall from grace, a form of schadenfreude. With regard to micro-celebrities, because they are "just like us," we may actually hold them to a higher standard. To that end, they may not get the same "pass" as a bona fide celebrity who may be forgiven for some transgression or another in the same way that we might not forgive a friend with whom we have a close relationship. Paradoxically, as we do not know micro-celebrities more than we know celebrities, it is the very strength, as Mark Granovetter put it, of weak ties that allow people to comment or tweet in degrading and disparaging ways. Not that we don't do similar things with celebrities as evidenced by a recurring segment on the Jimmie Kimmel late night talk show in which he has celebrities reading "mean tweets." But these are delivered with the wink of an eye, whereas when micro-celebrities are disparaged, they do not have the protection that allows them to defend against "haters." We think of micro-celebrities as more real and less perfect, which makes them vulnerable. That vulnerability is the price of authenticity. Therefore, when micro-celebrities violate the trust of their fans, it raises questions of ethical authenticity. Where micro-celebrities are monetizing their brand through efforts like those cited above, it may raise questions in some of their fans and followers as to whether it is ethical to commercialize the adventure by selling merchandise, offering a chance to ride along based on patronage and receiving money from Amazon-affiliated programs and other commercial enterprises, like 23andme.com, among others. Simply put: do their fans think they are selling out?

Disclaiming Inauthenticity

When the couple on Curiosity uploaded a video that was for all intent and purpose a commercial for 23andme.com, a service that provides analysis of one's DNA, 477 comments were posted based on almost 40,000 views.

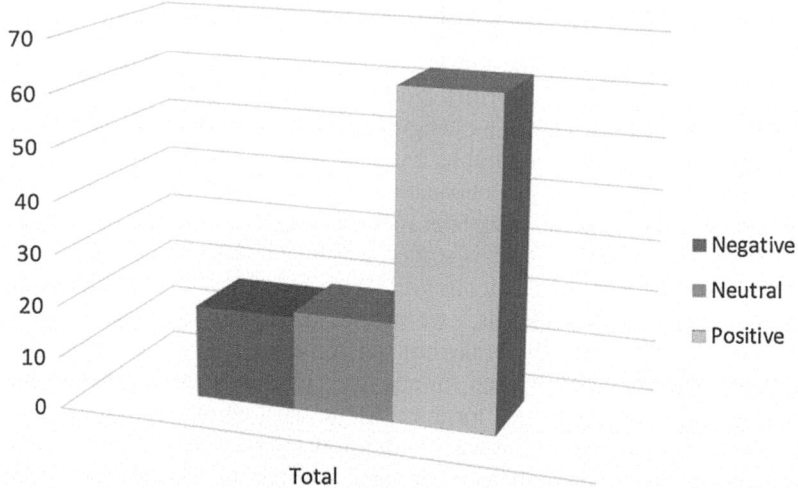

Fig. 5.3 Sentiment analysis of Gone with the Wynns' 23andme video comments

Almost 10% of the comments were very negative and 18% were moderately negative, compared to the remainder of the comments which were either moderately positive (32%) or very positive (24%) (see Fig. 5.3).

Among the comments and replies, the following cluster emerges:

sherrie gassaway
Infomercial. ya… about that…lets [sic] get back to sailing now?
Dilly Dally
sherrie gassaway – I like the personal touch in the videos too
James Frizzell
Get back to sailing, that's free right? You don't have to make money to sail, right?
RV Cruza
And you don't have to comment on every thread do you. Maybe you should go sailing and get a life.
sherrie gassaway
Dilly Dally i like the personal touch, but not an infomercial that has NOTHING to do with sailing… it is, afterall [sic], a "sailing" channel, no?

sherrie gassaway
James Frizzell its [sic] youtube, not the discovery channel...geeez....
sherrie gassaway
RV Cruza i comment on every thread? Hummm... someone forgot their
meds. Cant [sic] help stupid.

This a broader interconnected network of people who are fans and followers of the travel vloggers like those described here suggests that there is
symbiosis as well as discord that shifts with the changes in the discourse
that accompanies changes in scene and situation. The individual vloggers
network is not monolithic, as fans and followers are not a school of fish
that react or respond in unison. Rather, the social network of these travel
vloggers is made partially of clusters of individuals that see themselves as
protectors of the domain, defending the vlogger along the way. But even
these clusters may grow in size or become smaller, as niches may emerge
to degrade or denigrate the vlogger. To put it another way, while haters
are gonna hate, likers are going to like and lovers are going to love, and as
such a hate-fest may go on at the same time as a like- or love-fest. Social
networks are complex and reflect the kinds of human discourse people
experience away from digital media.

Micro-celebrities labor to establish and maintain trustworthiness by
demonstrating their authenticity and sincerity through routine postings
and excessive disclosure. As audiences engage in mediated social connections, they join a fan community and establish groups that may cluster
around various aspects of their affinity or disdain for the micro-celebrity
that range from hater to friend, to mentor or idealized other based on
extreme admiration. The social media exchanges—comments and replies,
for example—are not only between the micro-celebrity and the fan or follower, but also between fans themselves as they participate in a social network that may extend beyond one micro-celebrity to include references to
others who fans follow on social media. These interactions over time build
connection that may create a panoply for the micro-celebrity when they
cross a line in which some might perceive them as "selling out" to commercial interests. While some fans may declare that they will abandon the
micro-celebrity, others demonstrate through their interactions a willingness to understand and accept the "system" as presented or they react
strongly against other commenters who attempt to degrade the
micro-celebrity.

CONCLUSION

The musician and blogger Momus published an essay in 1991 that is apropos to micro-celebrity in which he offered a corrective to Andy Warhol's famous statement: "In the future, everyone will be famous for fifteen minutes." Momus countered that "In the future, we will all be famous to fifteen people."[43] If we take Momus' quote within the context of self-branding, that is to say, buying into the need to establish and maintain an online brand, well then perhaps Momus was onto something. But it turns out that such a glib statement may miss the point: niches, cliques and groups are as important as crowds, clusters and networks. In an era of digital media, they all work in connection to form a celebrity and micro-celebrity network, even if the network is loosely connected or not connected at all. While the social practices may differ between the two, micro-celebrity doesn't change the game of celebrity; rather, it adds to or extends the game so that others may play. As such digital media have to an extent democratized the ability of diverse people to participate in the celebrity economy. Consider, for example, the phenomenon of "micro-merch" in which micro-celebrities market products like T-shirts, mugs, key chains, coloring books and tissue boxes, not for the masses, but for a dedicated few.[44] What has made this possible is one's ability to develop a following on a platform like Instagram through self-branding, the ability to manufacturer small amounts of goods lending an air of exclusivity and the ability to deliver those goods in an economical and efficient manner. The micro-celebrity phenomenon brings new meaning to the phrase "small is beautiful." Not only do the traveler vloggers described in this chapter sell mugs and T-shirts, among other goods, many other micro-celebrities based on their personal interests or brand may appeal to relatively small numbers, by mass marketing standards, of engaged people. These micro-celebrities may represent nascent businesses that operate in the celebrity economy, and while they may never grow to reach the sales figures of Kim Kardashian's micromerch Post-it notes shaped like her derrière, among other items she sells, they are part of the personal branding that takes part in the postmodern economy, often referred to as late capitalism, in which everyone is required to be an entrepreneur. Micro-celebrity fits well within such a neo-liberal framework.

Whether the sale of merchandise is a primary objective of one's personal branding, micro-celebrities can develop numbers of fans, friends and followers that, while not at the levels of Selena Gomez's Instagram account, do provide enough "market share" to keep their brand growing and, in the case of the sailors described in this chapter, keep them traveling. After all, a highly rated cable television program may have a viewership in the low hundreds of thousands; in the case of some micro-celebrities, they reach those numbers and beyond. There is intense labor associated with building and maintaining a brand. The work done by a micro-celebrity requires them to be "always on," creating a public presence of their private experiences, all managed through various social media channels. The requirements are not only cultural—playing by the rules of the game—but labor intensive, as micro-celebrities have to digitally film, photograph and write about their experiences. They also have to edit the material into a digestible and in that a highly readable or viewable (entertaining) format with special effects, including drone footage and music, along with titling. They also have to upload their videos to one of the Internet channels—YouTube or Vimeo—which takes a great deal of time, given the spotty and slow Internet connections while traveling in various parts of the world. They also have to maintain cross-channel communication utilizing multiple social media platforms, writing blog posts, posting photos and so on. Such intensive labor diminishes their actual experiences, as there is little time for reflexivity.

While all of this perhaps began with the idea of keeping friends and family informed of the whereabouts of these adventurers, as the audience builds something else begins to take hold. In other words, they didn't set out intentionally or consciously to create a personal brand. However, commercialism creeps in as these micro-celebrities learn to successfully utilize a platform like Patreon.com to raise money from fans; it is now a standard feature of these and other micro-celebrities who are engaged in creative endeavors, which extends from teaching music lessons online to selling art. Selling merchandise—hats and T-shirts, among other items—emblazoned with their logo is another way of raising money to keep the adventure going. Co-branding with equipment manufacturers is yet another, as is co-branding with companies like audible.com and 23andme. com. In addition, these micro-celebrities engage directly with their fans by offering the opportunity to actually go sailing with them. In this way, their fans become, at least for a time, micro-celebrities too. And, several who came along for the proverbial ride have since started their own channels in hopes of sustaining their nascent micro-celebrity status.

The adventurers upon whom this chapter is based represent a niche among micro-celebrities, appealing to those who already sail locally, far offshore and those who dream of doing so. There is tremendous appeal to the latter that use the experiences of others to live vicariously and create mediated social connections that extend to the possibility of interaction by liking or commenting or even for the lucky few to join the adventure. It is the niche or narrow interest that draws people who find great meaning as followers and fans. The audiences are engaged, as evidenced by the amount of income generated by these travelers. As the audience for this category of video adventurers is based on a rather narrow interest, it is incumbent upon these micro-celebrities to create and maintain a sense of closeness, perhaps intimacy with their fans, whether that means directly replying to their comments on social media or inviting fans to join the adventure for short periods of time. The maintenance of a social media presence for these micro-celebrities is a form of labor; however, unlike some other forms of internet labor for which there may be no financial reward, this particular breed of micro-celebrity uses their regular appearance on YouTube and blog posts, Instagram photos, Tweets, among others to help support the continuation of their adventure. In this way fans are not only contributing to the micro-celebrities production of content but also engaged in keeping this world metaphorically afloat.

In this chapter, we have looked at the celebrity economy vis-à-vis travel vloggers, exemplars of how micro-celebrity operates in the digital age. Chapter 6 adds another layer to our understanding of the ordinary/extraordinary binary as it explores the use of celebrities in promoting prescription drugs. The thread that binds these chapters is not only the presence of celebrities but the ways in which ordinary people engage deeply as they form and maintain mediated social connections.

NOTES

1. Rose, R. & Wood, S. (2005). Paradox and the Consumption of Authenticity through Reality Television. *Journal of Consumer Research*. 32:2, pp. 284–296.
2. Boorstin. D. (1962). *The Image: A Guide to Pseudo-events in America*. New York: Vintage Books, p. 324.
3. Gamson, J. (2011). The unwatched life is not worth living: The elevation of the ordinary in celebrity culture. PMLA, 126(4), pp. 1061–1069. doi:https://doi.org/10.1632/pmla.2011.126.4.1061
4. Ibid., p. 1062.
5. Ibid., p. 1063.

6. Marwick, A. (2015). You May Know Me From YouTube: (Micro)-Celebrity in Social Media. In *A Companion to Celebrity*, Marshall, P.D. and Redmond, S., Eds. Hoboken, NJ: John Wiley & Sons Inc.
7. Ibid.
8. Socialblade.com (n.d. a). Top Ranked YouTubers. Retrieved from: https://socialblade.com/youtube/
9. Andrejevic, M. (2002). The Work of Being Watched: Interactive Media and the Exploitation of Self-Disclosure. *Critical Studies in Mass Communication.* 19:2 (June), pp. 230–248.
10. Senft, T. (2008). *Camgirls: Celebrity and Community in the Age of Social Networks.* New York: Peter Lang Publishers, p. 25.
11. Op cit., p. 237.
12. Krotz, F. (2009). Mediatization: A Concept with Which to Grasp Media and Societal Change. In *Mediatization: Concept, Changes, Consequences,* edited by Knut Lundby, pp. 21–40. New York: Peter Lang.
13. Turner, G. (2006). The Mass Production of Celebrity 'Celetoids', Reality TV and the 'demotic turn.' *International Journal of Cultural Studies.* 9:2: pp. 153–65.
14. Khamis, S. L. Ang, L. & R. Welling, R. (2016). Self-branding, 'micro-celebrity' and the rise of Social Media Influencers, *Celebrity Studies,* 8:2, pp. 191–208. Retrieved from: https://doi.org/10.1080/19392397.2016.1218292
15. Senft, T.M. (2013). Microcelebrity and the branded self. In J. Hartley, J. Burgess, and A. Bruns, eds. *A companion to new media dynamics.* Chichester: Wiley-Blackwell, pp. 346–354.
16. Peters, T. (December 18, 2007). The Brand Called You. *Fast Company.* Retrieved from: http://www.fastcompany.com/magazine/10/brandyou.html
17. Senft, T. (2013). The Branded Self. P. 3.
18. Marwick, A., & boyd, d. (2011). "To See and Be Seen: Celebrity Practice on Twitter." *Convergence* 17:2, pp. 139–58.
19. Marwick, A. (2013). *Status Update: Celebrity, Publicity, and Branding in the Social Media Age.* New Haven, CT: Yale University Press.
20. Marwick, A. (2015). You May Know Me From YouTube: (Micro)-Celebrity in Social Media. In *A Companion to Celebrity*, Marshall, P.D. and Redmond, S., Eds. Hoboken, NJ: John Wiley & Sons Inc.
21. Senft, T. (2008). Camgirls: *Celebrity and Community in the Age of Social Networks. Digital Formations.* New York: Peter Lang.
22. Marwick, A. (2015). You May Know Me From YouTube: (Micro)-Celebrity in Social Media. P. 16.

23. Shah, B. (2017, October 20). From Shondaland to Lenny Letter, Celebrity Platforms stretch to Find Fans. Ad Age. Retrieved from: http://adage.com/article/media/makes-celebrity-media-platforms-succeed/310965/
24. Rosenbloom, S. (2014, August 23). Dealing with Digital Cruelty. The New York Times. Retrieved from: http://nyti.ms/1qAXuKO
25. DeFino, J. (n.d.). Celebs Who Were Caught with Fake Followers on Social Media. Ranker.com. Retrieved from: https://www.ranker.com/list/celebrities-who-have-fake-followers-on-social-media/jessica-defino
26. Poniewozik, J. (2016, October 13). Review: In 'Haters Back Off!' a Cringe-Worthy Star Is Born. *The New York Times*. Retrieved from: https://www.nytimes.com/2016/10/14/arts/television/review-in-haters-back-off-a-cringe-worthy-star-is-born.html?_r=0
27. Gray, J. (2005). Antifandom and the Moral Text: Television Without Pity and Textual Dislike. *American Behavioral Scientist*. 48, pp. 840–857. DOI: https://doi.org/10.1177/0002764204273171
28. Miranda Sings YouTube Channel. (n.d.). Retrieved from: https://www.youtube.com/channel/UC1OFDlfdRb6ma1ZGZd07gWA
29. Dictionary.com (n.d.). Selling out. Retrieved from: http://www.dictionary.com/browse/sellout
30. Schoenberg, N. (2016, February 24). Movie stars in TV ads: Are they worried about 'selling out'? *The Chicago Tribune*. Retrieved from: http://www.chicagotribune.com/lifestyles/ct-movie-star-sellouts-0224-20160224-story.html
31. Abercrombie, N. & Longhurst, B. (1998). *Audiences: A Sociological Theory of Performance and Imagination*. Washington, D.C.: Sage Publications Inc.
32. Longhurst, B. (2007). *Popular Music and Society*. Cambridge: Polity Press, p. 261.
33. Leasca, S. (January 9, 2018). How This Couple Is Getting Paid to Sail Around the World. Travelandleisure.com. Retrieved from: https://www.travelandleisure.com/trip-ideas/couple-sailing-around-world
34. Caughey, J. (1984). *Imaginary Social Worlds: A Cultural Approach*. Lincoln, NB: University of Nebraska Press.
35. McCrae, S. (2017). Get Off My Internets: How Deconstruct Lifestyle Bloggers' Authenticity Work. Persona Studies. 3:1, pp. 13–27
36. YouTube Partner Program Overview. (n.d.). Retrieved from: https://support.google.com/youtube/answer/72851?hl=en
37. Gonewiththewynns.com (n.d.a). Retrieved from: http://www.gonewiththewynns.com/travel-money-wynns
38. Experticity. (n.d.). Research Shows Micro-Influencers Have More Impact Than Average Consumers. Retrieved from: http://go2.experticity.com/rs/288-azs-731/images/experticity-kellerfaysurveysummary_.pdf

39. Gonewiththewynns.com (n.d.b). Domestic Portable Electric Fridge/ Freezer - Gone With The Wynns. Retrieved from: http://www.gonewith-thewynns.com/product/dometic-portable-electric-fridgefreezer
40. Gonewiththewynns (2017, September 17 c). Nomads & Settlers - Diving into our Backstory. Retrieved from: https://www.youtube.com/watch?v=8LLJBMmpouc&t=5s
41. Sailing Lavagabond.com (2015a). Blog post. Retrieved from: http://sailing-lavagabonde.com/yesterday-someone-called-me-an-e-begger/
42. Sailing Lavagabond.com (2015b). How I Bought a Yacht and Afford to Sail. Blog post. Retrieved from: http://sailing-lavagabonde.com/money-money-money/
43. Momus. (1991). Pop Stars? Nein Danke! Retrieved from: http://imomus.com/index499.html
44. Caramancia, J. (April 17, 2018). The Dawn of Micromerch. *The New York Times*. Retrieved from: https://www.nytimes.com/2018/04/17/style/micromerch-niche-fandom.html

CHAPTER 6

Skin Wars: Building Mediated Social Connections to Promote Prescription Drugs

Should he tell her? Would it, by making her share the shame, wed them inextricably; make her, by bondage of pity, his slave? Can he, so young, afford a slave? (John Updike, writing about psoriasis in the novel *The Centaur*)

On September 2, 1985, *The New Yorker* magazine published a story by celebrated author John Updike titled "At War with My Skin."[1] In the story, Updike recalls his mother saying that he showed signs of psoriasis at age six. The disease played a significant role in his personal life as well as his creative life. The condition drove him inward and in part accounts for his desire to become a writer, working in isolation. He shares this story later in life, after he has come to reconcile the disease, treatment and flow of his existence as a sun chaser (because the sun helps to diminish the effects) with the rest of his social life as a student, husband and father. Updike wrote about not only the physical aspects of the disease, but the psychological affects.

In an Updike novel *The Centaur*, the character Peter Caldwell has psoriasis.[2] In the book, Updike, speaking through Caldwell, considers his disease as he decides whether or not to tell his girlfriend, expressed in the quote at the beginning of this chapter. In this sense this popular fiction is a reflection of the writer's reality. Updike was not the only author to write fiction about this disease of the skin; as such, personal lamentations are reflected in the fiction of other authors like Dutch novelist Connie Palmen's 1992 book *The Laws*.[3] Television writer Dennis Potter was

© The Author(s) 2019
N. M. Alperstein, *Celebrity and Mediated Social Connections*,
https://doi.org/10.1007/978-3-030-17902-1_6

known to include characters with psoriasis, such as Philip Marlow in *The Singing Detective*, in which case Marlow portrayed by actor Michael Gambon is confined by psoriasis to his hospital bed.[4] Whether in fiction or personal reflection, there are only a few instances where psoriasis is discussed or depicted in popular culture, despite the fact that seven and a half million people in the United States suffer from the disease.

On the Internet, there is a website devoted to fictional characters with skin conditions: skinema.com. A dermatologist Dr. Vail Reese, who has an interest both in skin diseases and in cinema, created the site.[5] Dr. Reese reports on various types of skin conditions that are reflected both in movies and in actors in their real lives. Under the banner "evil," for example, the site categorizes scars, baldness, albinism, albinopecia, itchy skin, and tattoos and piercings. Under the heading realism, the site categorizes various skin conditions as realistic scars, HIV/AIDS, skin conditions (in general), psoriasis and leprosy. However, Dennis Potter's Marlow character in *The Singing Detective* is the only report of a character with psoriasis. In other words, psoriasis has been shunned by the movies and there is only scant reference to the disease in popular culture in general.[6]

For more than 25 years, direct-to-consumer prescription drug advertising (DTCA) has been the venue through which people are likely to learn about disease treatments as marketers spent $6.4 billion on related promotions in 2017.[7] In recent years that information and related promotion of prescription drugs has spilled over from legacy media into social media, muddying the promotional landscape. Advertising on television is one-way communication, but in our participatory culture, the Internet plays an important role, not only through Internet advertising, but through blogs, dedicated web pages and ePatient participation through social media platforms, like Facebook, Instagram and Twitter, or dedicated websites like patientslikeme.com. Celebrities as well as social influencers, including ePatients, play an important role in direct-to-consumer prescription drug advertising and promotion serving as key influencers, especially when they can establish their own connection to a disease or ailment.

This chapter explores the role that digital media play in the medicalization and pharmaceuticalization of culture, in particular the ways in which people participate in social media platforms through which prescription drugs are promoted, sometimes by celebrities or other social influencers. In the process, participants engage in mediated social connections with media figures that participate in those social networks. Such connections may be based on long-term admiration of a celebrity who has a special focus on disease and medications. Direct-to-consumer prescription drug advertising and related exposure to prescription drug messaging extend the narrative of a celebrity or media figure that is well known outside of a disease circle. Participation by celebrities is a kind of punctuation for more traditional forms of prescription drug promotion on television or in print media. Social media serve a different purpose than legacy media: the latter are one-way communication, and social media hold the potential for interactivity. Celebrities and other social influencers play important social roles in this process, as the level of self-disclosure has the potential to bring forth a sense of closeness when a celebrity expresses their own connection to a disease or ailment. And criticism of a celebrity's appearing in prescription drug promotions may be suspended if their expression is one of sincerity (honesty), but people are also quick to call out celebrities who lack credibility or who are perceived to be selling out to commercial interests. It is a narrow path through which the celebrity threads their way. We can view this process through the lens of the broader social network promoted by corporations, nonprofit cause-related organizations, celebrity spokespersons, micro-celebrities and other social influencers who may have a stake in a disease, medical issue or related cause. The convergence of direct-to-consumer prescription drug advertising, celebrities, media figures and social media platforms is an ideal place to see the web of crowds, clusters and networks in action. In particular, this chapter will focus on psoriasis, a campaign for a particular drug to treat the disease and the various social roles that are played by all those who choose to be involved, including celebrities and ordinary people that suffer from the disease.

Psoriasis, which affects millions of Americans and many more people worldwide, is steeped in mythical cures; we can trace homeopathic cures to diet, exercise and mental well-being. It was approximately 50 years ago that a shampoo, Tegrin, whose chief ingredient was coal tar, was advertised and offered as a remedy for psoriasis. In addition to treating skin conditions eczema and seborrhea, it was also offered as a treatment for "the heartbreak of psoriasis," which may have spawned a number of references in various forms of popular culture, including the 1978 film "Grease."[8,9,10] More recently there have been a number of prescription medications that have come to market, making the treatment of psoriasis a multibillion dollar industry. However, before moving onward to better understand psoriasis medications and the role that various types of media figures play in promoting them, a little background is in order.

DIRECT-TO-CONSUMER PRESCRIPTION DRUG ADVERTISING

The first direct-to-consumer prescription drug TV commercial was aired in the United States in 1981.[11] The advertisement was for Rufen, a painkiller from Boots Pharmaceutical. Within 48 hours of airing the commercial, the US government forced Boots to withdraw the ad. In the aftermath, advertisements in consumer publications and on television really didn't begin to appear again until the late 1980s, but the regulations governing such advertising were pretty narrow. By agreement with the Food and Drug Administration (FDA), drug marketers at that time could mention the name of the drug but not describe what the drug was used for, or alternatively, the advertisement could describe the condition but not provide the drug's name, setting up a very convoluted system. A television advertisement for Claritin, a prescription allergy medication at the time, provides a good example, as it mentions the name of the product, but does not inform consumers about the drug, not even what the medication is used for.[12] However, as Claritin was the only prescription allergy medication on the market at that time, not mentioning what the medication was for posed little risk to the manufacturer. If you are a drug marketer, life is good if there is only one choice, and it's your product that gets to the market first.

DTCA AND CONTRACEPTIVES

There is an interesting connection to those initial regulations regarding direct-to-consumer prescription drug advertising (DTCA) and the marketing of contraceptives. There is a legal doctrine—learned intermediary—that says that the doctor is the best person to provide a patient information about the risks of a prescribed drug. In that sense, she or he operates between the pharmaceutical company and the patient—an intermediary role. Operating within that doctrine, drug companies avoided liability, because it was the doctor's responsibility to provide adequate warnings to the patient, not the responsibility of advertising. That changed with a 1985 court case—MacDonald v. Ortho Pharmaceutical Corporation—in which the court ruled that contraceptives were an exception to the learned intermediary rule, because of the particular prescribing practices; the doctor would likely see the patient but once a year. In other words, the pill wasn't associated with an acute sickness that needed to be treated immediately or on an ongoing basis and the women to whom the contraceptives were being prescribed actively engaged in requesting the prescription. Therefore, the court ruled that the physician was playing more of a passive role; hence she or he was not the learned intermediary. Rather, it was the pharmaceutical company's obligation to warn the patient of the risks that might be associated with the drug.

According to an article appearing in the *International Journal of Business & Law*, "Arguably, DTC advertising has an impact similar to that of oral contraceptives on a patient's self-involvement in her own health care decisions." Patients who see an advertisement and recognize their own symptoms or risk factors may then contact their physician to discuss their treatment options, thus participating more fully in their own medical care. The learned intermediary doctrine was seen as an exception for contraceptives and some immunizations as well. Then, in 1999, the New Jersey Supreme Court, in *Perez*, created the DTC advertising exception. Specifically, the court denied prescription drug manufacturers marketing their products directly to consumers the right to use the learned intermediary doctrine to shield themselves from liability if their advertising failed to provide adequate warnings and information about the side effects of the product. As a result, the DTC advertising landscape began to change. At that time, advertisers were allowed to mention the product by name and describe the condition that the drug was designed to treat, but the advertiser had to include what was referred to as "fair balance," including the risks as it described the benefits of the prescription drug. An advertiser simply could not include all the risk information in a 30- or 60-second television commercial. So, the TV ads had to contain a 1–800 telephone number and a web address where consumers could obtain more information. At that point the floodgates opened as DTCA expenditures increased from $1.3 billion in 1998 to a peak of over $6 billion in 2016.[13]

It is important to note, there are only two countries in the world that permit direct-to-consumer prescription drug advertising: the United States (pop. 318 million) being one, the other is New Zealand (pop. 4.4 million). Prescription drug advertising flourished in New Zealand not because of the doctrine of learned intermediary, but through what I would characterize as benign neglect. Simply put, the New Zealand Medicines Act of 1981 simply failed to consider direct-to-consumer prescription drug advertising. According to the *New Zealand Medical Journal*, it was "seemingly more by accident than design." The article goes on to say: "Prescription medications were simply not being advertised in 1981, so DTCA had little visibility at a time when the ethical frameworks governing relationships between the pharmaceutical industry and health care sector were but inchoate concepts." Therefore, in New Zealand, they just didn't have their thinking caps on and failed to recognize that a tsunami of prescription drug advertising was about to engulf them. And, as for the United States, it was a court ruling related to prescribing oral contraceptives that led to the opening of the floodgates for direct-to-consumer prescription drug advertising.

In 2016, the FDA considered extending the reach of pharmaceutical marketers by allowing them to advertise prescription drugs for "off-label" uses. Off-label refers to the use of a drug to treat an ailment or condition for which it has not received FDA approval. Doctors are already prescribing drugs for off-label use, but the regulatory change would allow for the promotion of drugs for such off-label uses. The rationale for the change in policy is that 20% of prescriptions written by physicians are already off-label. But there is a fairly long leap from what doctors and patients discuss during an office visit to promoting drugs through television and magazines for uses for which the drugs have not been approved. The impetus for this regulatory change came not from the FDA; the pharmaceutical industry was pushing for this change, as two court cases make this a first amendment issue. The plaintiffs in those cases argued that off-label marketing is protected free speech as long as the information in the ads is truthful and not misleading. In other words, the courts determined that the pharmaceutical industry has the same right to free speech as any other individual or corporation. Advertising is partially protected under the first amendment based on the FTC regulation regarding false and deceptive advertising.

While the pharmaceutical industry spent billions on advertising in 2016, they spent a greater amount on sales and marketing of prescription drugs. If the FDA's regulations are changed to allow for advertising of off-label use of prescriptions drugs, we can anticipate additional direct-to-consumer prescription drug advertising, as advertising sales and promotion expenditures will increase to support the demand. It is important to emphasize that advertising is not neutral communication; rather, it is inherently persuasive, and its persuasive ability is further enhanced by the presence of celebrities and other media figures.

REGULATING DTCA ON SOCIAL MEDIA

It's not difficult to determine that a print advertisement or a TV commercial is a paid message when you see one. These are forms that we routinely see and avoid if we choose. To an extent, we live in an attention economy, as marketers vie for our eyeballs. In response, consumers have developed a cultural practice when it comes to Internet advertising—banner blindness. This refers to the ability to selectively look at content on a screen, avoiding the ads. The equivalent with regard to traditional television advertising might be getting up to go to the bathroom when the commercials come on. There is ample evidence that consumers have never paid close attention to what is before their eyes either in print or on television, whether it be page flipping or channel surfing, consumers practice avoidance when it comes to commercial messages. In the book, *Advertising in Everyday Life*, consumers are described has having their eyes on the screen, for example, but their minds elsewhere. In Chap. 1, I utilized the metaphor of driving to work on a daily basis using the same route. In such a situation, drivers become very familiar with the route they take, so familiar that people will often report that they arrive at their destination not remembering how they got there: a rather shocking thought, given the possibility of causing an accident. The fact is, driving to work, which some describe as routine and in that boring is not that different from the ways we consume media. People have become enculturated into the viewing patterns or structure of commercial television programming in which commercial pods are presented at intervals during scheduled program. As such watching television becomes a regular route through which viewers travel, and there are associated routine behaviors that go along with that viewing experience. Such familiarity with commercial pods breeds the ability to leave the presence of the television for a bathroom break, phone call, to talk to the person with whom we might be watching a program, or to get something to eat, among other possibilities. But even if viewers are present with eyes on the screen, the routine experience of TV viewing allows individuals—perhaps promotes this behavior—to shift the mind elsewhere. As a result of repeated experiences, individuals engage in stream of consciousness thoughts, fantasy behavior and self-talk.[14] Whether it is the shift of one's physical presence as a means to avoid commercials or a mental activity, avoidance is something that is practiced and becomes ingrained in the cultural experience of consuming commercial media. Legacy media are, as one business magazine put it, in a "state of flux," as consumers shift away from traditional forms of media consumption to newer ways on consuming content.[15] That shift is exacerbated by, among other things "cord cutting," as individuals spend more of their time with non-commercial streaming services, like Netflix, which allow them to watch visual content on any device, smart TV, mobile device or tablet, commercial free. The implications are significant, if for no other reason, traditional media—television, print, including magazines and newspapers, and radio—are based on an advertising-supported business model, as opposed to a subscription-based model or free. With regard to Internet advertising, people have developed their own avoidance strategies, like banner blindness mentioned above. Celebrity appearances in television, in magazines or on the Internet are attention getters. It makes sense in the attention economy to utilize those who are likely to get consumer eyeballs to stick on the ad or related social media post.

It may be easy to identify when a celebrity appears in an advertisement promoting a prescription drug. It is, however, more difficult when a celebrity appears on a talk show, for example, and promotes a drug or merely raises awareness for a particular condition or disease. Oftentimes, their appearance is for a good cause, the public good. Katie Couric, for example, after her husband died in 1998, became an advocate for colorectal screenings.[16] In other words, it's difficult to know if that celebrity is getting paid to say whatever it is they are saying about a drug or condition. But how does one determine if a blog post, an Instagram post, tweet or YouTube video of a celebrity is paid sponsorship for a prescription drug? Not only is it difficult if not impossible to determine whether sponsorship is paid or not, commenters on social media platforms are likely to let their feelings be known about a celebrity's presence in drug promotions. For several years, marketers clamored for clarification from government regulators regarding the "rules of the road" when it comes to online promotions, and the FDA has provided some guidance; those rules are not as clear as they might be and marketers are still testing to determine the limits.[17]

CELEBRITIES IN DTCA

The 1950s represented the golden age of television, where a program like *I Love Lucy* would have garnered 50 million viewers. Comedian Milton Berle, host of a popular NBC program, who was referred to as TV's first superstar, would often joke about how good the prescription drug Miltown made him feel, so good in fact he referred to himself as "Uncle Miltown." Comedic references to this prescription drug were made by other television stars of the time: Red Skelton, Jerry Lewis and Perry Como, among others. Even popular comedian Bob Hope joked, "Doctors call Milton the 'I don't care' pill. The government hands them out with your income tax blanks."[18] Andre Tone writes in the book, *The Age of Anxiety: A History of America's Turbulent Affair with Tranquilizers*, that the celebrity endorsements for Miltown became so pervasive that the FDA eventually stepped in to investigate whether celebrities were being paid to endorse the product; however, the FDA never did find a connection.

Although celebrity endorsements of prescription drugs may have inadvertently begun in the 1950s, they are pervasive in today's media-saturated society. The list of celebrities who appear in advertisements for prescription drugs is extensive, including actors, musicians, sports figures and personalities. In 1997 the FDA relaxed the rules regarding direct-to-consumer prescription drug advertising, and shortly thereafter Joan Lunden, perhaps best known as a TV talk show host, began to promote Claritin, a medication to treat allergies. However, the manufacturer, Schering, was called out by the FDA for not including the side effects and contraindications for the drug in their advertising; as a result, the ad was removed.[19]

Jennifer Aniston in 2016 became the spokesperson for the Shire pharmaceutical's product, Xiidra, which treats dry eye syndrome.[20] Using the theme "Eyelove," the campaign featured Aniston directly addressing the consumer and confessing her personal experience with dry eye syndrome. "What they (my friends) didn't know is how much my eyes were bothering me." The voiceover at the end of the commercial encourages viewers to have a "chat" with their doctor about the condition and the video includes a link to the Eyelove website, myeyelove.com.[21] What makes this particular campaign unique is that it never mentions the name of the drug Xiidra, only making reference to the condition and encouraging consumers to ask their physician about the condition and visit the website. Prior to 1997, before the FDA relaxed the rules regarding DTCA, pharmaceutical marketers had two choices: either mention the name of the product in the ad only, but not describe the condition it treated, or describe the condition it treated without mentioning the name of the product. The campaign for Xiidra is unique in that it harkens back to the pre-1997 regulations for prescription drug advertising. In this case, the marketer chose a TV and movie star whose popularity far exceeded the potential name recognition of the drug. This approach stands in contrast to a competitive drug Restasis, which is supported by a $20 million advertising budget, but does not feature a celebrity spokesperson. Beyond Jennifer Aniston, there are at least 50 celebrities who in recent years have endorsed prescription medications ranging from politicians like Bob Dole and sports figures like Phil Mickelson to pop singers like Jon Bon Jovi and personalities like Kim

Kardashian.[22] Nancy Baym, in her book *Playing to the Crowd*, claims that "the further musicians are away from commercial pressures the more authentic them seem to be."[23] This would seem to apply to other celebrities as well, as they too seek to demonstrate their authenticating selves to their audiences and in the process express themselves as real as they would when communicating with their friends. Advertising campaigns like the one for the prescription drug Xarelto are indicative of the controversy surrounding celebrity appearances in direct-to-consumer prescription drug advertising. One such advertisement for Xarelto features several celebrities including basketball player Chris Bosh, comedian Kevin Nealon and the recently deceased golfer Arnold Palmer. It's worth noting that in 2015 $106 million was spent on advertising for this drug, which is made by Bayer and marketed in the United States by Janssen Pharmaceuticals, a division of Johnson & Johnson. The advertisement included references to the use of Xarelto for nonvalvular atrial fibrillation. And, it included additional references to the drug's ability to treat deep vein thrombosis and treatment of pulmonary embolisms. There is a lot at stake, as this is a drug that generates over a billion dollars in revenue. Although the drug continues to be widely advertised, there have been several thousand lawsuits levied against the manufacturer. The commercial more recently, however, has been modified—the message now delivered by basketball great Jerry West focuses solely on treating atrial fibrillation.[24]

One of the more egregious violations of FDA guidelines took place in 2015 when Kim Kardashian posted a photo on Instagram and Facebook promoting the drug Diclegis, which is prescribed to alleviate the symptoms of extreme morning sickness. She made an error that the FDA did not think was minor when she posted her promotional comment for the morning sickness drug by claiming the drug carried no risks, violating the regulation by not including the major contraindications along with the potential benefits of the drug. Also, she failed to disclose she was a paid spokesperson for the prescription drug. It was, however, the drug's manufacturer, Duchesnay, that received a warning letter from the FDA. As a result, Kardashian took the social media posts down, but garnered massive publicity for the drug. Less than a month later, she reposted a promotion for the drug, but this time included the risks.[25] While the drug company was held accountable by the FDA, the rules regarding promoting prescription drugs on social media are not all that clear, as the FDA requires that any direct-to-consumer drug promotion not only include the benefit of the drug, but also the risks. Balancing the two becomes difficult when it comes to posting on social media, especially those platforms that limit the length of their content to limited number characters or those that are image based. A promotion for a drug on Twitter would have to follow this example taken from a draft of the FDA's guidelines for dealing with new media:

> NoFocus for mild to moderate memory loss; may cause seizures in patients with a seizure disorder www.nofocus.com/risk [117/140]

In this example, in addition to naming the drug and what it may be used for, there is a risk message, as well as a website where consumers can obtain additional information. Kardashian in her initial promotion did not include the risk message in her Instagram and Facebook posts. And there was no clear indication that she was a paid spokesperson for the company. It is, however, the drug's manufacturer that is being held in violation by the FDA guidelines. There is a paradox at work: the controversy surrounding Kardashian's post on behalf of the drug gained wide notoriety, much greater than if the company placed an advertisement in traditional media. On the one hand, the manufacturer's reputation has to a degree been sullied, because they violated FDA guidelines, but the publicity was worth perhaps millions of dollars. In other words, as the old adage goes: any publicity is good publicity. As the online publication Media Marking & Media reported: "Online conversations around the drug increased by 500% after she [Kim Kardashian] became the brand's spokesperson, according to data-mining firm Treato, which also found that 29% of all online conversations around Diclegis mentioned Kardashian and that the drug was discussed three times more than its competitor, Phenergan."[26]

While expenditures for direct-to-consumer prescription drug advertising actually declined between 2005 and 2009, one category of expenditure is up significantly—digital DTCA. According to a recent study, expenditures for digital advertising of prescription drugs, or eDTCA as it is referred to, have risen 109%.[27] It makes sense for marketers to shift their expenditures to digital media as a Pew Internet Research study determined that the majority of Americans turn to newer digital media to search for health information. "Thirty-five percent of U.S. adults say that at one time or another they have gone online specifically to try to figure out what medical condition they or someone else might have."[28] One problem with eDTCA is the difficulty of packing in sufficient information regarding benefits as well as risks within the confines of particular social media platforms. Regulations have not kept up with the technologies through which prescription drug advertising is communicated. This is exacerbated by the use of hashtags like #ad or #sponsored, a requirement of sponsored content, which may be hard to identify among other hashtags present in a post. It may be that the issue regarding Diclegis caught the eye of the FDA because of Kim Kardashian's extraordinary popularity.

Kardashian's appeal is to a relatively young crowd; Millennials being a prime mover regarding the switch from traditional to digital media. Paradoxically, there has existed for some time now a tacit agreement among drug marketers to avoid promoting prescription drugs to those under 18 years of age. There is a well-known incident where President Obama remarked while watching a Super Bowl game that he and—at the time—his young daughters were being exposed to advertisements for Viagra. There is a demonstrated tendency for drug marketers to reach for younger and younger audiences, what I have referred refer to as ad creep.[29] Kardashian's notoriety brought momentary focus to eDTCA. The ways in which consumers obtain health information continue to change. Digital platforms extend and enhance legacy media, like TV and print. Consumers of every age are driving this shift through changing media habits. In fact a lot of direct-to-consumer prescription drug advertising is directed not at the person who may be suffering, but to their caregivers or family members. It has been pointed out that direct-to-consumer prescription drug advertising is legal in two countries: the United States and New Zealand. However, as eDTCA bleeds across borders, the implications are not only for the two countries that allow for prescription drug advertising, as the Internet can reach consumers all over the world who can access health information that may not be within regulatory compliance in their country or where there may be little or no regulation at all.

MICRO-CELEBRITIES, THOUGHT LEADERS AND SOCIAL INFLUENCERS

Word of mouth, it has been said, is the oldest form of advertising. Indeed, it is in many instances the most persuasive form of advertising. The influence that friends and family have with regard to persuading us to use a product or a service has much greater potential than traditional forms of advertising, which is to a great extent anonymous. This power of social influence is embodied in a theory of opinion leadership developed many decades ago by Elihu Katz and Paul Lazersfeld. The theory contends that particular individuals pay closer attention to media content than others; in other words, they are better informed. Opinion leaders pass on information to others through their social network, hence the two-step flow theory of communication. Although the theory is decades old, in contemporary society, it still plays out on a day-to-day basis on social media. Marketers understand how this theory may be applied, and so it is preferable if one wants to influence others to utilize opinion leaders in the process, as they tend to be much more effective than standard marketing messaging. In the present day, in an era of new media, thought leaders and social influencers play a similar role as opinion leaders. A social influencer builds relationships with people through blogging and posting on social networks. Social influencers can do this in ways that are different than traditional forms of advertising. Similarly, thought leaders establish their expertise through being well informed and sharing their knowledge that may lead to increased trust among followers. They may constitute the strength in weak social connections. Although the concept of opinion leadership has been around a long time, thought leaders and social influencers have in more recent times become a billion dollar industry. The types of influencer marketing tactics include ongoing ambassadorships, product reviews, brand mentions, event coverage and sponsored content. According to eMarketer, in 2016 advertisers spent $570 million on Instagram influencers.[30]

With the growth and popularity of social media platforms ranging from Pinterest to YouTube.com or dedicated platforms like WebMD, the notion of who is a celebrity has been disrupted. There are major celebrities like pop star Selena Gomez, who tops the list with more than 100 million Instagram followers; however, an analysis of cost versus reach suggests that top-tier celebrities may not be the most effective way to spend advertising dollars, as there are other tiers of celebrity influencers who may yield higher levels of engagement, including micro-influencers or nano-influencers on social media platforms.[31,32] In 2001 media scholar Theresa Senft was writing about "camgirls" who utilized newer media, like video and blogging, to "brand" themselves to their online fans. Senft maintains that all the changes that have taken place since the advent of the Internet decades ago are rooted in the development of the branded self. Individuals now have the tools to create and distribute media content like never before, and they have the opportunity to participate in the cultural economy through newer iterations of celebrity; this holds true for promoting prescription drugs.

ePATIENTS

The term celebrity or micro-celebrity may have negative connotations, but in a world of interactive media where individuals with significant interest can become producers and distributors of content, the process and nature of communication has changed. For example, Regina Holliday became a health activist in 2009 after her husband was diagnosed with metastatic kidney cancer. Unfortunately in June of that year he passed away. Frustrated by the inaccessibility of his electronic medical records, Holliday eventually directed her energy toward an ongoing art project in which she along with more than two-dozen patients paint their stories on the backs of jackets. Her movement called The Walking Gallery of Healthcare is now more than six years old and has a presence in 15 countries as well as more than 400 members. She maintains an Internet presence on her blog site,[33] Twitter,[34] Vimeo,[35] Google+[36] and Facebook.[37] Holliday may not be a celebrity in the traditional sense, but her ability to communicate in a unique and creative way established her as a thought leader on health issues.

Around 2004, we entered an era of Web 2.0, which has been referred to as a participatory stage of web development, marked by interactive social media platforms. This technological change not only made the web more accessible, it offered ordinary citizens the opportunity to more fully engage in and participate in various aspects of everyday digital life. For example, we can point to the "citizen journalists" who serve as primary or ancillary purveyors of news. In the healthcare field, we can point to ePatients. According to the Society for Participatory Medicine, the term ePatients was coined by Tom "Doc" Ferguson, who described them as "individuals who are equipped, enabled, empowered and engaged in their health and health care decisions. He envisioned health care as an equal partnership between e-patients and health professionals and systems that support them."[38] ePatients can take several forms, as they may be medical activists based on their own health issues or they may be health advocates on behalf of a loved-one, as is the case for Regina Holliday. They are in most cases ordinary people—micro-celebrities—who have taken to electronic media in order to make the medical system work better on their behalf. And ePatients, who may be perceived to have greater authenticity may experience elevated social status when their blog, Facebook page, Twitter feed, among others grows in popularity. The website patientslikeme.com is a platform that is intended to empower individuals with regard to their own healthcare. Their mission for the more than 600,000 people living with 2800 conditions is to put patients first.[39]

It was Lou Gehrig, the 1930s' New York Yankees' famous first base-man, that was perhaps the first well-known patient whose experience with disease took place on the public stage. Gehrig suffered from what is now been shortened to the acronym ALS, then known by its full name, amyo-trophic lateral sclerosis.[40] The disease became so closely associated with the baseball star that it is to this day often referred to as Lou Gehrig's disease. In recent memory, the most famous celebrity whose illness was taken pub-lic was the cyclist Lance Armstrong, who chronicled in a book his experi-ence with and recovery from testicular cancer, *It's Not About the Bike: My Journey Back to Life,* published in 2000. Seven years later Armstrong left the cycling world and his charity, best known for the yellow Livestrong bracelets, as a disgraced "doper." Armstrong represents a case in which we can see the development of a connection with him as an outstanding sports figure and a cancer survivor. Meaning comes from the fans who deeply admired his prowess as a cyclist on the international stage, winning the Tour de France six times. And, others for whom cycling is not a meaning-ful sport admired his tenacity to deal with his disease and persevere through treatment and return to championship form. In other words, he developed a complex and ongoing narrative. Until his fall from grace, he became a role model for other cancer patients and their families, and this led to the development of the Livestrong Foundation and the wildly popular yellow wristbands that millions of people wore in support of the cause. It is the feeling of closeness that develops over a period of time that leads to a feel-ing of "knowing" the celebrity, as opposed to knowing about the celeb-rity—the distinction should not be lost. But we can also see that subsequent to his exposure as a cheat, as someone who took performance-enhancing drugs in order to further his cycling career and perhaps jeopardize his chances of reoccurrence of cancer, that many of his fans and supporters abandoned him. He became a pariah and was forced to resign from the Livestrong Foundation. It is the abandonment coupled with extreme dis-appointment that led people to reconsider his place in their lives.[41]

There is an expectation that people have regarding celebrities and other types of media figures with whom they feel closeness; that expectation has to do with sincerity—honesty. This is echoed in the results of an analysis of online discussions about celebrities and their health conditions con-ducted by Treato that concluded, "patients expect celebrities to use their platforms to advance the cause of their disease, and resent them when they choose not to."[42] But the research claims that celebrities that demonstrate trustworthiness and in that credibility provide a positive role model, while those like Armstrong or Kim Kardashian, who has spoken about her struggle with psoriasis, only serve to increase the stigma surrounding the disease. The Treato research was based on an analysis of 700 online discussions about celebrities and their diseases. Among them were discussions regarding Kardashian's expressed worry on an episode of her cable TV program, *Keeping Up with the Kardashians*, that her psoriasis would impact her livelihood, as she publicly worried how the press would treat her less-than-flawless appearance. The Treato analysis reported: "We didn't come across a single positive discussion among psoriasis patients about Kim Kardashian…50 percent of the patients in the discussions [we looked at] didn't think she could be a good advocate even if she tried."[43] Kardashian isn't the only celebrity to publicize their struggle with psoriasis, as she was joined during National Psoriasis Awareness Month by model and actress Cara Delevingne, country singer Leann Rimes and pop singer Cyndi Lauper, who is the spokesperson for the National Psoriasis Foundation.[44,45] In this digital age, there is an interlacing between nonprofit organizations that support a cause, commercial enterprises—namely, drug companies—celebrities and ePatients who suffer from a disease or ailment or their advocates. Convergence around a disease may begin in traditional media, and extends to various social media platforms, what might be referred to as the network of social networks. In the case of psoriasis, all of these—medication, cause and celebrity—converge in a well-orchestrated campaign launched during National Psoriasis Awareness Month.

One of the unique twists to the ways in which people communicate about prescription medications and treatments is based on the particular qualities of social media. Curtis et al. view the use of social media as a great equalizer. They say: "By creating direct communication, social media can be seen as an equalizer, giving everyday people access to individuals and institutions with whom they would be unlikely to communicate otherwise."[46] These researchers add that we are only now beginning to understand the relationship between digital media and healthcare communication. The researchers studied more than 700,000 social media posts on networks such as Facebook and Twitter, as well as discussion forums and blogs. Their data showed a threefold increase in posts following televised direct-to-consumer advertisements. However, those posts on social media expressed concern for medication safety: negative posts were significantly more frequent than favorable posts. But their research did not look at the following four qualities of a mediated social

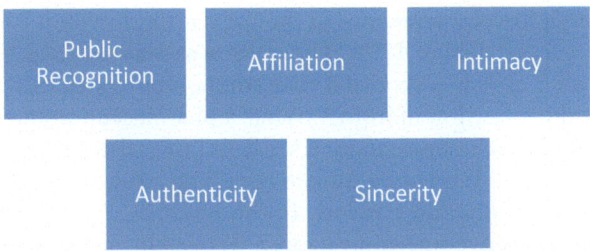

Fig. 6.1 Five qualities of mediated social connections

connection: public acknowledgment or recognition, affiliation, intimacy, authenticity and sincerity. Public recognition or acknowledgment is a measure of loyalty that may lead to a feeling of closeness. Affiliation refers to the "we are in this together" mentality. Over time the connection may lead to a feeling of knowing the celebrity. Intimacy is based on exclusive content, information and news. And finally, authenticity and sincerity refer to both the backstage disclosure of a celebrity's true self and the honest expression of their experience with a disease (see Fig. 6.1).

Cedric Kyles, perhaps better known as Cedric the Entertainer, serves as a prime example of how someone with broad notoriety can serve a public good and create a partnership with a particular prescription drug. In this instance, the comedian and actor, the American Diabetes Association and Pfizer Pharmaceuticals joined to create the *Step on Up* campaign that is intended to create awareness of diabetic nerve pain. In a 30-second commercial disseminated both through legacy and digital media, Cedric the Entertainer establishes his credibility by letting the audience know that he witnessed his father suffering from this diabetes-related disorder. While there is no mention of a particular drug, viewers are urged to see their doctor to get treatment. The campaign was first launched in 2014 and continues with a series of television spots that have boosted traffic to the Diabetes Pain Help website, StepOnUp.com, by 107%.[47] Somewhat hidden is the connection—never directly mentioned on the website—to Lyrica, a prescription drug marketed by Pfizer to help alleviate the symptoms of diabetic nerve pain.[48] In this instance, Kyles doesn't personally suffer from the condition, but is close to someone who does. This is not dissimilar to the way in which then *Today Show* host Katie Couric in 2000 actually underwent on-air a colonoscopy. She wanted to raise awareness of the need for colorectal screening in the prevention of colon cancer from which her husband died in 1998. The effort was referred to as "The Katie Couric Effect," as it was reported that colonoscopy rates increased substantially in the following months.[49] While a pharmaceutical manufacturer did not fund Couric's appearance, actor Rob Lowe also participated in an awareness campaign funded by Amgen regarding a side effect that is common among chemotherapy patients. In this instance, it was Lowe's father who had been recovering from cancer. While the name of the drug, Neulasta, was not mentioned during Lowe's appearances, the campaign was not entirely altruistic.[50]

Since the early promotions of prescription drugs, like Claritin, which at the time was the only allergy prescription medication available, advertisers didn't have to compete the way they do in today's marketplace. Celebrities play an important role in distinguishing one brand from another, which may apply to all sorts of consumer products and prescription medications as well (see Table 6.1). Ethical issues arise when celebrities are paid for their endorsements, while at the same time they may be doing good by raising awareness for an important cause. Such conflicts are present in the mind of the consumer who has to consider both the "do-gooder" nature of celebrity drug promotions and the celebrity's for-profit motivations. Such a conflict plays out as individuals grapple with the authenticity and sincerity of the celebrity spokesperson.

Table 6.1 A partial list of celebrities promoting prescription drugs

Celebrity	Related disease	Company	Drug
Marcia Cross	Migraines	GlaxoSmithKline	Imitrex
Kathleen Turner	Rheumatoid arthritis	Wyeth	Enbrel
Lauren Bacall	Macular degeneration	Novartis	Visudyne
Kelsey Grammer	IBS	GlaxoSmithKline	Lotronex
Cybill Shepherd	IBS	Novartis	Zelnorm
Brooke Shields	Thin eyelashes	Allergan	Latisse
Sally Fields	Postmenopausal osteoporosis	Sanofi-Aventis	Multaq
Phil Mickelson	Arthritis	Amgen	Enbrel
Paula Deen	Diabetes	Novo Nordisk	Victoza
Paul and Mira Sorvino	Diabetes	Sanofi-Aventis	Lantus
Mike Ditka	High cholesterol	Merck	Zocor
Jack Nicklaus	High blood pressure	King	Altace
Ricky Williams	Social anxiety	GlaxoSmithKline	Paxil

CASE STUDY: CYNDI LAUPER AND PSORIASIS

Pop singer Cyndi Lauper is perhaps most famous for her 1983 song "Girls just wanna to have fun" and 1984 hit song "Time After Time." More recently she is noteworthy as the composer for the Broadway show "Kinky Boots." Lauper holds long-standing celebrity status, with deep roots supporting LGBLT causes. Her presence on social media is not significant in numbers by contemporary celebrity standards, but along with micro-celebrities and other social influencers, she plays an important, perhaps more focused, role in the communication that takes place through social media, as mediated connections extend the traditional boundaries between celebrity and fan or supporter that existed in a world based solely on the celebrity's main talent. The case being presented in this chapter regarding a particular prescription drug, Cosentyx, illustrates how people go about making sense of their world through interactions on social media and the social roles that media organizations, corporations, nonprofit organizations, journalists, private persons and in particular celebrities play in the process of developing a neural-like network or an interconnected group of nodes, which in many ways are similar to the network of neurons in the brain.[51]

The site of the investigation is the network formed through interactions of media, both legacy in the form of direct-to-consumer prescription drug advertising and various social media platforms, like Facebook, Twitter, Instagram, Pinterest and web, and news and blog sites like Tumblr. Pharmaceutical marketers, patients, advocates, professionals and celebrities form the interconnected nodes. The focus here is on the ways in which those nodes (inputs) and the social media that provide the conduit or circuitry through which a network of cross channels is formed, through which individuals—in this case people who suffer from psoriasis and those who advocate on their behalf—make sense (outputs) of the disease and potential treatments and the impact the convergence of messages has on the individual fan or follower.

DTCA researcher Bret Rollins believes that with so many celebrities endorsing prescription drugs advertising fatigue can set in. The antidote, Rollins says, is that celebrities need to demonstrate high involvement with a disease.[52] As discussed earlier in this chapter, writer John Updike expressed his distress regarding his personal experience with psoriasis through his creative writing. Today personal involvement is conveyed through social media, not so much as a confessional where one expresses guilt or remorse, although it may be utilized in that manner, but rather as a form of excessive disclosure—the transgressive intimate self—as public (celebrities) and private persons present aspects of their lives that heretofore would have been considered too personal to share with others outside of one's closest social circle, if at all; what may be referred to as a public-private person. In this case I am referring to the merger of a public persona that encases the private person. In this way identity is more integrated and layered. For instance, Kim Kardashian spoke of her struggle with psoriasis on her cable TV program *Keeping Up with the Kardashians*, and she posted a photo of her psoriasis on Twitter (see Fig. 6.2).

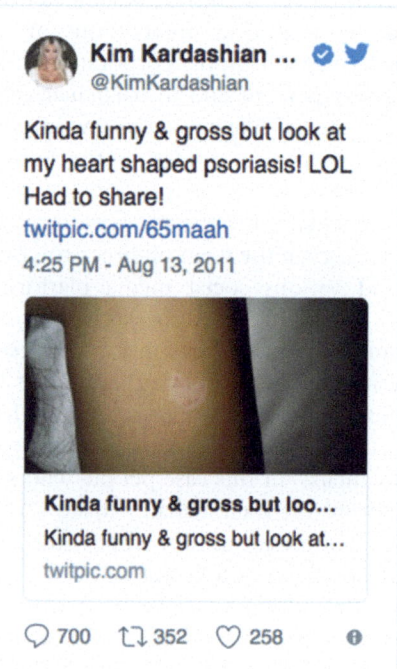

Fig. 6.2 Kim Kardashian's psoriasis tweet. (Kim Kardashian Psoriasis Tweet. https://twitter.com/KimKardashian/status/102490867327176704?ref_ src=twsrc%5Etfw&ref_url=https%3A%2F%2Fwww.healthline.com%2Fhealth%2Fp soriasis%2Fcelebrities-with-psoriasis)

The concept of the public-private person also relates to Goffman's dramaturgical metaphor regarding frontstage and backstage behavior. The metaphor, even though he developed the notion in the late 1950s, is applicable in today's social media environment. Today, however, the distinction between the two has become blurred, which is especially so when it comes to prescription drug promotion and promotion of disease-related causes.[53] Digital media offer a new set of requirements: creating the feeling of direct address in the guise of greater intimacy between the celebrity and viewer, reader or listener, opening up opportunities to interact with the media figure and perhaps brands or issues they represent. Celebrities, micro-celebrities or other social influencers attempt to manage their media presence, sometimes with the intention to create a bond and perform a role in the lives of their audience through digital media platforms, operating within a code of authenticity. With social media like micro-blogging site Twitter, as Marwick and boyd (2011) point out, there is no backstage.[54] Therefore there is no place for the media figure to metaphorically rehearse; what takes place takes place on the "stage" of social media. Moreover, what is created through the collapse of the front and back stages creates the illusion of intimacy. Film critic Richard Schickel wrote in his 1985 book *Intimate Strangers* that each new development in communications has increased our illusion of intimacy with the celebrated. Writing about celebrities in the pre-Internet era, Schickel said: "Not only do we think we know them, we think we know what makes them tick, which makes us want to tick as they do."[55] The illusion of intimacy does not, however, consider that in today's era of interactive social media, including user-generated content, the illusion is negotiated among all those who participate in the network.

As an example of how social media attempts to invoke the illusion of intimacy, a National Psoriasis Foundation blog post cites "5 Ways Cyndi Lauper is Just Like You." The post relates concerns in common with Cyndi and "other people" who have suffered from the disease like finding the right treatment, possible side effects of medications, impact on job performance, the condescending way other people might look at someone with psoriasis, and wanting to build community with others who suffer from this disease.[56] The message, which is part of a campaign co-sponsored by the National Psoriasis Foundation and the pharmaceutical company Novartis, under the banner, "I'm Pso Ready," is echoed in an accompanying 2015 video posted on YouTube.com in which for 3 minutes and 56 seconds, Lauper directly addresses the viewer as she describes her personal experience with the disease.[57] The empathy expressed in the video is emblematic of the ways in which many participants approach social media in order to suggest that Lauper is in it with you (the psoriasis sufferer), or to put it another way, all psoriasis sufferers are in this together; this is a collective movement that is being created, coalescing around a celebrity. In this instance, more than 21,000 people viewed the video. The National Psoriasis Foundation does not allow commenting on their videos, which stymies the ability to measure engagement or gauge sentiment for this campaign. It also might explain why the viewing numbers are low by YouTube standards and represent a very small percentage of those who suffer from psoriasis.

Beginning August of 2017 Cyndi Lauper participated in a second campaign, also co-sponsored by the National Psoriasis Foundation and Swiss drug manufacturer Novartis (see Fig. 6.3). This campaign is part of a promotion for Cosentyx, under the banner, "See Me." The market for psoriasis drugs is quite competitive, as Eli Lilly's Taltz, Valeant's Siliq and Johnson & Johnson's Tremfya, among others, join Cosentyx. Cosentyx alone accounted for over $1 billion in worldwide sales in 2016.[58] This campaign is unique in that it places Lauper within the context of ordinary people who suffer along with her with the disease. The campaign takes

Fig. 6.3 Cosentyx Twitter launch

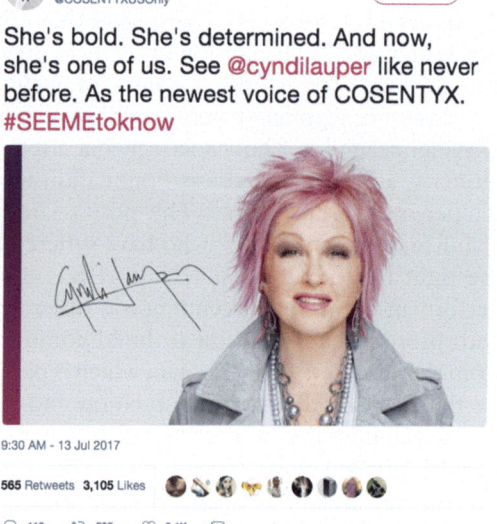

COSENTYX®secukinumab ✓
@COSENTYXUSOnly   Follow ⌄

She's bold. She's determined. And now, she's one of us. See @cyndilauper like never before. As the newest voice of COSENTYX. #SEEMEtoknow

9:30 AM - 13 Jul 2017

565 Retweets **3,105** Likes

113   565   3.1K

place across legacy media through direct-to-consumer prescription drug advertising and it extends to social media platforms including Facebook, Tumblr and YouTube, but there is scant evidence of the campaign on Instagram or Pinterest. As social media can be interactive, individuals have the opportunity to steer the discussion in whatever direction they choose; for instance, on Pinterest posts are related to the hairstyle Lauper wore in the Cosentyx commercials, mentioning nothing positive or negative about the drug or the campaign. Furthermore, this elaboration on the part of individuals illustrates how the conversation on social media is beyond the control of the marketer. There is risk associated when consumers can generate their own commentary and steer the conversation in a direction other than the one the marketer intended, as the marketer gives up a certain amount of control over the key message in order to play in the social media sandbox. In one example of user-generated content on the Cosentyx Facebook page, a young woman who suffers from psoriasis posts a self-produced video. Her post says:

> My quick take of a COSENTYX comercial [sic]. I #seethem all the time and am inspired by their words. Was in a hotel and decided to throw this together. Hope you like ♥♥♥ #seeme #dontstareatme #seemeonmyway with #cosentyx[59]

A closer look at the Facebook community page for Cosentyx reveals that members use the page to discuss the pros and cons of their experience with this medication as well as their experiences with similar medications, like Humira.[60]

At times individuals use this newer medium to respond, react to or just vent their emotions regarding something they have seen or read on the Internet. As you can see in Fig. 6.4, Cosentyx, in this tweet, positions Cindy Lauper as "one of us." A sentiment analysis reveals that the majority of comments are neutral and about a third positive. There were no negative comments. The Twitter feed is from the Cosentyx US-only site. The direct messaging that can be seen in Fig. 6.4 is between the brand and consumers, not Cindy Lauper. In such a controlled arena, the brand is able to respond to and manage the messaging as one person after expressing her extreme admiration for Cyndi Lauper is encouraged by the brand to contact her healthcare provider if she is interested in using this prescription medication. In this chain, another person expresses his admiration, and the direct response is a confirmation of his feelings.

Fig. 6.4   Direct messaging Cosentyx

Outside of this controlled Twitter arena, there may be a distrust or rather lack of forthrightness, regarding the campaign that can be seen in a post on Reddit.com under the heading, "I am sick to death of commercials for psoriasis drugs that don't actually show people with psoriasis."[61]

by j0npau1:

I think the worst offender is Cosentyx, with their "See Me" commercials, featuring a bunch of people without any visible signs of psoriasis just frowning a bunch. Or that new one, Taltz, where the commercial is just a woman with clear skin twirling around in a sleeveless dress.

Where's the psoriasis? These people are not suffering. I mean I'd understand if these were supposed to be "after" versions, but it's the same for the "before" versions too. The closest they ever get to realistic is the one where a guy with a little patch on his elbow is at a salad bar and a woman gives him a dirty look.

I'm glad there are more drugs on the market, and I'm glad to see these commercials bringing some attention to the condition. But if I didn't know what psoriasis was, I would have no clue based on the ads. I'd think it was depression or social anxiety or something.

There's definitely a stigma around the condition. I have near total coverage and have gotten every look and comment you can imagine, so it's extra irritating for me when these ads are like, look at how much this totally normal and attractive person is suffering. Dude, let me tell you something about suffering.

I think the best thing these commercials can do is show psoriasis as it actually is, and maybe desensitize people to it so sufferers might not get stared at as much in public. You know, in case anyone in the medical marketing industry regularly checks this sub.

A discourse unfolds through 40 comments through which individuals express their dismay regarding what they perceive to be the lack of honesty in the Cosentyx campaign. One comment, however, stands out, as it is from one individual who appears in the Cosentyx commercial. She says:

Dana_lou:
I assure you every patient in the Cosentyx commercial has psoriasis in some form or another. Psoriasis is not JUST a visible disease! The plaques are just affects [sic] of what's going on in our bodies. I myself without a biologic medication am 85 % covered and it is difficult to function on a daily basis! During film in I was almost completely clear and they did use makeup to try and show lesions on my arms as to show the healing of my psoriasis.

Such disparagement is echoed on the site commercialsihate.com. As the title implies, these are not going to be positive comments. One poster says, "Another celebrity endorsement for some medication. I can never take Cyndi seriously with that f'ing accent." And, another post says the following: "The accent has always sounded fake and exaggerated to me. How old is she now anyway, about 65? I wonder how much cosmetic surgery she's had. Looks like probably a lot. Or else the camera might've had some kind of filter or film over the lens to soften the lines and wrinkles."[62] Writing in DTC Perspectives, Bob Erlich says "Celebrities are a mixed bag when promoting a drug. They can be effective or polarizing depending on how they are used." He adds, "Here, Cyndi Lauper is being used as a member of a community that suffers from an embarrassing condition. She is not even identified with her last name but most of us would remember her, at least those over 40 years old."[63] And a blog post in the Pharma Marketing blog adds its critical assessment: "But it's unlikely that we will ever see Cindy responding to plain Janes...After all, like so many pharma social media activities, it's not really a community, it's a combination market research tool and marketing campaign," which echoes the idea that social networks are not monolithic, rather they are likely made up of smaller clusters or crowds of both promoters and dissenters.[64]

The nature of mediated social connections on and through social media represents a complex network that crosses platforms, as individuals, celebrities and marketers intersect to affect the discourse regarding a prescription drug. Within such complexity, the five qualities of mediated social connections described earlier in this chapter are difficult to manage or control. Moreover, sincerity—the ability to determine truth from falsity—as evidenced in the discourse above exemplifies such complexity—there is degradation and admiration. The celebrity, represented by her personal experience appears empathetic, concerned and passionate, which is a hallmark of authenticity. However, she is the spokesperson for a commercial interest—a drug marketer, and likely being paid for her effort. Consumers/audiences/fans have to work through those two positions—what Baym refers to as dynamic tension—to find their own meaning in all of this. While the celebrity is displaying aspects of her life that are private and personal, she seeks to establish affiliation at a distance. There are no comments allowed, for example, on the Cosentyx YouTube.com videos. Affiliation comes in the form of others like the young woman who produced her own "See Me" video while in her hotel room, posting it on the Facebook Cosentyx page. This and other examples of affiliation operate in tandem with the celebrity appearances in traditional and social media, but the direct address and the possibility of interaction are in this case not present. Instead there is the illusion of intimacy and that so-called intimacy takes place at a distance. It is as if the celebrity and others are operating on parallel planes; the closest one gets to the celebrity is through the voyeuristic nature of observing the celebrity interact with other celebrities. I want to emphasize the importance of this aspect of the mediated social connection, as there is a feeling of privilege, being an insider when a fan gets to witness such interactions even if the interactions are not directly with them. Having said that, there is also an inequality to the connection: the fan or follower is not a direct participant, but rather an observer. Within the social hierarchy, the fan is on a lower rung of the relationship ladder. There may be pleasure and some satisfaction in being an insider, but it does not constitute the other qualities associated with intimacy, even at a distance. In other words, the fan may appreciate Cyndi Lauper's appearance in Cosentyx commercials and her self-presentation in social media; however, it is on the "she is like me level." What fans or followers are left with is the ability to communicate with one another, to in this case commiserate about their experiences with this and other medications. There is social value in such a connection, but the connection to the celebrity is left purely to the imagination.

CONCLUSION

This chapter focused on prescription drug advertising, a widespread form of advertising that extends from legacy media to digital media where the rules are not particularly clear. A brief history of this unique form of advertising was presented, along with the vague rules regarding the use of social media to promote prescription medications. The chapter presented a case study regarding Cosentyx that features pop singer Cyndi Lauper. She appears in television commercials and in other social media platforms on behalf of the prescription drug, but Lauper's celebrity persona is made up of all that we know about her. She is re-presented to us within the context of all that makes up who she is in our minds: singer and pop culture icon. Furthermore, her celebrity persona becomes interlaced with, in this case, prescription drug advertising, pharmaceutical marketers, ePatients and other advocates, bloggers, consumers and other celebrities to create a complex network that allows fans and followers to create or maintain mediated social connections with celebrities they admire and with whom they feel a sense of closeness. In addition to the admiration we see, there is room for a critique to develop through which the fan must make their way as they engage directly or stay on the periphery of the interaction that takes place on and through social media. That engagement is particularly acute in this age of digital media where individuals get to participate and in that sometimes steer the discussion. However, the mechanism offered to us as a means to best control the direction of the discussion is based on the five qualities of mediated social connections and what has been referred to here as the illusion of intimacy; the illusion is not unique to social media, as it has always been a part of the carnivalesque and the beginnings of fame, topics discussed earlier in this book. In the case of Cindy Lauper and Cosentyx, authenticity can be summed up in the lyrics her song "True Colors" in which she speaks of revealing our true selves, our authentic selves. And she offers herself up as one who is not "afraid to let them show." This is the truth and realness that she shares in an intimate manner, letting us in to the backstage of her life. And as a result, fans, and in particular psoriasis sufferers, are brought closer to her private unguarded world, to which under other circumstances we would not be privy.

How Little We Know of Each Other

While the disclosure may feel like we are being drawn closer to the celebrity, she is never really disentangled from her celebrity persona—her voice, hair, music, political stance and so on. Because of this complexity, individuals get to pick and choose aspects of the persona—or none at all—which to admire and which perhaps to show disdain. Engagement with celebrities on and through legacy and digital media both disrupts the imagination and encourages or enhances it. Humanizing the celebrity does not absolve them of their celebrity status; she (they) is to us first and foremost a "star." As the celebrity "opens up" to us about more intimate aspects of their life, we are expected to use that as a marker of authenticity. However, as authenticity in contemporary society is not a static proposition—we are always authenticating ourselves—so too is revealing our true colors, nothing but another ingredient in the illusory mix that makes up persona and fuels the mediated social connection. No matter how much we know or think we know about a celebrity, we really know very little. Authenticity is merely a chess move in the game of celebrity. There is great pleasure to be had in this game, and in a world dominated by digital technologies that allow and encourage us to feel closer to one another. In a simplistic way, it makes sense that authenticity would play an important role. We can't know Cindy Lauper's true colors, nor can we know any other celebrity's true colors. It's not authenticity or truth we seek, it is connection. We can certainly feel like we know them, establishing and perhaps maintaining a sense of closeness, and from time to time even interact with them. Direct messaging notwithstanding, we can also become voyeurs as we follow celebrities as they operate in the world of celebrity. We live in a medicalized and pharmaceuticalized society where being part of a network regarding drugs and diseases is an important part of everyday life. As participants, people can engage with one another and confer status on the celebrity, and along the way we ground ourselves in our own reality.

Chapter 7 takes us beyond the micro-celebrity, celebrity and media figures who are at the center of mediated social connections to explore the qualities of mediated social connections through broader social movements and the ways in which those movements impact and are impacted by diffuse audiences. In a similar vein, as has been demonstrated in this and previous chapters, social networks are not monolithic; rather, they tend to be made up of smaller units operating within the network. While social connections may be based on broad interest in a product, topic, issue or person, connections are more likely to form within clusters or communities that represent more localized views or interests. This is particularly so of social movements that are addressed in Chap. 7.

NOTES

1. Updike, J. (1985, September 2). At War with My Skin. *The New Yorker*, pp. 30–67.
2. Updike, J. (1963). *The Centaur*. New York: Alfred A. Knopf Publishers.
3. Palman, C. (1992). *The Laws*. New York: George Braziller.
4. Newton, M. (2014, May 30). Under the skin of Dennis Palmer. *The Guardian*. Retrieved from: https://www.theguardian.com/culture/2014/may/30/under-skin-dennis-potter-michael-newton
5. Skinema.com. http://www.skinema.com/
6. Beiler, S. (2016, February 23). Psoriasis on the silver screen: The one place where your spots disappear. National Psoriasis Foundation. Retrieved from: https://www.psoriasis.org/blog/psoriasis-silver-screen
7. Horovitz, B. & Appleby, J. (2017, March 17). Prescription drug costs are up; So are TV ads promoting them. USA Today. Retrieved from: https://www.usatoday.com/story/money/2017/03/16/prescription-drug-costs-up-tv-ads/99203878/
8. Chang, M. (2012 August). The heartbreak of psoriasis: It's more than merely skin deep. ASBMB Today. Retrieved from: http://www.asbmb.org/asbmbtoday/asbmbtoday_article.aspx?id=17471
9. Dave's Psoriasis Info (n.d.). Psoriasis and the Arts. Retrieved from: http://www.psorsite.com/art.html
10. Vintage Tegrin advertisement. (1963). Retrieved from: https://www.vintage-adventures.com/vintage-healthcare-medical-dental-ads/3077-1963-tegrin-ad-heartbreak-of-psoriasis.html
11. Rufin TV commercial (1983). Retrieved from: http://content.jwplatform.com/previews/Pf6xTNMk-jEuQjxp9
12. Claritin Commercial. Retrieved from: https://www.youtube.com/watch?time_continue=9&v=oQFS3c-5xYM
13. Medical Marketing & Media. (n.d.). Pharmaceutical industry direct-to-consumer media spending in the United States in 2016, by media type (in million US dollars). In *Statista—The Statistics Portal*. Retrieved September 26, 2017, from https://www.statista.com/statistics/317788/pharmaceutical-dtc-media-spending-medium-usa/
14. Alperstein, N. (2003). Thinking About Advertising: Making, Unmaking and Remaking Meaning. In *Advertising in Everyday Life*. New York: Hampton Press. pp. 43–62.

15. Ingram, M. (2015, August 12). The attention economy and the implosion of traditional media. Fortune. Retrieved from: http://fortune.com/2015/08/12/attention-economy/
16. Couric, K. (2005). A message from Katie Couric about colon cancer. Today.com Retrieved from: https://www.today.com/news/message-katie-couric-about-colon-cancer-wbna7210595
17. Drugwatch (2015, November 9). Celebrities Team with Big Pharma to Promote Drugs, Disease Awareness. Retrieved from: https://www.drugwatch.com/2015/11/09/celebrity-and-big-pharma-drug-promotion/
18. Tone, A. (2012). *The Age of Anxiety: A History of America's Turbulent Affair with Tranquilizers*. New York: Basic Books, pp. 65–66.
19. Drugwatch.com. (November 9, 2015). Celebrities Team with Big Pharma to Promote Drugs, Disease Awareness. Retrieved from: https://www.drugwatch.com/2015/11/09/celebrity-and-big-pharma-drug-promotion/
20. Bulik, B. (2016, August 31). Shire snags eye-drop 'addicted' Jennifer Aniston as new dry eye spokeswoman. FiercePharma.com. Retrieved from: http://www.fiercepharma.com/marketing/actress-jennifer-aniston-s-eye-drop-addiction-leads-to-gig-as-shire-spokeswoman
21. Jennifer Aniston's chronic dry eye story | it's time for eyelove™. (2016). Retrieved from: https://www.youtube.com/watch?v=n_w6VjnB87k
22. Medical Marketing & Media (2016, February 9). 50 celebrity healthcare endorsements. MM&M.com. Retrieved from: http://www.mmm-online.com/campaigns/50-celebrity-healthcare-endorsements/article/471671/
23. Baym, N. (2018). *Playing to the Crowd: Musicians, Audiences, and the Intimate Work of Connection*. New York: New York University Press.
24. Jerry West Xarelto Commercial. (2016). iSpot.tv. Retrieved from: https://www.ispot.tv/ad/ARh_/xarelto-high-risk-of-stroke-featuring-jerry-west
25. Elkins, C. (2015). Celebrities Team with Big Pharma to Promote Drugs, Disease Awareness. Drugwatch.com. Retrieved from: https://www.drugwatch.com/2015/11/09/celebrity-and-big-pharma-drug-promotion/
26. McCaffrey, K. (2015, September 15). Kim stands corrected: the limits of corrective promotion. MM&M.com. Retrieved from: http://www.mmm-online.com/campaigns/kardashian-diclegis-duchesnay-corrective-advertising/article/438723/
27. Mackey, T. K., Cuomo, R. E., & Liang, B. A. (2015). The rise of digital direct-to-consumer advertising: Comparison of direct-to-consumer advertising expenditure trends from publicly available data sources and global policy implications. *BMC Health Services Research*, 15, 236. https://doi.org/10.1186/s12913-015-0885-1
28. Fox, S. & Duggan, M. (2013). Health Online 2013: One in three American adults have gone online to figure out a medical condition. Retrieved from: http://www.pewinternet.org/2013/01/15/health-online-2013/

29. Alperstein, N. (2014, August 26). Ad Creep: How DTC Prescription Drug Advertising Seeks Younger and Younger Audiences. Medium: Retrieved from: https://medium.com/@NeilAlperstein/ad-creep-how-dtc-prescription-drug-advertising-seeks-younger-and-younger-audiences-3a6d07dc18ba
30. eMarketer.com (2016, December 13). Marketers to Boost Influencer Budgets in 2017. Retrieved from: https://www.emarketer.com/Article/Marketers-Boost-Influencer-Budgets-2017/1014845
31. eMarketer.com (2016, December 13). Marketers to Boost Influencer Budgets in 2017. Retrieved from: https://www.emarketer.com/Article/Marketers-Boost-Influencer-Budgets-2017/1014845
32. SocialBlade.com (n.d.) Top 100 Instagram Users by Followers. Retrieved from: https://socialblade.com/instagram/top/100/followers
33. Holliday, R. (n.d.). Regina Holliday's Medical Advocacy Blog. Retrieved from: http://reginaholliday.blogspot.com/
34. Holliday, R. (n.d.) @ReginaHolliday Twitter. Retrieved from: https://twitter.com/ReginaHolliday
35. The Walking Gallery (n.d.). Vimeo. Retrieved from: https://vimeo.com/80009527
36. Holliday, R. (n.d.). Google+. Retrieved from: https://plus.google.com/+ReginaHolliday
37. Holliday, R. (n.d.). Facebook. Retrieved from: https://www.facebook.com/regina.holliday
38. Society for Participatory Medicine. (n.d.). Retrieved from: https://participatorymedicine.org/epatients/about-e-patientsnet
39. Patientslikeme.com (n.d.). Retrieved from: https://www.patientslikeme.com/
40. Lerner, B. (2006). When Illness Goes Public: Celebrity Patients and How We Look at Medicine. Baltimore: The Johns Hopkins University Press.
41. Gwynne, S. (2017, September 15). The Road Goes on Forever and the Story Never Ends. Outside magazine. Retrieved from: https://www.outsideonline.com/2237386/road-goes-forever-and-story-never-ends
42. Nobel, D. (2016, March 10). Treato.com. What Patients Want From Celebrities With Health Conditions. Retrieved from: https://treato.com/articles/What_Patients_Want_From_Celebrities_With_Health_Conditions/
43. Ibid.
44. Dovey, D. (2017, August 11.) Kim Kardashian's Psoriasis, And 3 Other Celebrities With Chronic Skin Condition. Medicaldaily.com. Retrieved from: http://www.medicaldaily.com/kim-kardashians-psoriasis-and-3-other-celebrities-chronic-skin-condition-421258

45. Famous people with psoriasis. (n.d.) *Disabled World.* Retrieved from: https://www.disabled-world.com/artman/publish/famous-psoriasis.shtml

46. Curtis, J. et al. (2017). Social media for arthritis-related comparative effectiveness and safety research and the impact of direct-to-consumer advertising. *Arthritis Research & Therapy* 19:48 DOI https://doi.org/10.1186/s13075-017-1251-y

47. StepOnUp Campaign (n.d.). Retrieved from: http://www.anjaamanda.com/step-on-up-1/

48. Lyrica.com (n.d.) Retrieved from: https://www.lyrica.com/diabetic-nerve-pain

49. Cram, P., Fedrick, M., Inadomi, J., Cowen, M.E., Carpenter, D., & Vilan, S. (2003). The Impact of a Celebrity Promotional Campaign on the Use of Colon Cancer Screening: The Katie Couric Effect. Arch Intern Med. (July 14). 163:13, pp. 1601–1605. Retrieved from: https://www.ncbi.nlm.nih.gov/pubmed/12860585

50. Thepharmaletter. (April 29, 2002). Thepharmaletter.com. Amgen's celebrity marketing of Neulasta. Retrieved from: https://www.thepharmaletter.com/article/amgen-s-celebrity-marketing-of-neulasta

51. Puljic and Kozma state: "Neural and social networks have several common features. In both networks, the individual entities mutually influence each other as participants in a group. While a social network is made up of humans, a neural network is made up of neurons. Humans interact either with long reaching telecommunication devices or with their biologically given communication apparatus, while neurons grow dendrites and axons to receive and emit their messages." Puljic, M. and Kozma, R. (2004). Activation Clustering in Neural and Social Networks. Retrieved from: https://pdfs.semanticscholar.org/ea1f/4257b7374f6296c64849314957871bea2c5f.pdf

52. Rollins, B. (2015, November 9). Seen in: Celebrities Team with Big Pharma to Promote Drugs, Disease Awareness. Drugwatch.com. Retrieved from: https://www.drugwatch.com/2015/11/09/celebrity-and-big-pharma-drug-promotion/

53. Goffman, E. (1956). *The Presentation of Self in Everyday Life.* New York: Random House Publishers.

54. Marwick, Alice, & boyd, d. (2011). "To See and Be Seen: Celebrity Practice on Twitter," *Convergence.* 17(2), 139–158.

55. Schickel, R. (1985). Intimate Strangers: The Culture of Celebrity. New York: Doubleday, p. 29.

56. Leavitt, M. (2016, March 7). 5 ways Cyndi Lauper is just like you. NPF Blog. Retrieved from: https://www.psoriasis.org/blog/5-ways-cyndi-lauper-just-like-you

57. Cyndi Lauper Says "I'm PsO Ready" To Talk about My Life with Psoriasis. YouTube.com. Retrieved from: https://www.youtube.com/watch?time_continue=89&v=wtpPe53dnRw
58. Helfand, C. (2017, July 21). Cyndi Lauper showcases backstage psoriasis woes in Novartis' new Cosentyx spot. FiercePharma.com. Retrieved from: http://www.fiercepharma.com/marketing/cyndi-lauper-showcases-back-stage-psoriasis-struggles-novartis-latest-cosentyx-spot
59. A Facebook user creates her own version of a Cosentyx commercial. Retrieved from: https://www.facebook.com/emilieazalea93/videos/1915919515337783/
60. Cosentyx Community Page. Facebook. Retrieved from: https://www.facebook.com/pg/Cosentyx/community/
61. Reddit.com. (n.d.). I'm Sick to death of commercials for psoriasis. Retrieved from: https://www.reddit.com/r/Psoriasis/comments/5ibpmh/i_am_sick_to_death_of_commercials_for_psoriasis/
62. Commericalsihate.com (July 22, 2017). Cosentyx—Featuring Cyndi Lauper. Retrieved: http://www.commercialsihate.com/cosentyx-featuring-cyndi-lauper_topic25086.htm
63. Ehrlich, B. (July 31, 2017). DTC in Perspective: Cyndi Lauper and Cosentyx. Retrieved from: http://www.dtcperspectives.com/dtc-perspective-cyndi-lauper-cosentyx/
64. Pharma Marketing Blogspot.com (July 29, 2015). For Pharma Marketers, Celebrities + "Social Media" = Gold Mine! Retrieved from: http://pharmamkting.blogspot.com/2015/07/for-pharma-marketers-celebrities-social.html

CHAPTER 7

Social Movements: Our Virtual Collective Consciousness

The world is a cacophony of screeches and honks and hums and stinks and sweetness and reds and grays and blues and yellows and rectangles and poly-hedrons and weird irregular shapes of all sorts and cold surfaces and slippery, oily ones and soft, squishy ones and sharp points and edges; but somehow all of this resolves crisply into an orderly landscape of three-dimensional objects whose qualities we remember and whose uses we understand. (Larissa MacFarquhar on Cognitive Scientist Andy Clark, MacFarquhar, L. (April 2, 2018). The Mind Expanding Ideas of Andy Clark. *The New Yorker*. Retrieved from: https://www.newyorker.com/magazine/2018/04/02/the-mind-expanding-ideas-of-andy-clark)

It was half way through 2006 when the microblogging site Twitter first emerged as a social media platform in which users could post 140 characters of whatever was on one's mind. But it wasn't until Twitter was formally introduced at the 2007 South by Southwest Interactive conference that its popularity increased exponentially. Within a year of its launch, about 100 million tweets had been posted, certifying Twitter as a serious social media player, along with Facebook and YouTube. The now-ubiquitous hashtag was not part of the initial launch of Twitter, but again in 2007, Chris Messina brought the idea to Twitter, and the rest is history, as hashtags have become an integral part of Twitter as well as other social media platforms.[1] The history of Facebook is more well known as it has been documented in the movie *The Social Network*. As Mark Zuckerberg and friends, while students at Harvard University, created Facebook in 2004, access was

© The Author(s) 2019
N. M. Alperstein, *Celebrity and Mediated Social Connections*,
https://doi.org/10.1007/978-3-030-17902-1_7

first limited to students at the university and later entre was open to anyone with an .edu email address. But by late 2006, the platform was open to all, not just college students, and as of 2017, over two billion people world-wide use the platform, although in recent years other platforms have come along to compete with this dominant player like WhatsApp, Instagram (both owned by Facebook) and Snapchat, as the demographics of new media users continues to shifts toward younger generations eager to try the newest digital platforms. YouTube came on a bit earlier, and Google, the owner of YouTube, soon after introduced the Android operating system in 2007. And, Amazon began to market the Kindle that same year. There was another important technology shift that took place in 2007, as that was the year that Steve Jobs announced the iPhone. Simply put: the iPhone made the Internet more valuable, because it was more accessible.

This chapter begins with these watershed moments in the development of digital media and the fast pace at which technologies have proliferated and changed the ways in which we communicate. Accompanying those technological changes are social and cultural shifts that impact the ways in which people connect and in that communicate with one another through social movements. In order to better understand those connections, the chapter addresses three important social movements: the Arab Spring, Me Too and March for Our Lives. In doing so, the chapter describes the role that celebrities and ordinary individuals play as they are thrust into the foreground of a social or political movement. Then the chapter describes the excessive nature of participating in social media and the ways engagement plays in the process of popularizing events and issues on digital media platforms and the mind/technology connection that manifests as a virtual collective consciousness (VCC). The chapter provides an under-standing of how participants come together as clusters and crowds within social networks that may be loosely or tightly connected and whose medi-ated social connections may be weak or strong. The chapter will look at community building on social networks as it considers the longevity of connections, various roles within social networks and the active/passive nature of participants—clicktivists and slacktivists—in social movements as they are embodied in social networks.

2007 A Watershed Moment in Digital Media

While technological advancements, like the smartphone, and social media platforms liker Twitter, Facebook and YouTube were revolutionary, their introduction also led to significant changes in the ways in which people began to use them. From a user perspective, it was also in 2007 that Adam Nyerere Bahner, perhaps better known as Tay Zonday, made his first appearance on YouTube singing a song he wrote, "Chocolate Rain." The video built a viral following after some well-known celebrities mocked it, but has since garnered over 116 million views. Zonday says he never set out to become a celebrity, but YouTube certainly made him one.[2] Zonday refers to himself as "patient zero," because there was no one else before who could have prepared him for instant fame. He says, "In 2007, the Internet was a novelty economy, and now it's a loyalty economy." Several years later the same thing happened to an aspiring pop singer, Rebecca Black. Her music video, "Friday," has garnered over 118 million views since it first appeared on YouTube in 2011, but has also been criticized for being the worse song ever. Writing in his book *Contagious*, author Jonah Berger claims that the title of the song, Friday, serves as a trigger that gets something talked about and, in this case, causes the video go viral.[3] Perhaps the same thing could be said for Zonday. In a sense, it doesn't matter whether something is good or bad, funny or unamusing; apparently fan communities just want to be part of the conversation and perhaps along the way take on celebrity status of their own. A trigger, therefore, offers a simple entre into the conversation as the network builds. In this case Berger points out that the song, Friday, is searched for mostly on Fridays, hence the simple connection between the title and a day of the week. The potential for postings to go viral by individuals or the gathering collection of memes and other forms of engagement relate not only to individuals who seek to entertain, but also to social movements as well. And, just like the videos and memes that go viral, some have greater longevity than do others. The same could be said for social movements that, too, are difficult to sustain in the age of digital media.

THE ONLY THING CONSTANT IS CHANGE

In an age where technology develops and changes so rapidly, society has little time to catch up and internalize new norms that are at work. In other words we don't fully understand why or how these things operate in everyday life, and by the time we do, people may have moved on to a newer technology or social media platform. People who use digital media and related technologies often are ill equipped to handle such rapid changes in societal mores. Culture has little time to catch up and develop a code of behavior through which we learn to differentiate, for example, right from wrong when it comes to dealing with mediated connections. In a related twist, fake news has been around since the invention of print technology some 500 years ago, when news became a concept. Indeed, the idea of objective reporting is only about a century old.[4] But in more recent years, as television became the dominant medium for news delivery—a regulated medium—the nature of news reporting changed as well. No such regulations exist in the wild west of today's Internet. Fake news played an important role during the 2016 US presidential election; for example, one man with an AR-15 rifle in hand took it upon himself to fire shots outside a Washington, DC, pizza restaurant, because he read fake reports about a Democratic-led child abuse ring operating there. And, in the Netflix documentary *The American Meme*, Josh Ostrovsky describes how he created faux sneakers and promoted them on his Instagram account to his ten million followers.[5] He claims that people actually tried to purchase them, even though they weren't real. Furthermore, even if digital literacy is integrated into the education system, by the time students obtain an understanding of how to operate within a socially acceptable set of mores based on new technological developments, the technology changes, making re-education a constant effort, which is not a practical solution. "Real news is not coming back in any tangible way on a competitive local level, or as a driver of opinion in a world where the majority of the population does not rely on professionally reported news sources and so much news is filtered via social media, and by governments."[6] The same goes for other aspects of participating in an era of digital media, as we no longer have time to play catch-up, because change is constant. The era of "truthiness," a term proffered by talk show host Stephen Colbert, needs to be considered within the context of what Ulmann, among others, would call "media imaginaries," the "production and validation of the truth (how things are put in order) and the realization of the possible (how things are made)."[7]

Beyond fake news and related issues, digital media and related technologies will always have a good and bad side. On the one hand, more and more people around the world have access to the Internet, which holds the potential to break down political barriers and lead to more democratic governments, as people engage and participate in uncensored ways. However, even though about 47% of the world's population has access to the Internet, geographic and economic disparities remain.[8] In some cases, according to a UN report, the Internet may be available, but because of economic conditions people do not have access to technology, like mobile phones or computers. In the parts of the world where people do have access, they tend to rely on the so-called influencers who may have a great impact on decision-making. Here I'm referring to celebrities and micro-celebrities that account for about a third of decision-making on the part of consumers. Tim Berners-Lee, father of the World Wide Web, said on the occasion of its 29th anniversary in March 2018 that things have not turned out as he imagined. The Web is too centralized, controlled by a few very large corporations, like Google and Facebook. Beyond the business aspects of the Web, Lee states that one of the most important goals should be to make the Internet accessible and affordable for all, but he maintains that billions of people are denied this basic right even though in 2016 the UN "declared internet access a human right, on par with clean water, electricity, shelter and food. But until we make Internet access affordable for all, billions will continue to be denied this basic right."[9]

Emiliano Treré writes in his book *Hybrid Media Activism* about what he calls the grammar of protest. Related to social movements, Treré describes five binaries of media hybridity: online/offline, old/new, internal external, corporate/alternative and human/nonhuman, the latter referring to the use of algorithms and social bots to drive either repression or resistance.[10] Starting in the mid-2000s, Treré studied the Anomalous Way student movement in Italy, the Movement for Peace and Justice and Dignity in Mexico, and later the #YoSoy132 movement also in Mexico, as well as the Five Start (5SM) political movement in Italy. He also studied the 2015 Indignados (5M) political movement in Spain. Although often attributed to digital media as a driver of these movements, Treré maintains that the media landscape is more complex in which legacy media and social media coexist. Ultimately, he claims that the purpose of digital media is to move people from clicktivists to activists offline. We can see this play out with the Arab Spring movement of 2011.

The Arab Spring

Access is certainly one part of the equation, but even in those societies where there is access, how the technology is utilized has come into question. Reflecting on the uprising that led to the overthrow of the government of Egypt, Internet activist and computer engineer Wael Ghonim once said, "If you want to liberate a society, all you need is the Internet." He changed his mind, however: "I said those words back in 2011, when a Facebook page I anonymously created helped spark the

Egyptian revolution. The Arab Spring revealed social media's greatest potential, but it also exposed its greatest shortcomings. The same tool that united us to topple dictators eventually tore us apart." If the goal of a social movement is to use digital media to turn out supporters or protesters, then the expectation is that those supporters or protesters will show up in the flesh somewhere. A paradox emerges, however, as digital media are non-locative in nature, as anyone can participate from anywhere; ultimately what may have begun as an imagined community must take on some physical manifestation like a protest rally. Otherwise, participation in such a digital revolution is nothing more than slacktivism, where one feels good for "liking" or commenting on a post, but nothing more.

The revolution to which Ghonim referred was a leaderless one, or to use contemporary parlance, it was crowdsourced, but not by a homogeneous crowd. On the surface, many of those engaged on social media found situational relevance in their political opposition, or to put it another way, they connected through a common goal, which was to overthrow the Mubarak government. It may be that the kinds of connections to which Ghonim refers are based on the ultimate local connections necessary for social movements to succeed in which weak ties are more likely to link members of a movement. The Arab Spring of 2011 provides just such an example of the ways in which digital media can fuel a social movement through weak ties. During the Egyptian uprising, there were more than one million tweets that some suggest provided motivation to join the movement. However, and I think this illustrates the difference between strong and weak ties, despite one million tweets, much smaller clusters formed around specific traditional news organizations Al Arabiya and Al-Jazeera. In other words, Twitter served to disseminate information, but it did little to congeal those engaged into monolithic networks of interconnected individuals.

In general, social media serve two structural functions: information dissemination and direct communication. In the case of Arab Spring, social media's primary role may have been framing the discussion. I don't want to dismiss framing the discussion as unimportant; however, I do want to stress the difference between direct communication and information dissemination. To that point, Rob Schroeder, Sean Everton and Russell Shepherd concluded in their study "Mining Twitter Data from the Arab Spring" that one of the most influential Twitter accounts, under the handle Hosni Mubarak, was a fake account. "This account's tweets attracted a large audience, and may have helped disseminate a portrayal of Mubarak as a corrupt leader who should resign, both of which were goals of the Egyptian revolution."[11] The authors maintain that three things must be present for social media to affect social change. First, a situation must be framed in a way that others recognize its importance and share it with others, including a belief that something can be done about the situation. Second, people need access to appropriate resources, like smartphones. And third, they need to perceive that the situation can be changed through collective action.

ROHINGYA OF MYANMAR

While the end results may have been a mixed bag of outcomes, engagement with social media may have initially injected energy into the Arab Spring, helping to bring down the governments of Egypt and Tunisia; however, unfettered access to digital media can cause harm as well. In the case of the Rohingya Muslims massacre that took place in Myanmar during 2017, UN investigators placed a significant amount of blame on hate spewing on Facebook, a widely utilized social media platform in that country. The United Nations chief investigator said, "Everything is done through Facebook in Myanmar...Facebook had helped the impoverished country but had also been used to spread hate speech."[12] Social media posts are expressions of an individual's state of mind, their thoughts and beliefs, but in sum represent a collective. Uprisings like the Arab Spring, which developed without a leader or central authority, demonstrate how digital media has the potential to play a critical role in developing a social network, one that may be tightly knit or one that is polarized. Marzouki and Oullier, who coined the term "virtual collective consciousness" (VCC), state: "the possibility of a leaderless revolution is likely to be (at least partially) explained by the spontaneity, the homogeneity and the synchronicity of the actions of these cyber-activism networks that were catalyzed by social media. This explanation is supported by what we coined virtual collective consciousness (VCC) referring to an internal knowledge shared by a plurality of persons. Coupled with 'citizen media' activism, this knowledge emerges as a new form of consciousness via communication tools."[13] Social media operated in a similar way in the "yellow jacket" movement in France that was motivated by both an increase in a gasoline tax and unhappiness with French President Macron's economic policies in general. Some would argue that movements do not begin with social media; rather, they begin as political movements and spread to social media.[14] Some have argued, however, that Facebook unwittingly may have caused the *gilets jaunes* protest in France. I say unwittingly as in an effort to diminish the presence of fake news on its platform, Facebook privileged memes and vitriol from populist groups that would become the organization of the movement.[15]

ME TOO MOVEMENT

Although the power of the virtual collective consciousness can be viewed through the lens of recent political revolutions and social upheaval, the same collective consciousness takes place in everyday life among fans, friends and followers that are liking, disliking, commenting, tweeting or re-tweeting, posting photos and memes, vlogs or blogs in response or reaction to trending topics or issues. The #MeToo movement that became viral toward the end of 2017 serves as an example of the development of global communities based on personal stories of women and some men regarding their experiences of sexual harassment and assault. The movement became a cause célèbre on the heels of the public disclosure of sexual misconduct allegations against movie mogul Harvey Weinstein. The hashtag was first popularized by actress Alyssa Milano, who encouraged women to tweet "Me Too" to give voice to the issue (see Fig. 7.1). The reference to Me Too, however, pre-dated the hashtag. Since that time the hashtag has been posted over a million times, along with personal stories of sexual harassment and assault, both in the United States and in many other countries. Other celebrities joined in including Gwyneth Paltrow, Ashley Judd, Jennifer Lawrence and Uma Thurman. However, the Me Too movement was actually started 10 years ago by civil rights activist Tarana Burke, "in order to spread awareness and understanding about sexual assault in underprivileged communities of colour."[16] This exemplifies how movements may begin as political or social movements, but may spread based on the use of social media and further promoted when celebrities become involved. Burke describes how celebrities to a degree usurped a movement she started. She expressed her frustration with the media in particular that selected "leaders," referring to Hollywood celebrities who have erased her work that focused particularly on women of color.[17] The Me Too movement on social media has become a gathering storm of global proportions. Some

Fig. 7.1 Actress Alyssa Milano, October 15, 2017, "Me Too" tweet. (Alyssa Milano "Me Too" Tweet. (October 15, 2017). Retrieved from: https://twitter.com/Alyssa_Milano/status/919659438700670976/photo/1?ref_src=twsrc%5Etfw&ref_url=http%3A%2F%2Fwww.independent.co.uk%2Fnews%2Fworld%2Famericas%2Fme-too-facebook-hashtag-why-when-meaning-sexual-harassment-rape-stories-explained-a8005936.html)

have referred to the movement as "the power of testimony," while others have criticized the movement, as just another example of women having to bare their pain in public. Men are by and large the objects of the movement, but some male celebrities have joined the movement to declare their own experiences of sexual harassment. Actor Terry Crews, for one, let it be known that he was groped by a Hollywood agent, and prior to the Me Too movement, he railed against what he referred to as "toxic masculinity" in Hollywood.[18] Other prominent men have come to defend and support the movement. Regardless of a particular position taken on the issue, the global nature of the campaign represents how a virtual collective consciousness forms and operates within the era of celebrity-driven digital media movements.

While the political uprisings in Tunisia and Egypt were what might be referred to as bottom-up or leaderless revolutions fueled by social media, in the case of the #MeToo movement, the social movement, while not driven by a single leader, certainly gained much impetus from the celebrities that brought light to an issue that had not earlier gained widespread public attention, even though "Me Too" had been around for some time. Whether bottom-up or top-down, new media provide a vehicle for what Marzouki and Oullier called "emergent behavior," the complex interconnectivity of individuals that yields patterns of "accumulating change."[19] A leaderless revolution is based on those three qualities, spontaneity, homogeneity and synchronicity, all of which take place on and through social media. What also needs to be considered is the structure of a movement's hierarchy, whether it is horizontal or vertical. Leaderless movements, those that tend to be horizontal, provide opportunities for greater participation and a stronger feeling of democracy in that anyone can choose to participate. Whether movements suffer from or gain traction through the involvement of celebrities or other media figures has not been determined. A celebrity-initiated movement is not likely to gain momentum over a long period of time unless the movement grows through both clicktivism and activism to encourage others who are not celebrities or media figures into the movement. Opinion leadership should not be confused with true leadership, as ordinary people may take the role of the latter, but celebrities based on the mediated social connections we have with them and the roles they play in our imaginary social worlds help movements gain traction in a competitive world of trending hashtags.

Virtual Collective Consciousness

If the individual's thoughts and beliefs expressed on social media merge with other people's thoughts and beliefs, in sum they form a collective consciousness, as one's inner world is turned outward to become part of a network, including membership in a cluster or crowd. To a degree the virtual collective consciousness represents the expression of our inner mind wandering, stream of consciousness, daydreams and nocturnal dreams, turned outward in a spontaneous, synchronous manner within a social network, based partially on mediated social connections with celebrities and other people who are present and active on the social network. This shift represents a significant change in human expression. And while such a change in the expression of thoughts and feelings may not lead people to become less thoughtful, the need to act spontaneously may impact critical thinking, as people become less reflective and discerning. And, the virtual collective may reflect a false sense of consciousness that may impact public opinion. There may also be a tautological effect in which visceral reactions and responses on social media become a model for practice in actual social relationships. The spontaneous requirement of reacting and responding as a collective on social media is to a degree a function of emotional impulse. Additionally, digital media operate as an echo chamber in which our ideas reverberate within themselves as we limit access to our thoughts and ideas and limit others ideas to those that are consistent with our own, although there is a lot of leakage when the unintended tweet or post goes viral and as messages become distorted through memes.

The virtual collective consciousness is represented within digital media as data, as both social network analysis and artificial neural networks are developed and utilized in order to better understand how people think and feel about various topics and issues. That data may be utilized by governments and other organizations to control the wily beast of social media. We can see the attempt to control social networks through the work of Cambridge Analytica that utilized deep learning in order to shape the messaging for the 2016 Trump presidential campaign and the vote on British Brexit. The company came under fire from many quadrants of society, along with Facebook from whom they gathered the data under the pretext of taking an academic personality survey of Facebook users, but captured data of those users and their friends to form psychographic profiles through which they subsequently shaped messages to appeal to various clusters of people based on their political beliefs.[20] Social media require users to operate at speed; ideas flow rapidly requiring an immediate response or reaction, one that may not be steeped in deep thought, in consideration for others and in that civility. Perhaps responses are a function of FOMO, fear of missing out. But spontaneous responses or reactions also present the opportunity to become noteworthy, taking on at least for a time increased social status, as indicated by the number of likes or re-tweets accumulated. In this way everybody gets to participate, albeit unwittingly, in the data game. I refer to the ways that organizations manipulate social networks as bridging the gap; the gap is the distance between groups or clusters within a social network. Bridging the gap refers to the ability to use data to adjust messaging in an attempt to influence the direction of a social network. In this way social movements operate in the same attention economy as do celebrities. Celebrities, micro-celebrities and media figures are interested in their social media analytics. As well, the ultimate response that many fans, friends and followers seek is to be acknowledged by a celebrity or many others within the social network. In the celebrity economy, the more extreme or outrageous the post, the more attention it is likely to garner, a measure of notoriety, actually one of the more superficial measures of social media analysis. Therefore notions of reflective thought and consideration of others runs counter to the way participation in digital media is presently structured. In other words, rumor and vitriol are easy; thoughtfulness is hard; the end result for both, however, is data that reflect acknowledgment of one's presence and participation in a digitally mediated society.

It would be impossible to legislate reflection, and thoughtful and considerate behavior, as that's the role of culture. As culture is a social practice, learning is variable and volatile. A culture cannot operate in the direction of humaneness when the speed of change is such that society is always playing catch-up. The Internet thrives on chaos, and the attention economy within which it operates it is agnostic as to whether users are complicit or resistant to its messaging.[21] The fact of the matter is that the system in which digital media operate holds us captive, unless we opt out. Therefore, rather than considering issues of complicity or resistance to celebrity influencers or political tweeters and everyone else in between, consideration needs to be given to uncertainty, ambiguity and chaos upon which the system is based. It is not so much that digital media are inclusive, although their reach may be broad; they are, however, always available, and as such, information moves rapidly through the system or network. To that end, the Pew Research Center found that 26% of Internet users are online "almost constantly." And, almost 40% of people of ages 18–49 years report being online "almost constantly."[22] Within such an interactive and in that participatory media system, outcomes are difficult if not impossible to predict, because meanings are indeterminate. The indeterminacy of meanings is actually the great hope, as our consumption of content concerning political and social issues, brands and popular culture in general may open us up to elaboration, that is, thinking and wondering about things, in which case reference is made to relational or item-specific processing and affect. With regard to affect, consideration is given to emotional states and specifically liking, disliking, commenting, among other ways to express one's emotions in the interactive environment of digital media. Social media are feeling media, not so much thinking media. By that I mean that participants in social media tend to react viscerally and respond in the most sparing way possible, a "like" is merely an expression of sentiment.

A condition that fits well within a chaotic Internet is known as the butterfly effect, which may be applied to social movements through their engagement with digital media and the ways in which individuals participate in a culture of excess, including transgressive disclosure about one's self. The butterfly effect literally refers to the flapping of a butterfly's wings, which may cause some unrelated atmospheric change. In other words, change in one state can result in differences in another. The term first appeared in a paper authored by MIT mathematician and meteorologist Edward Lorenz. In his paper titled, "Predictability: Does the Flap of a Butterfly's Wings in Brazil Set Off a Tornado in Texas?" Lorenz demonstrated how the flapping of a butterfly's wings, a small event, might lead to a large-scale alteration of future events. What he described as a domino effect with regard to changes in the weather can be applied to social movements when a tweet, post or comment enters into the collective consciousness. But how such content goes viral, through which platforms it travels, how long the trending message or meme is sustained and whether or not the original intent is carried forward or modified can lead to a much larger consequence, one that may be unintended by the originator. Although it applies to a single individual, the case of Justine Sacco serves as just one example, as someone else with a large Twitter following picked up a naïve tweet she posted, and the rest is history—she was fired from her job.[23]

THE NEVER AGAIN MOVEMENT

In the aftermath of the 2018 Parkland Florida school shooting at Marjory Stoneman Douglas High School in which 17 people died, survivors mobilized to launch the #NeverAgain movement. Unlike past efforts to stop gun violence in schools and elsewhere, this effort is driven by high school students. Students from Parkland appeared on local and national media to bring awareness to the issue of gun violence, and they lobbied the Florida legislature to pass a bill limiting access to guns. In the midst of their lobbying efforts, the students launched the March for Our Lives rallies that took place on March 24, 2018, in Washington, DC, as well as in other cities in the United States and around the world.[24] As with any movement in the age of digital media, the students' efforts permeated social media under the banner hashtag #NeverAgain. Celebrities played an important role in the effort by funding the movement, including George and Amal Clooney, Steven Spielberg and Kate Capshaw, Jeffrey Katzenberg, and Oprah Winfrey. Other celebrities lent their support via social media, including Kim Kardashian West, Justin Bieber, Bette Midler and Debra Messing.[25] And, several popular singers from Molly Cyrus to Jennifer Hudson appeared on stage at the Washington, DC, rally.

UNWILLING OR UNWITTING CELEBRITIES

With regard to the Arab Spring, some have placed social media, like Facebook and Twitter, in the forefront, elevating these platforms to celebrity status. Additionally, women have been lauded for the active role they played in the political uprisings, elevating the role of gender in political change. And there are politicians who also took on celebrity status in the course of these recent movements. But ordinary people, too, can be thrust by circumstances to the forefront of a social movement. Jaclyn Corin is one of the student organizers of the March for Our Lives. At the time of the incident, she was a 17-year-old Stoneman Douglas High School student and along with two other students started a social media campaign around the hashtag #NeverAgain to bring prominence to the issue of gun violence.[26] That campaign grew into the March for Our Lives rally. Corin cast herself as an activist, but in the process became an unwitting celebrity. Participants in these movements discussed in this chapter utilized social media to spread the word and build an audience of followers as well as employing more direct tactics like lobbying legislators. And like Wael Ghonim of the Egyptian uprising, Corin and her fellow organizers knew intuitively how to effectively utilize social media, as these are platforms that both felt comfortable with, the latter being a so-called digital native and the former operating with a background in technology. Corin and other event organizers also understand the need to operate in the celebrity economy in order to sustain the movement over time.

Among the things these movements have in common is that their audiences comprised of fans, friends and followers are diffuse. Social movements may begin prior to the use of social media, but the power of a revolution, protest or movement comes from the force multiplier effect of digital media. In the case of the Arab Spring, the promise of liberation has faded as Libya and Syria, among other Middle Eastern countries are at war. Only time will tell whether or not the Me Too movement or the student-driven March for Our Lives rallies and associated Never Again movement will remain forces for change. Messages of change promoted through social media will have to sustain motivation and in that maintain their relevance in order to turn crowds into communities and communities into large connected networks if they are to remain a social and political force. Moreover, those who utilize digital media to further their cause need to understand the difference between thousands of tweets or retweets and getting people to actually do something about a social issue or cause. In the case of #NeverAgain, a nationwide voter registration drive was launched to encourage young people to vote during the 2017 midterm elections. It is difficult to sustain such messaging through digital media, but the requirement for success is embedded in the excessive everyday.

The Excessive Everyday

The excessive everyday operates outside the realm of complicity or resistance. Rather the excessive everyday is one aspect of limitless flux of ideas or variability within which users of digital media operate. Here I'm referring to the multiplicity of meanings that individuals make of the content they consume and the various things they do with that content both in their imaginary worlds and as expressions on social media. Memes are one example of limitless flux. What engagement leads to is an unstable system based on uncertainty, ambiguity and chaos. However, people are inherently stability seekers; terra firma is a more comfortable place to metaphorically stand. Celebrities and social influencers play a role in helping people seek meanings and in that help them find the firm ground to which I refer. Celebrities may come to digital media with a single purpose in mind, like furthering a cause or issue, or for that matter building a brand, although they operate in an excessive manner that spills over into all of this. Other media figures thrust into the limelight by circumstance have little purpose or intent, unless it is to begin building or extend a nascent following. And yet others come to digital media with specific intentions, but without an accompanying narrative. Yet fans, friends and followers, as well, come with varied interests and intent. They may want to become popular too and elevate their social status by participating in the celebrity economy, or they may merely be lurkers; in other words, the system is complex, uncertain and ambiguous.

LOSS OF IMAGINATION

When he published *The Private Death of Public Discourse* in 1998, critic Barry Sanders, who was primarily concerned with the loss of literacy, could not have imagined how the explosion of digital media in the years to come would change the nature of public discourse. In the book, the author claims that our interior space, in the form of private ideas, without reflection or discernment, began to show up in public discourse. He placed the blame squarely on electronic media.[27] By electronic media, he was referring to technology like the word processor, a term that now has become antiquated, and to place such blame on today's technology is naïve. But around the same time of the book's publication, a new word entered the lexicon, weblog, which was used to describe a personal homepage where individuals could within a Web 2.0 participatory environment present their ideas to others, perhaps reaching large audiences and have their followers directly respond to them and each other. In a society whose public communication is based on haptics like swiping, tapping and pressing the "like" or "dislike" button or "share" button, there remains the question as to whether our ability to discern and reflect has diminished, being replaced by an impulsive need to react quickly, perhaps with vitriol. When people participate in the excessive everyday, they don't have time to reflect; immediate response is necessary or else the hashtag may pass you by. Under such circumstance, coupled with the need to be constantly connected, it is difficult for people to find terra firma, much less a place to rest temporarily to catch their metaphoric breath in order to take the time to engage in some critical thinking. Ultimately, the cure for the problem, introduced by Sanders and echoed in a more contemporary sense by others, is not about liberating the Internet; rather, the question for the future is can we liberate our imaginations. Participation in a celebrity economy based on the broad-spread of popularity coupled with the illusion of intimacy has gone so far that our mediated social connections distract from issues that are really before us, but celebrities may provide the terra firma we seek.

PERSONAL IS POLITICAL

There is a second-wave feminist argument from the 1970s embodied in the slogan, the "personal is political," political referring to power relationships, not the electoral process.[28] What is meant by that phrase is that exposure of the personal is a pathway to a better world. But it is doubtful that the originators of that idea could foresee a celebrity culture that operates within the chaos of the excessive everyday. The idea that the "personal is political" requires us to look more closely at what makes up an image or other content delivered on digital media, to be more self-reflective and discerning. Significance of the personal becoming public foreshadows the era of digital media and the ways in which people engage through mediated social connections with people they do not actually know but to whom they are drawn and feel a sense of closeness. One space in which to see this at work is through social and political movements and the excessive forms of expression associated with such movements. Mediated social connections present themselves with great variability, especially when they take place without leadership or direction. It is in this way that communicating through digital media often is nothing more than shooting arrows into the wind, where content—images or words—floats in space; often that content never lands, or if it does land, we often don't know to whom we are connecting, making outcomes difficult to control or predict. This should suggest that the excessive everyday is superficial, lacking significance and meaning, but measures of engagement may be indicators of popularity through the number of views or likes. Such superficial engagement, based on the terseness of likes and dislikes, lacks the kind of dialogic that the creators of the Web envisioned for digital media. The #MeToo movement may provide a forum for personal disclosure that may lead to feelings of empowerment. And celebrities, and their fans and followers, become unwitting participants in the uncontrolled ecosystem of digital media. In the course of participating in social and political movements on digital media, networks, clusters and crowds form that may have both polarizing and tightening effects, and both connections may take place simultaneously. Digital media are agnostic, based on a system of excessive disclosure within the chaos of everyday digital life.

MAPPING CLUSTERS, CROWDS AND NETWORKS

While demographics as well as psychographics play a role in understanding how mediated social connections are formed and maintained, viewing how people connect and in that come together around social movements through social media, the degree to which they connect and the nature of the connection cannot be explained by such social constructs. Professional communicators, like those in the public relations industry, look more closely at the ways in which people find situational relevance between themselves and issues or causes. While demographics are the social categories by which we classify people based on age, income and education, among other social variables, situational relevance is based on the theory of publics. Publics are demographically agnostic, as they represent how people come together around an issue: the meanings they ascribe to the issue, what they take away from an issue and what they feel they can do regarding a cause or social issue. In that sense, an issue like gun violence will cut across different age or income groups. Some publics for whom a situation is quite relevant may become stakeholders having a vested interest in the outcome. Accompanying this perspective and with a mind toward bringing order out of chaos, James Grunig and Todd Hunt developed what they called a "linkage model" that helps to explain how publics and stakeholders come together around an issue—who affects an issue and who is affected by an issue. The model doesn't go far enough, however, in explaining how people cluster within larger digitally based social networks or the nature of connected crowds.

The Grunig and Hunt model describes four linkages: enabling, functional, normative and diffused.[29] Enabling linkages, for example, may provide the financial base for an issue or they may hold some regulatory control that enables the issue to go forward. As an example, in the March for Our Lives rally celebrities played a role by lending their names, providing a significant amount of funding and appearing at the rallies. Corporations like Ben & Jerry's and the owner of the New England Patriots, Robert Kraft, provided air travel for some of the students to come to Washington. But a GoFundMe campaign encouraging ordinary people to engage also served as an enabling linkage to the event. By all reports the student organizers did the work, but as with any issue or cause, there are going to be other stakeholders who enable the movement to go forward.[30]

Another type of linkage is one that is normative, referring to organizations that have similar or corresponding interests. In other words, they have a stake in similar values, goals or problems. With the March for Our Lives rally, organizations like the Gabby Giffords Gun Safety Group, Every town for Gun Safety and Moms Demand Action for Gun Sense in America joined in. Diffused linkages like community activists may not have close ties to the movement, but given the nature of the crisis or event, they become involved. We can see this in the Me Too movement with Tarana Burke's participation. Also, news media are considered a diffused linkage within the model. In the case of March for Our Lives, legacy or mainstream media played an important role both in the run-up to the rallies and subsequently as student organizers appeared on major networks and were featured in print publications. But social media played an important continuous role as well, as participants utilized their own channels through which to engage others based on their own interests and perceived levels of relevance of the movement.

Functional linkages divided between input and output are those that provide the labor to get things done. The student organizers are key functional linkages to the March for Our Lives event. And, those who attended any of the rallies, watched on television or other digital device, or followed on social media in this way become linked to the event. The linkage model provides a way of framing the varying ways in which networks are formed based on the level of interest of various publics. It is in this way that people come together based on the relevance of a situation. And, that relevance is based on infinite semiosis or multiple meanings that people ascribe to a situation and through which they form connection to one another. In this sense, connections may be loose or they may be tight, weak or strong depending on the extent to which people feel a personal sense of involvement and empowerment. In other words, if people believe they see there is a problem, and perceive they have a personal stake in the issue that they can do something about, they would be considered active on that issue. Others, however, may feel constrained for many reasons, and while they are aware of the issue and agree with the position being taken by the movement, they may not feel they can do much about it, while still others may just go about their business because they see little relevance of the issue to themselves. And finally, there are people who may feel fatalistic regarding the issue, situation or problem—they may feel there just isn't anything that can be done about the issue.

While this model provides a way of organizing stakeholders and nonstakeholders and those that are active or passive on an issue, such a model is made more complex when digital media are considered within the concept of clusters and crowds within social networks, as the complexity becomes more apparent regarding how digital media play a role in developing and maintaining mediated social connections. Sentiment expressed through digital media tends to be bipolar, by which I mean we like or dislike something, admire or hate something, among other responses. And, the assumption is that if individuals perceive they have something at stake—that is, find situational relevance—and therefore form an "activist public" around a topic or issue that this translates into a network of connected individuals and groups. But in reality that is not the case, as participation is much messier than such organizing principles allow.

Most social scientists attempt to describe predictable phenomena, for example, cause and effect in communication. Chaos theory, as applied to social systems, views them as nonlinear and therefore, like the weather or traffic, difficult to predict or control. In fact, if you look at a visualization of social networks, they often look very much like the spaghetti strands of everyday life. Some of the strands are stuck together and may form a cluster of strands. Some connected strands might represent a niche, or clique, and sometimes those small groups are connected, perhaps loosely, to other small groups that operate within a complex communication system. Therefore, what we generally refer to as a social network is more likely to be a complex web of crowds and clusters loosely or tightly connected or disconnected individuals, some of whom are on the sending end and others on the receiving end of communication, while yet others are both sending and receiving messages. Chaos in this sense does not mean out of control or for that matter chaos representing the lack or absence of something. Rather, chaos is conceived of as the complex ways in which we participate in mediated social connections that constitute in and of themselves a sort of order. Therefore participation in social networks is an attempt to bring order to disorder. It is the chaotic nature of networked systems that drives those who want to understand and perhaps control processes and outcomes to grasp at models like linkages, in order to help frame the ways in which people engage in social movements.

The Extended Mind

Consistent with the ideas presented in this book, the philosopher and cognitive scientist Andy Clark believes that the mind extends into the world and is regularly entangled with a whole range of devices. If we take him literally, digital media and related technologies would be included in that range of devices. Based on that entanglement, haptic technologies like an iPhone and associated social media platforms serve the same function as parts of the brain; liking and swiping are in this sense extensions of our thoughts into the world. It is in this way that Clark would identify all of us as cyborgs, being of both organic and biomechanical parts. Such a view offered by cognitive science provides additional ground upon which to understand mediated social connections, as it links our unconscious systems with the virtual collective consciousness of social movements that has been addressed in this chapter. Clark takes his cue from the psychologist Vygotsky, who described how children learn as a form of scaffolding: in the case of writing, one might write something, read it, think about what was just written and write again. Clark saw this process, which could also be applied to drawing, as "integral components of certain kinds of thought."[31] He theorized, "if thinking extended outside the brain, then the mind did too." He referred to this phenomenon as "the extended mind," the connection to the ways in which we utilize haptic technologies, and the extended mind moves the idea beyond paper and pencil to consider our relationship to digital media. There is an important connection between a chaotic media ecology in which individual participants based on the vagary of meanings contribute to the virtual collective consciousness based on Clark's idea of the extended mind. The extended mind is one that is like a cyborg in that it is represented by our multiple embodiments and social complexity, the former referring to the melding of individuals and technologies. An in-game marriage that takes place in the game World of Warcraft or the ways in which we engage with social movements and celebrities would all serve as examples of multiple embodiments and social complexity vis-à-vis digital media.

The discussion of the extended mind raises the question regarding the "inside" or backstage connecting to the "outside" or frontstage that can be applied to digital media. Beyond the mind/technology connection, based on the transgressive intimate self that was described in Chap. 4, there exists an electronically mediated intimacy. Jiang, Bazarova and Hancock, who studied the disclosure-intimacy link, concluded, "computer-mediated interactions intensified the association between disclosure and intimacy relative to face-to-face interactions and this intensification effect was fully mediated by increased interpersonal (relationship) attributions observed in the computer-mediated condition."[32] In this way disclosure of intimate details is not merely a symbolic expression of closeness or intimacy; rather, it exemplifies the extended mind. There is complexity at work, as those on the other end of the communication may over-interpret the cues they receive. Intimacy is uniquely tied to self-disclosure with regard to a mediated relationship, even if it is an imaginary one.

FROM THE PARASOCIAL TO MEDIATED SOCIAL CONNECTION

I began this book by discussing how the idea of parasocial interaction developed by Horton and Wohl gave way to imaginary social relationships, a theoretical framework presented by John Caughey in his book *Imaginary Social Worlds*. I have sought in these chapters to move the discussion forward by extending those ideas to consider the role of digital media in our everyday lives, what I have referred to as mediated social connections. While parasocial interaction was originally conceived of as taking place through the direct address of the media personality and the subsequent bonds that were created, within imaginary social relationships, celebrities and other media figures were described as entering into our daydreams, stream of consciousness, mind wandering, fantasies and nocturnal dreams, and play a role in helping us to better understand our world and in that our selves. Both parasocial interaction and imaginary social relationships are at work today, but they have been extended in the age of digital media to mediated social connections. Within this newer framework, the connection between the celebrity and our imagination is intensified through both the excessive disclosure that is required of those who utilize digital media and the possibility of actual interaction with a celebrity. The imagination plays a vital role in helping us to make sense of things on the outside, and the extended mind leads to connections we establish and maintain on digital media that can both help and hinder us. Those connections, both weak and strong, can lead to admiration or degradation with many other stops in between. In addition to the importance of celebrities and new media figures in our imaginations, we sometimes use what we have learned and processed internally to re-present those ideas to others as a way of confirming our own beliefs, changing our minds or perhaps convincing others to change their minds. With the swift-moving changes in technologies and platforms, the rules of the engagement changed as we entered an era of mediated social connections. As social media play a significant part in our everyday lives, there is the possibility of interacting directly with not only a bona fide celebrity but also ordinary people because of their adventurous spirit, like the world travelers, ePatients or those individuals who because of their social or political consciousness described in this book open themselves up to engage with people they don't actually know. Within this newer framework, the connection between the celebrity and our imagination is intensified through both the excessive disclosure that is required of those who utilize digital media and the possibility of actual interaction with a celebrity. In a world of digital media, we get the false feeling that anyone can become a celebrity of sorts. Of course some people for a time may be thrust into public light, becoming famous not of their own accord, but because of surrounding circumstance. But celebrity, micro-celebrity or ordinary/extraordinary citizen, in a world in which anyone can tweet or re-tweet, post a video, write a blog post, comment, like, dislike or share, may play by the ever-changing rules set forth in the celebrity economy as what may have been in the past considered private and kept inside our heads becomes public. And, the need to respond swiftly, before a topic quickly loses its luster, may compel people to engage without much forethought. This is the dilemma of mediated social connections in the digital age.

THE DILEMMA OF MEDIATED SOCIAL CONNECTIONS

There is a growing body of criticism regarding the effect that digital media is having on our imaginations and in general the influence of new technologies in our everyday lives. To that end a group of Silicon Valley technologists has formed the Center for Humane Technology and along with Common Sense Media launched an anti-technology addiction lobbying group and plan a public service advertising campaign aimed at public schools.[33] The group claims that Google, Facebook, Twitter and Instagram, the major social media platforms, use increasingly competitive means to encourage users to stay connected.[34] However, keeping us connected is only part of the problem, as the struggle exists between attention and in that focus on the screen and the inward turn toward the imagination. Even the American Academy of Pediatrics chimed in with guidelines regarding children's screen time. They see a correlation between screen time and diminishment of imagination and wonder.[35] Others have raised similar issues regarding the use of digital media and the diminishment of the imagination in children.[36,37,38] Caughey posits that "ordinary human life is not, as it seems, an obvious, natural, or simple phenomenon, but rather a problematic, complex process in need of exploration and explanation."[39] He furthermore says that it is through "in-context investigations of everyday life that we can best frame an adequate understanding, not only of particular human groups, but of human thought and behavior generally."[40] It is relatively easy to observe the amount of time that a young person or adult spends with digital media and make assumptions about the loss of imagination and creativity. But such assumptions are based on the simple idea that it is the time devoted to digital media and related technologies that causes a disconnection from our inner worlds. Screen time may not be the most important correlate, as what should be of concern under most circumstances and what is so difficult to access is the inner world of the individual. But mediated social connections within a media ecology that extends the inner world into the objective world offered by digital media, we can see ourselves turned inside out. As Tim Berners-Lee said: "Today, I want to challenge us all to have greater ambitions for the web. I want the web to reflect our hopes and fulfill our dreams, rather than magnify our fears and deepen our divisions."[41] I would stop short of Berners-Lee's statement to say that I just want us to be able to dream, revel in our thoughts, fantasize and to do so in the privacy of our own mind, not an extended version.

CONCLUSION

It has been said that human beings are social animals, an evolutionary condition based on the need for protection and cooperation in order to survive. But from a practical point of view, in contemporary society being social may simply refer to getting together with friends. On digital media, the idea of friending was based on the prospect of creating or strengthening ties with others. The Dunbar Number, a concept developed by anthropologist Robin Dunbar, suggests that based on the evolutionary structure of social networks we can maintain no more than 150 meaningful relationships at a time. That's still a lot of relationships, but all relationships are not equal. As there are acquaintances, which can number in the hundreds, but also intimate friends, which may be limited to just five. Challenges to Dunbar's theory in the era of social media have suggested that in a collaborating environment such as Facebook or Instagram one can have more "friends." It turns out that it is not the case, as Dunbar maintains that what binds us together is shared experience, and digital media lacks the synchronicity of shared experience.[42] Having said that, as technology continues to evolve and as we enter an era of virtual, augmented and mixed reality, what constitutes being social and what constitutes a friend on and through social media and related technologies may change. The original idea from which the Web evolved was rooted in connecting people, encouraging discourse and sparking creativity through things like crowdsourcing embodied by the famous quote referring to our collective consciousness: "everybody is smarter than anybody." And as we have seen, diverse movements like the Arab Spring, Me Too and March for Our Lives were driven largely by digital media. This despite the fact that in 2018 Facebook and Google in particular had come under greater government scrutiny because of the ways in which they collect and re-sell user data. Moreover, people are tiring of Facebook the same way they moved on from MySpace and a slew of other early platforms. And, while these media behemoths will likely come under greater regulation in the United States and increased scrutiny abroad, technologies will not remain static, as the only constant in the world of digital media is change. As the media through which we communicate continues to evolve, so too will the ways in which we utilize those media, including celebrities that make up much of mediated culture.

NOTES

1. Cooper, B.B. (September 24, 2013). The Surprising History of Twitter's Hashtag Origin and 4 Ways to Get the Most out of Them. Buffer.com. Retrieved from: https://blog.bufferapp.com/a-concise-history-of-twitter-hashtags-and-how-you-should-use-them-properly
2. Scutti, S. (March 16, 2018). Accidentally famous: The psychology of going viral. Cnn.com. Retrieved from: https://www.cnn.com/2018/03/16/health/social-media-fame/index.html
3. Beger, J. (2015), Contagious: Why Things Catch On. New York: Simon & Shuster.
4. Zoll, J. (December 18, 2016). The Long and Brutal History of Fake News. Politico.com. Retrieved from: https://www.politico.com/magazine/story/2016/12/fake-news-history-long-violent-214535
5. Radulovic, P. (December 10, 2018). Netflix's doc The American Meme challenges the reality of social-media stars. Polygon.com. Retrieved from: https://www.polygon.com/2018/12/10/18131141/netflixs-the-american-meme
6. Ibid.
7. Uhlmann, A. (1997) Introduction: What are "media imaginaries." Continuum: Journal of Media and Cultural Studies. Retrieved from: http://www.tandfonline.com/doi/pdf/10.1080/10304319709359431
8. Taylor, A. (November 22, 2016). 47 percent of the world's population now use the Internet, study say. The Washington Post. Retrieved from: https://www.washingtonpost.com/news/worldviews/wp/2016/11/22/47-percent-of-the-worlds-population-now-use-the-internet-users-study-says/?utm_term=.3081bdabb612

9. Berners-Lee, T. (March 11, 2018). The web can be weaponised—and we can't count on big tech to stop it. The Guardian. Retrieved from: https://www.theguardian.com/commentisfree/2018/mar/12/tim-berners-lee-web-weapon-regulation-open-letter

10. Treré, E. (2018). *Hybrid Media Activism: Ecologies, Imaginaries, Algorithms.* New York: Routledge.

11. Schroeder, R., Everton, S. & Shepherd, R. (2012). Mining Twitter Data from the Arab Spring. Combating Terrorism Exchange. 2:4, pp. 54–64. http://hdl.handle.net/10945/53058

12. The Guardian (March 12, 2018). Myanmar: UN blames Facebook for spreading hatred of Rohingya. The Guardian.com. Retrieved from: https://www.theguardian.com/technology/2018/mar/13/myanmar-un-blames-facebook-for-spreading-hatred-of-rohingya

13. Marzouki, Y. & Oullier, O. (December 6, 2017). Revolutionizing Revolutions: Virtual Collective Consciousness and the Arab Spring. Huffpost.com. Retrieved from: https://www.huffingtonpost.com/yousri-marzouki/revolutionizing-revolutio_b_1679181.html

14. Wolfsfeld, G.,Segev, E. & Sheafer, T. (2013). Social Media and the Arab Spring: Politics Comes First. *The International Journal of Press/Politics.* 81:2, pp. 115–137. Retrieved from: https://journals.sagepub.com/doi/pdf/10.1177/1940161212471716

15. Read, M. (December 8, 2018). Did Facebook Cause Riots in France?. Intelligencer.com. Retrieved from: http://nymag.com/intelligencer/2018/12/did-facebook-cause-the-yellow-vest-riots-in-france.html

16. Shugerman, E. (October 17, 2017). Me Too: Why are women sharing stories of sexual assault and how did it start? The Independent. Retrieved from: http://www.independent.co.uk/news/world/americas/me-too-facebook-hashtag-why-when-meaning-sexual-harassment-rape-stories-explained-a8005936.html

17. Read, B. (February 22, 2018). Me Too Founder Tarana Burke: "Watch Carefully Who Are Called 'Leaders' of the Movement." *Vogue.* Retrieved from: https://www.vogue.com/article/me-too-tarana-burke-frustrations-mainstream-twitter-thread

18. Bennett, A. (March 15, 2018). Terry Crews Is Not Going Down Without A Fight. Buzzfeed.com. Retrieved from: https://www.buzzfeed.com/alannabennett/terry-crews-and-hollywood?utm_term=.ur7YDkeKK#.dhWMxw766

19. Marzouki, Y. & Oullier, O. (December 6, 2017). Revolutionizing Revolutions: Virtual Collective Consciousness and the Arab Spring.

20. Thompson, N. & Vogelstein, F. (March 20, 2018). A Hurricane Flattens Facebook. Wired.com. Retrieved from: https://www.wired.com/story/facebook-cambridge-analytica-response/

21. Ang, I. (1994). In the Realm of Uncertainty: The Global Village and Capitalist Postmodernity. Seen in Crowley, D. and Mitchell, D. *Communication Theory Today*. Calif.: Stanford University Press. Pg. 193–213.
22. Perrin, A. & Jiang, J. (March 14, 2018). About a quarter of US adults say they are "almost constantly" online Pew Research Center. Retrieved from: http://www.pewresearch.org/fact-tank/2018/03/14/about-a-quarter-of-americans-report-going-online-almost-constantly/
23. Pilkington, E. (December 22, 2013). Justine Sacco, PR executive fired over racist tweet, 'ashamed'. The Guardian. Retrieved from: https://www.theguardian.com/world/2013/dec/22/pr-exec-fired-racist-tweet-aids-africa-apology
24. March For Our Lives website (n.d.). https://marchforourlives.com/
25. Aggeler, M. (March 18, 2018). Everything You Need to Know About the March for Our Lives. TheCut.com. Retrieved from: https://www.thecut.com/2018/03/march-for-our-lives-for-gun-control-will-be-on-march-24.html
26. Rodriguez, V. (February 20, 2018). Florida School Shooting Survivors Announce Nationwide March. *Seventeen*. Retrieved from: https://www.seventeen.com/default/a18364071/march-for-our-lives/
27. Sanders, B. (1998). *The Private Death of Public Discourse*. Boston, MA: Beacon Press.
28. Hanisch, C. (2006). The Personal is Political. Retrieved from: http://www.carolhanisch.org/CHwritings/PIP.html
29. Grunig, J. & Hunt, T. (1984). Managing Public Relations. Boston, MA: Cengage Learning Publishers.
30. Blinder, A. Bigood, J. and Wang, V. (March 25, 2018). In Gun Control Marches, Students Led, but Adults Provided Key Resources. The New York Times. Retrieved from: https://www.nytimes.com/2018/03/25/us/gun-march-organizers.html
31. MacFarquhar, L. (April 2, 2018). The Mind Expanding Ideas of Andy Clark. *The New Yorker*. Retrieved from: https://www.newyorker.com/magazine/2018/04/02/the-mind-expanding-ideas-of-andy-clark
32. Jiang, L. C., Bazarova, N. & Hancock, J. (2011). The Disclosure–Intimacy Link in Computer-Mediated Communication: An Attributional Extension of the Hyperpersonal Model. *Human Communication Research*. 37, pp. 58–77.
33. Midkiff, S. (February 4, 2018). A Group Of Former Facebook & Google Employees Issue Warnings About Tech. Refinery29.com. Retrieved from: http://www.refinery29.com/2018/02/189888/former-facebook-google-employees-start-anti-tech-group

34. Human Tech Website. (n.d.). Retrieved from: http://humanetech.com/problem/
35. Bernstein, M. (October 26, 2016). How We're Endangering our Kids' Imaginations. Time. Retrieved from: http://time.com/4544654/how-were-endangering-our-kids-imaginations/
36. Rettner, R. (August 12, 2011). Are Today's Youth Less Creative & Imaginative? LiveScience.com. Retrieved from: https://www.livescience.com/15535-children-creative.html
37. Greenfield, S. (April 6, 2006). 'We are at risk of losing our imagination'. The Guardian. Retrieved from: https://www.theguardian.com/education/2006/apr/25/elearning.schools
38. O'Regan, J. (March 1, 2016). Social Media Vs. Imagination. TheOdysseyOnline.com. Retrieved from: https://www.theodysseyonline.com/social-media-vs-imagination
39. Caughey, J. (1982). Ethnography of Everyday Life: Theories and Methods for American Culture Studies. *American Quarterly*. 34:3, pp. 222–243.
40. Ibid., p. 222.
41. Berners-Lee, T. (March 11, 2018). The web can be weaponised—and we can't count on big tech to stop it. The Guardian. Retrieved from: https://www.theguardian.com/commentisfree/2018/mar/12/tim-berners-lee-web-weapon-regulation-open-letter
42. Konnikova, M. (October 7, 2014). The Limits of Friendship. *The New Yorker*. Retrieved from: https://www.newyorker.com/science/maria-konnikova/social-media-affect-math-dunbar-number-friendships

CHAPTER 8

Conclusion: What About Us?

In this chapter, I want to explore the mediated connection with one of my informants. Sara a 40-something administrator has a long-held fascination with ballroom dancing that goes back to her early childhood, and in more recent years she has developed a keen interest in ice dancing. In addition to being a fan of US ice dancers, she developed a more focused and involved interest in the 2018 Canadian ice dancing gold medalists from the Pyeongchang Winter Olympic Games in South Korea. In carrying out this analysis, I want to highlight some of the unique qualities of her mediated social connection with the Canadian ice dancers and how it extends our understanding of an imaginary social relationship based on parasocial interaction. We spoke using Zoom, an online video conferencing tool to delve into more detail about her feelings and online and offline experiences with the skating couple, as she had told me enthusiastically that she recently drove several hundred miles from her home to Canada, where she met up with other fans of the skaters and saw the skaters perform as well. Several weeks later in October 2018, she flew to Nashville to again see the skaters perform and to hang out with members of the social network that has formed around the Olympic skaters. What began through viewing on television a sport that provides great emotional satisfaction led to online searches for more news and information about the skaters and eventual engagement with other fans of the skaters on various social media platforms, but primarily on Twitter, where the social network utilizes direct messages to communicate.

© The Author(s) 2019
N. M. Alperstein, *Celebrity and Mediated Social Connections*,
https://doi.org/10.1007/978-3-030-17902-1_8

TESSA VIRTUE AND SCOTT MOIR

It is important, I think, to establish some background to better understand the skaters and some of the meanings that their fans ascribe to these
celebrities. Scott Moir and Tessa Virtue have been skating partners since
the age of seven. They have won many medals in the past representing
their home country of Canada and briefly gave up the sport only to return
as a skating couple during the 2018 South Korean Olympic Games. Scott
Moir generally shuns social media in an attempt to keep his and their lives
private. Tessa Virtue, however, directly engages with fans on social media
viewing it as her duty and obligation in order to build the skaters' brand.
For example, she serves as Canadian brand ambassador for Nivea, among
other brands. In her online activities, Virtue seeks to establish her authenticity; for example, one magazine reported on her viral tweet referencing
"the struggle is real." Further indication of her authenticity, the article
states: "She isn't flawless—and when I suggest she is, she insists that 'it's
your flaws that make you so special'—but sitting next to her is the closest
I've ever been to an angel. She radiates kindness, enthusiasm, comfort,
grace and every other positive personality trait that warms you from the
inside."[1] Flawless versus flawlessness is the binary that creates tension for
fans who seek identification with the celebrity. The same goes for her relationship with her male partner, which both skaters have continuously been
coy about. Are they romantically involved or not, fans ask? It is through
such binaries that fans have to work through in order to develop their own
meanings and perhaps significance as they seek to admire if not closely
identify with one or both of the skaters.

SARA: THE FAN

Sara is an avid consumer of popular culture and includes many celebrities
with whom she is familiar. Indeed she chuckled at my request to name
only ten celebrities with whom she is familiar and has a strong connection.
In addition to American ice skaters like Adam Rippon, whom she follows
on social media, Sara listed Stephen Amell, the lead character from her
current favorite CW network TV program *The Arrow*, Colin Donnell, one
of the lead actors on *Chicago Med*, and his wife (Patti Murin), who is playing Anna in the Broadway show *Frozen*. She mentioned Oliver Queen and
Felicity Smoak, fictional characters from *The Arrow*. She says she doesn't
follow musicians or politicians; the people she tends to follow are TV

celebrities, in particular those from her favorite genre, Sci-Fi. Her interests in these characters are furthered as she traverses the TV screen to "fill in the blanks" by scouring social media sites. As she engages in fan communities, sometimes indulging in fan fictions, she moves from observer to participant. What may have begun as TV viewing moves forward as she engages her imagination to consider her feeling of admiration for these actors and characters, and this conception of engagement regards the imagination as the celebrity enters into the imaginary world of the individual. But participation can be conceived of differently in the age of digital media, as participation may be redefined as forms of engagement to include all of the things I have discussed in this book ranging from liking, commenting, direct messaging, friending and the like. Furthermore, digital media provide opportunities to engage in social networks that include not only the celebrity but also the celebrity's fans and followers as well. I want to stress that these latter forms of participation do not take place within the mind of the individual, as they are examples of the extended mind in which what was once the domain of the imaginary seeps out into the objective world.

I Could Never Be an Olympic Skater

For Sara, engagement in social networks began after the skaters' appearance at the Winter Olympics in February 2018 as Sara scanned sites for news and information about the skaters. But she describes Twitter as the platform through which she has engaged in a social network of fans that began with direct messaging and continues as a way of staying in touch and developing what appears to be friendship at a distance. Several members of the network have attended events together and extended to experiences that reach beyond the digital network into real life. For instance, when Sara attended a skating charity event in Nashville, Tennessee, she met up with several friends initially established on Twitter to tour the city.

Sara expressed a long-term interest in figure skating, especially pairs skating and in recent years ice dancing at the Olympic level. Her introduction to Scott and Tessa goes back to the 2010 Vancouver Winter Olympics, and she recounts watching them win a silver medal at the Sochi Winter Games. Sara's involvement includes her niece who, she says, "got into figure skating and we were watching (separately) but talking via Facetime. She loved the costumes, but I was first attracted because they skated to the music of Moulin Rouge, one of my favorite movies." It was the music that served as a trigger stimulating her desire to see the video of the skaters performing to this musical piece. As she says, she began to watch their videos and follow them more closely on social media, not only because of their physical prowess on the ice, performing moves that Sara says she will never be able to do, but because they told a story. That the couple exude passion and romance on the ice is the key quality that Sara admires in the couple. As she watched them perform to Moulin Rouge, she "second screened," meaning she got on Twitter, which she says was "exploding" with people from all over the world who described the couple as "Canadian Royalty" and there were other people who were seeing them for the first time as they were just coming to prominence. People tweeted about their routines and their chemistry; at that point, Sara says, it was "down the rabbit hole for me."

She started looking around to find more about their background, and learned that they had been together for 21 years. "I kind of thought about what intrigued me about them and I think it is their story, that they have been together for that many years, since they were seven and ten years old." She read about their ups and downs both personally and profession-ally. As she gathered more and more information about them, Sara says she started watching videos of their performances. Then she began to reach out to people on Twitter through the Virtue/Moir hashtag to ask what would others recommend, as "I wanted to watch more." And she goes on to say, "that got me into starting conversations with five or six different people, like my friend Liz I met who is from the Philippines. And there is a friend of mine I met online, Luciana from Argentina, and there are others from all over America. I never met these people before, but through talking on Twitter after the Olympics were over, a group of 20 of us met online to watch a livestream performance by the couple in Japan." Sara described this as a "total social gathering" in which several of the people in addition to using Twitter during the performance were Facetiming. Baym referred to this as a performance based on "collabora-tive interpretation."[2]

Sara says that she has a long history of participating in fan communities, ever since X-Files, she says. So this gathering of disparate individuals from all over the world was nothing new or unusual to her. Fan communities exhibit a sense of closeness that comes from engaging in shared experi-ences, particularly in online groups. Baym identifies five qualities of online fan groups. These include a sense of shared space, shared identities, exchange of resources and social support, interpersonal relationships and rituals of shared practice.[3] Sara says she is the type of person that has no problem attending fan gatherings or conventions to meet like-minded people who are pop culture fans. But Moir and Virtue, Sara says, have become her latest fan obsession, although she backs off a bit to refer to it as "fan focus." And, there is a hierarchy in the network, as those fans who attend more events and tweet more at the skaters, and who are therefore more likely to get responses from the skaters, hold higher status within the group. Sara says that with the other celebrities in which she's interested, it is more about the individual or character they play; in this case it's about the couple. It's their story, she says, and the biggest intrigue is whether or not they are a couple, and the discussion among those active in the social network centers on what they determine to be with surety that the skaters most definitely are a couple. However, a big brouhaha started when it was reported that Scott was dating somebody else. This is an important moment as part of the romantic fantasy surrounds the couple's romantic involvement.

The degree and nature of the admiration she feels for Tessa is based on qualities she sees in the skater that she also sees in herself or those she would like to see in herself (emulation). There are also values through which there may be strong identification with the skater. It is in this way that the strong identification projects her own self onto the persona of the celebrity. This may be taking place within the spectator-media encounter, as it plays out within the individual's imaginary social world. And, the dynamics of identification may also take place outside of media consumption when the individual engages in daydreaming or perhaps the celebrity is present in a nocturnal dream. It is also possible that the individual may exude characteristics she gleaned from the celebrity as she engages with other people in the objective world, in other words acting like the celebrity through interactions with others. Their long-term connection and romantic involvement are idealizations of modern-day romance that play against a culture that "swipes" from relationship to relationship. Steadiness and in that continuity are important characteristics exuded by the couple and admired by their fans. There are good reasons why such characteristics would be important and appealing as they are the idealized image of a successful relationship. While the idealization of the romantic relationship may be internalized as part of a fantasy or daydream, it is also one that is shared emotionally and in that "processed" with others in the online network. In this way, Sara can consider both individually—in her own mind—and collectively whether or not Scott is a "cad" for dating someone other than Tessa. Sharing grows more complex when such beliefs about whether skaters are romantically involved or not are presented to the social network, as others may not agree with this subjective position (they are involved), subjecting themselves to isolation within the network or perhaps splintering off into a group of dissenters (he's cheating on her). But Sara is rather adamant saying that when you see them together and the way they are with one another, despite what they say and no matter how coy they are on camera or in media interviews, how can they not be together. This is a major discussion on social media as Sara as well as others in her circle attempt to reconcile their own beliefs with those that are presented to them by the couple. Sara says, "I've been wondering why I have stuck with them for so long, and I think what it comes down to is their story. Maybe it's the romantic in me." In other words, "if you can't find true love with the guy you've been skating with since you were seven years old, what hope is there for the rest of us."

Tessa Takes the Lead on Social Media

Sara points out that Tessa is the one that is on social media, not him. She's always posting things like "what makes you happy today?" and other aphorisms. She comments to fans and responds to their comments. Sara says she has never direct-messaged Tessa, but gets a kick out of watching her friends do so. There is satisfaction in lurking, she says. She did tweet at Tessa a couple of times and she "liked" her tweets. But she says, because "I'm more of a lurker," I really like seeing how my friends "go crazy" when she directly responds to them as they post or re-tweet Tessa's response to them. The few times that she has received responses, Sara mentions that it feels like being plucked out the crowd as if to acknowledge she has something important to say. There is status elevation in this experience that has been noted in many instances where a celebrity responds to a comment or post. Therefore, fans may experience enhanced status under these circumstances, but diminished status when they dissent from the group.

Sara is drawn to Tessa because of all the "stuff" she can do. "She's a dancer...I have no hand eye coordination and am awkward at everything. So, I really respect the talent....I know what it takes to be able to do that. She's pushed herself. She's trained through everything. She's had three leg surgeries and she has overcome so many things. And if you've followed her during this whole process the attitude she has, at least the way she comes across on social media is that she is pretty genuine." Sara goes on to say, "she just enjoys life. She encourages people to be happy with who they are and she is always posting uplifting comments." "Like if I see that she has posted something like 'greatness is from within,' I think to myself that is a nice affirmation of life." Sara goes on to say that Tessa understands that we as humans sometimes have bad days and seeing how she engages a lot with her fans by responding to their comments she takes on an added role. "That's a lot to take on," Sara says, "I respect that." At the same time, she says, she knows that it's all part of building a brand, but "I still enjoy that she still takes the time to engage." The duality of doing something for altruistic as well as selfish reasons relates to the work that fans have to do in order to find meanings that support their beliefs about the ways in which the world operates or the celebrity may present opportunities to alter those beliefs. As has been pointed out in this book, fans are empowered to disagree with a celebrity overtly through a tweet or comment or simply disconnect. "It's funny," Sara says, "as much as I like the thought that she is with Scott, when you look at her, she's a brand ambassador for Nivea, she's out doing videos…she is extremely empowering as a 29 year old with all that she has done…That she skates for three days in a row and then goes and does promotions is amazing." Sara says that, with all of the stresses of her job, watching Tessa is "stress relief." As I watch I think, "if she can do it, I certainly can deal with whatever…look at what she has gone through, I'm going through nothing compared to that… What do I have complain about?"

Scott as Prince Charming

As we turned to talk about Scott, Sara pointed out that he rarely engages in social media, except perhaps for the occasional Instagram post, like a shout-out to his hometown. And in the interviews she has seen or read, Sara mentions that he clearly respects women. But she did point out the stereotype of the male ice dancer, as she says that ice dancing may not be considered the most "manly" sport, but what they are doing physically is incredible. Sara mentions that Scott also in media interviews talked openly about personal struggles he underwent after the couple decided to retire after taking the silver medal at the Sochi games. His openness about excessive drinking and depression are acts of authenticity and sincerity that ingratiate the celebrity to the fan. There is a recurring theme that was initially expressed by Tessa whereby the idea of flawlessness plays against human frailty. It is the space or tension that exists between these two ideas where I have maintained culture does its work. Sara described how both skaters on podcasts and other interviews admit to having "issues." And to that point she talks about how the couple even at an early age, because they train so closely together, attended marriage counseling even though they are not married and were seeing counselors since they were teenagers. The skaters make fans aware that the two are different and sometimes get into conflicts and that they have to learn to figure things out together, and what has gotten them through is talking to therapists. They have been very open about that, Sara says. And, I think this speaks to the ideal of what that represents to fans as they map these experiences into their own lives. The chapters in this book have established that in the construction of persona, in the digital age, what heretofore may have been held privately becomes public. Moreover, a requirement of celebrity and micro-celebrity is excessive self-disclosure. On the one hand, excessive disclosure becomes an attention-getting device, and in the celebrity economy, attention is an important commodity. But in order to ingratiate one's self to fans, the excessive disclosures provide a sense of humanity that adds dimension and in that encourages elaboration on the part of the fan. That elaboration in thoughts and fantasies among fans also sometimes spills back out into social media through posts of empathy, admiration or denigration.

DOWN THE RABBIT HOLE

In addition to using the skater as a means to understand her stresses at work, comparing what they have to go through as a means to better understand her own stress, Sara also described how her mother became ill and this put additional stress on her everyday life. Watching the skaters on YouTube provided stress relief, but she is able to go beyond the vicarious experience of watching to engage with other fans online to chat, embellishing her knowledge regarding what is going on in the skater's lives. She found this use of digital media—staying up to date—calming, as such online interactions allowed her to distance herself from stressors that were before her. And she took a moment to emphasize that she could never be an Olympic athlete, but the fact that they are so driven to succeed and exhibit abilities that speak to all their accomplishments, she said, "why can't I do that in my life where I'm not competing." All the stress is why I "went down the rabbit hole," watching videos and engaging in online interactions with other fans, as she didn't have to think about things that were before her—mother's illness and job responsibilities. Generally, Sara says, she would immerse herself in one of her TV shows to escape reality, but watching the skaters or reading about them, because they are "real," made this different. "They are fun to watch and think about, and now that I have really met them (Sara's face lights up), I know them as real human beings." She added that she has met some incredible people on the fan side of this. The friendships she has made and the people she has met through this fan community make her feel connected. She added that members of the fan community instruct one another to use direct messaging rather than posting things to the general Twitter population. Because if they are talking about more personal things, isolating the conversation lends a feeling of intimacy to the mediated social connections.

DIGITAL MEDIA AFFORDANCES

Sara mentioned toward the end of the interview that when she was younger she would fantasize more about the actors or characters that she followed who appeared in television programs. She recounted how she would fantasize about being "swept away" by one of the stars. I have described this experience throughout this book as entering our imaginary inner worlds. But as she has gotten older there is less fantasizing of this nature, Sara says. There is ample evidence that imaginary social relationships are not age related, but over time the type, nature and direction of fantasies change. It may not be that we give up fantasizing with age, rather what Sara is experiencing is the way in which the imagination sometimes spills back out as fans, friends and followers engage in mediate social connections in the digital age.

The goal of this ethnographic interview is to investigate this individual's mediated social connection and to extrapolate how such connections to celebrities, micro-celebrities, and their fans and followers begin with a media encounter, whether it is legacy media, like in this case watching the skaters perform on television, or through digital media, like watching videos on YouTube or images on Instagram. This chapter provides understanding of the significance of the relationships we form with celebrities who we do not actually know. Digital media provides affordances to go beyond the admiration or other feelings we may internalize to connect outward to those celebrities we most admire with the possibility they may connect back to us. In the course of such engagement, we also connect with other fans, friends and followers within a social network. Mediated social connections work at the level of individual consciousness and operate at the level of collective consciousness as expressions of the extended mind that represent a significant shift in the ways in which we engage with one another in the age of digital media. In this case, not only does Sara use the information and news she has gleaned from media as part of her own meaning-making system, to imagine about ideas regarding romantic relationships in contemporary society, but also she is able to use her connection to these performers to diminish the stress in her everyday life. Beyond such a functional use, her inner experiences also turn outward as she connects with others digitally through social media. And, she demonstrates in her behavior how far people are willing to go to create and maintain connections, sometimes turning relationships with intimate strangers into actual social relationships.

So What About the Rest of Us?

As we engage with celebrities through media that I contend is an imaginary world itself, we sometimes internalize characteristics or qualities of the personas that we admire, whether they be "real" people or the characters they play. This imaginary world connects to our inner experiences to encourage imaginary relationships with people we do not actually know, but may know a lot about. We traverse our inner worlds to connect to our objective world and back in a dynamic process (see Fig. 8.1). The amount of time we spend in our stream of consciousness or self-talk imagining our past or anticipating our futures is considerable, and when you couple that with our always-connected lifestyle to digital media, there is little time left to dream. There was a time when the imaginary world was to a great extent walled off from the objective world, although the former may have been made up of people and places from our objective world. But in an age of digital media, seepage takes place in which the inner world is extended back into the objective world. In this way, some of our thoughts and fantasies spill out into the objective world of digital media.

The process takes place through identification with a celebrity while internalizing and perhaps taking on some characteristic the celebrity exudes. But in this digital age, the fluidity with which the content of pop culture and celebrity fills our imaginary world and the ways in which we integrate aspects of it into our thoughts and fantasies represent only part of the equation. We may take the thoughts we have conjured up, the

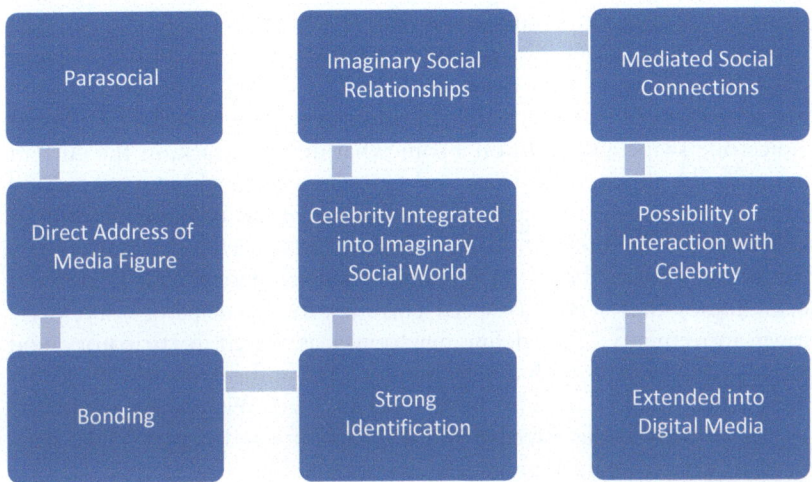

Fig. 8.1 From parasocial to imaginary to mediated connections

exaggerations and violations of norms that titillate us, and feed them back into the system through our engagement with digital media. There are cultural forces at work that could not have been anticipated in the dawn of the digital age. There is more at work here than the feelings that we may have formerly held inside because that was the custom, as our inner thoughts were our own. In a world of mediated social connections, pseudosocial interactions give way to the possibility of actual interaction.

Concurrent with changes taking place in digital media are the changing nature of the relationships we form and maintain. As examples of those changes, we witness the rise of the micro-celebrity and nano-celebrity, the social or brand influencer as extensions of what might now stand in for celebrity culture. The term digital native refers to someone who grew up with technology and therefore has a greater familiarity with media than perhaps other, nondigital natives. But if technologies are continually changing, along with the ways in which we utilize them, then there cannot be such a thing as a digital native, which assumes that digital media are somehow static or stable. To place this within another framework, in cultural studies we often say that people do culture long before they know it. I think the same thing can be said for digital culture. As digital technologies are in constant flux, what it means to be in relationship in the digital age, too, is in flux, as exemplified by the proliferation of dating apps that through a simple swipe encourage people to continuously choose. The compelling feeling one gets from participating in swipe culture suggests that relationships, at least those generated by dating apps, are always in flux, a product of endless choice. In other words, there is always a better choice one swipe away. Or, on a somewhat different tack, in the current digital media climate, Facebook and Google operate within a centralized Internet, but in time that centralization may give way to a more decentralized Internet. In their book *New Power*, Jeremy Heimans and Henry Timms make a case based on ubiquitous connectivity afforded by newer technologies that serves as social currency for participatory and peer-driven movements. They define new power as "open, participatory, and peer driven."[4] But as with any technology, the authors acknowledge that "new power" can be used for both good and bad. With regard to the latter, they point to the effective way ISIS has utilized digital media platforms to get across its message.[5]

The good and bad of digital media and related technologies notwithstanding, we should not assume that those powerful platforms of today will look and operate similarly in years to come. After all, the Facebook of 2004 looks and feels little like the Facebook of today. Over the years, Twitter introduced the hashtag and then direct messaging and, of late, increased the allowance for a tweet from 140 to 280 characters. It may be that a more distributive, that is decentralized, system will replace the current centralized Internet. Indeed many people feel that the large social media companies don't operate in their users' interests. The idea of a distributed Internet is not merely a resistance movement or a revolution that rejects the status quo; rather, a decentralized system places the ability to connect to one another in the hands of users. This idea is reflected in the 2018 season of the fictional HBO program *Silicon Valley*, in which the start-up featured in the show develops a peer-to-peer network connecting everyone's smartphone, "effectively rendering huge data centers full of servers unnecessary."[6] That's fiction, but in RL, techspeak for real life, as distinguished from VR, or virtual reality, we have seen how with movements such as Me Too and Never Again that there is strength in numbers rooted in the human desire to engage even at a distance. But we have also seen how social networks are diffused audiences, comprised of crowds and clusters and sometimes even smaller niches or cliques that come together to form a network, or perhaps part of the network is made up of a lot of individuals firing arrows, that is, unconnected messages, into the air. There are celebrities, micro-celebrities as well as ordinary people engaging to one degree or another through digital media. For example, ePatients comprise the half-million people who share information about thousands of diseases on an online community like patientslikeme.com.[7] It is important however, not to overemphasize the power of the crowd, as the crowd or cluster may in itself be diffused. And, among those who participate, the range of sentiment within those groups may range from admirers to haters.

Some critics of the Internet, like Nicholas Carr, maintain that we may be too connected in that we are being overloaded with information. His critique is not too different from the one offered by critics of the previous generation that claimed that we were all passive participants, that is, couch potatoes, in a TV-dominated media culture. In his book *The Shallows: What the Internet Is Doing to Our Brains*, Carr claims that it is the intensity of our use of digital media that is changing our brains that would relate to the almost-always-connected culture described in this book as evidence of that sensory overload. In this always-connected culture the extent to which technology envelopes our everyday lives extends from an issue like identity theft to consider attention capture. Attention capture, which is practiced by brands, political operatives and celebrities, among others, plays against the strategies individuals develop in order to practice avoidance and the overload to which Carr refers. Practiced avoidance is indeed a strategy in which individuals may turn away or turn inward to avoid direct contact with content on the screen. Theoretical physicist Leonard Mlodinow echoes this concern in his book, *Elastic: Flexible Thinking in a Time of Change*, in which he describes the need for individuals to practice nonlinear thinking, as opposed to executive function and reasoning that is built into the present more "rigid" world. What leads us to such a rigid and in that unbalanced approached to thinking? Technology. What we are left with is a kind of us versus technology dilemma, but ultimately what is called for is a more balanced approach in which the elastic mind works with, not against, the more rigid mind. What I have argued for in this book is a world that allows, if not encourages, people to daydream, engage in stream of consciousness thinking and fantasize about celebrities and media figures, as our inner world is as significant as our objective world. To suggest that we should build a proverbial wall between the two is an idea that runs counter to the reality of an always-on, always-connected culture in which we presently live. Recognizing that mediated social connections are not necessarily as social as we would like to think may allow us to step back from the idea that is being sold to us by companies, governments and organizations in whose interest it is to further such beliefs. If we step back from that position, then perhaps we can reengage our inner worlds, and spending more time in our heads might actually place us in a better position to deal with the outside world. The one thing we can be assured of is that new digital media, at least for the foreseeable future, will continue to emerge, offering enticing ways to engage and interact with those platforms and technologies. However, our immersion into a world of digital media as we presently know it is just the tip of the proverbial iceberg, as technology changes, rapidly moving us to a future that drives us toward artificial intelligence, digital assistants, and augmented and virtual reality. As such we will live in an expanded version of multiple realities, RL being just one of them. What we continue to experience as a culture is the fluid nature by which we traverse the multiple realities that make up our everyday lives.

NOTES

1. McKenna, M. (March 12, 2018). Tessa Virtue Talks Social Media, Self-Care and Yes, Scott Moir. Fashionmagazine.com. Retrieved from: https://fashionmagazine.com/beauty/tessa-virtue-nivea/
2. Baym, N. (2000). *Tune In, Log On: Soaps, Fandom, and Online Community.* London: Sage, p. 83.
3. Baym, N. (2010). *Personal Connections in the Digital Age.* Cambridge: Polity Press.
4. Heimans, J. & Timms, H. (2018) *New Power: How Power Works in Our Hyperconnected World—and How to Make It Work for You.* New York: Doubleday Publishers, p. 1.
5. Ibid.
6. Finley, K. (June 1, 2017). Pied Piper's New Internet Isn't Just Possible-It's Almost Here. Wired. Retrieved from: https://www.wired.com/2017/06/pied-pipers-new-internet-isnt-just-possible-almost/
7. Patients Like Me website. (n.d.). Retrieved from: https://www.patientslikeme.com/

Index[1]

[1] Note: Page numbers followed by 'n' refer to notes.

© The Author(s) 2019
N. M. Alperstein, *Celebrity and Mediated Social Connections*,
https://doi.org/10.1007/978-3-030-17902-1

The manufacturer's authorised representative in the EU is Springer
Nature Customer Service Centre GmbH, Europaplatz 3, 69115 Heidelberg,
Germany. If you have any concerns regarding our products, please
contact ProductSafety@springernature.com

Printed and bound by CPI Group (UK) Ltd, Croydon, CR0 4YY
29/04/2026
02099471-0005